ON THE RUN

"Their warts-and-all portrayal of the immense disruption to their lives caused by their father's criminal recidivism is often heartbreaking. Gregg's story is especially moving as he traces his personal evolution from model student to an adolescent forced to protect his mother from his father" *Publishers Weekly*

"Mob children are the hidden victims of organized crime . . . their story has never been told until now . . . A must-read for those who want the complete picture of life in the Mafia" Anthony Bruno, author of *Bad Guys*

"Remarkable . . . Only the children of Henry Hill could've written this intimate exposé, and they've done it with gut-wrenching honesty and incredible courage" Peter Earley, author of *Witsec: Inside the Federal Witness Protection Program*

"This account of life inside the witness protection program is more than just a riveting personal story. It also provides an unusual and revealing look at a part of the Mob world the public rarely hears about" Thomas Reppetto, author of *American Mafia*

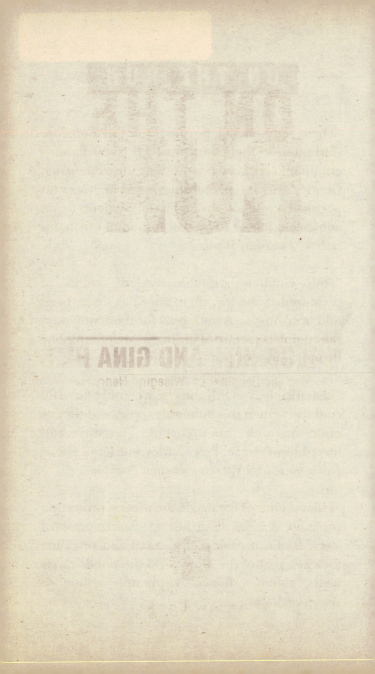

ON THE RUN

GREGG HILL AND GINA HILL

Son and Daughter of "Wiseguy" Henry Hill

arrow books

Published by Arrow Books in 2005

14 16 18 20 19 17 15 13

First published by Warner Books in the US in 2004

Arrow Books
The Random House Group Limited
20 Vauxhall Bridge Road, London SW1V 2SA

Random House Australia (Pty) Limited
20 Alfred Street, Milsons Point, Sydney
New South Wales 2061, Australia

Random House New Zealand Limited
18 Poland Road, Glenfield
Auckland 10, New Zealand

Random House (Pty) Limited
Isle of Houghton, Corner of Boundary Road & Carse O'Gowrie
Houghton 2198, South Africa

The Random House Group Limited Reg. No. 954009

www.randomhouse.co.uk

A CIP catalogue record for this book is available
from the British Library

Papers used by Random House are natural,
recyclable products made from wood grown in sustainable forests.
The manufacturing processes conform to the environmental
regulations of the country of origin

ISBN 0 09 947894 3

Printed and bound in Great Britain by
Bookmarque Ltd, Croydon, Surrey

For our mother, our grandparents,
Aunt Cheryl, and Aunt Ellen,
who sacrificed to make
our lives better.

ACKNOWLEDGMENTS

We're grateful to a number of people for their contributions to this book. Jerry Kalajian, our agent, encouraged us to tell our story and, together with Joel Gotler and Keith Fleer, he skillfully guided us. Rick Horgan, our editor, was a constant source of inspiration with his insights and his passion. Sean Flynn, an immensely talented writer, was invaluable. And retired FBI agent Ed Gueverra, retired U.S. marshal Alfie McNeil, and retired assistant U.S. attorney Edward McDonald helped us keep this book accurate.

AUTHORS' NOTE

This is a true story told mostly through our own recollections but also supported with interviews and official records. All of the dialogue is real, as are the names of our father's Mafia associates, the prosecutors, the people connected to the Boston College point-shaving scandal, and the federal agents we dealt with. Most of the other names and a few minor identifying details, however, have been changed to protect the privacy of those people who were only tangentially involved in our father's activities and our life on the run.

PROLOGUE

Gregg: I always thought the worst thing that could happen to my father was that he would go back to prison or get killed. It's not that I wanted either to happen; it's just that I expected it would be one or the other. By the time of my bar mitzvah, my father had spent more than one-third of my life locked up, and his friends—my family's friends, people I knew—were disappearing by the week. The way things were going, I wouldn't have been at all surprised if he had ended up gone too, one way or the other. But as bad as his options appeared—prison or death—at least those would have been things that happened to him. Not to me, not to my sister, not to my mother. To him.

My father was a criminal. I don't think I ever consciously thought of him with that precise term—*criminal*—but I knew he wasn't legitimate, that he wasn't like other fathers who went to work every day and paid their bills and showed up at their kids' track meets. My mother used to say he was a wangler, that he'd *wangle* this or *wangle* that or *wangle* his way out of some jam or another. I still cringe when I hear that word. *Wangle*.

In the spring of 1980, when I was thirteen years old and my sister, Gina, was eleven, my father's wangling consisted mainly of selling large quantities of drugs. Cocaine and marijuana, mostly, but also some heroin and all sorts of pills. It wasn't something my father talked to me about, but it wasn't a secret either. I'm sure my parents would like to believe that they sheltered Gina and me from the worst of it, but it was hard to miss the Hefty bags full of marijuana in the living room and the bricks of cocaine wrapped in foil on the coffee table. My father was a wreck, too, snorting three or four grams of coke every day and swallowing a dozen quaaludes to even it out. Plus, there were always people in the house getting high. My father would put Billy Joel's *Piano Man* on the stereo, light a bunch of candles, and drag out the oversized mirror from my closet or take the Miss Piggy mirror off my sister's wall to do lines. Some of his idiot friends would even offer me a snort. I guess they were trying to be polite, as if they were honoring some kind of drug etiquette, but they only made things worse: It's harder to ignore the drugs in the living room if your father's cokehead friends keep asking you to join the party. You know that feeling of being the only sober person in a room full of drunks? That was my life at thirteen. It took me years to get over the smell of candles. I still hate Billy Joel.

The drugs weren't much of a secret outside the house either. In the early spring of 1980, narcotics detectives in Nassau County, on Long Island, kept my father under surveillance for almost two months. They tapped the phones, they photographed all the people coming and going—including *my* friends—and they picked through the garbage, pulling out scraps of paper with notations of the flights that my dad's main courier, Amy Mulry, would take back and forth from Pittsburgh on drug runs. By the end of April, they had enough evidence for a warrant to search our house in Rockville Centre.

They came April 27, a Sunday night. I was on our big tan couch watching TV when the lights from their cruisers flashed through the living-room windows. I thought there must have been a fire at the apartments across the street, but there were no sirens. The silence was odd. Then someone started thumping on the front door.

They were coming to *our* house.

My muscles clenched and my heart raced,

making it hard to breathe. My mother, already nervous, unlocked the door, and more than a dozen men pushed in, four in plainclothes, the rest in uniform. It was like an invasion, all those men with guns pushing into the house, moving fast and shouting, securing the place.

We were in trouble. Big fucking trouble. *Holy shit,* I thought. *Our house is being raided.* We only lived a block and a half from the Rockville Centre police station on Maple Avenue, and it looked like the entire force was standing in our living room. They could have walked over. I didn't even get a chance to get off the couch, and I was shaking from the nerves. I never thought of myself as a macho kid or as particularly brave, but I thought I could handle anything—that was my strength. But no kid is prepared for a police raid.

When my mother recalls that night, she remembers being calm, even offering to make coffee for all those guys who'd come to tear up the house. That's a laugh. She was nearly hysterical. "We don't have anything you're looking for," she screamed at one detective, racing back and forth between him and another one, her face flushed. "There's nothing in the house."

"Karen, calm down," the detective told her. He used her first name, like he knew her, which he probably did, considering how often my father had been locked up.

"I won't calm down," she said. "You've got no right to destroy my house."

"We've got a warrant," the detective barked at her. "Now sit down and shut up."

I wondered if it was an act, my mother pretending to be hysterical to distract them. If it was, it seemed to be working because they left her alone and actually worked more quickly. I stayed on the couch, praying no one would ask me anything. Gina came out of her bedroom, red and trembling, and sat down next to my mother and me.

"What's happening, Mom?" she whispered.

"Not now," my mother snapped. Then she caught herself, like the way someone chokes off tears that are about to come spilling out. She softened her voice, realizing that Gina was crying. "Don't worry," she said. "Everything will be okay."

Even I knew this was not going to be okay. I'd never seen so many cops in one place. They'd caught us by surprise, so my mind was playing catch-up. *Okay, it's a raid. Dad's not home. What are they looking for?*

It took only an instant for it to hit me: drugs. My father had paraphernalia everywhere, and probably plenty of drugs hidden in the house. I'd always thought it was stupid to do drugs, to weigh drugs and count drugs and package drugs, in the open, right in our living room. Was I the only one—at thirteen—who understood that? Did my mother really think everything would be okay, that we'd get through this, too?

For my entire short life, my mother had been telling me and Gina that we'd get through one thing or another and then everything would be fine, at least until the next thing happened. What I couldn't understand, though, was why they couldn't just do things right. But no one ever listened to me. I was just a kid. What did I know? "Quit being such a fucking pussy," my father would say to me. "What are you, a fucking baby? Shut up already." So I did. I took no solace in being right this time, now that the next thing had happened. And I knew it was way more serious than anything that had come before. This wasn't something I had to endure from a distance or something Gina and I could watch from the sidelines—we were in the middle of it, surrounded, ambushed, trapped.

A police search does not happen quickly. It takes a while to flip over the mattresses and dump out the drawers and pull apart cabinets. They worked into the night, the detectives directing the uniformed men around the house. I could hear them pulling the fiberboard tiles from the basement ceiling, where my father once stashed a submachine gun. There was a scritching tear when they tugged up the carpet in my parents' bedroom that my father had refinished with pink satin and mirrored walls and a broad fan of stairs that swept up to a platform bed, the whole thing closed behind a heavy wooden door with an electronic lock and an intercom. My grandmother called it a brothel. I knew about the secret compartment in there, built into one of the steps but rigged in such a way that you had to reach in, back, and up to find whatever was hidden there. I waited and wondered if the cops would figure that out, or what else they would find.

Then they were in my room. I knew exactly what they'd find in there: I used to joke to my parents that I was the only kid at South Side Middle School with a triple-beam balance scale in my closet, the same kind we used in science class. My father had given it to me as a present, which I thought was strange—I'd never asked for a triple-beam balance—until he started using it to weigh out cocaine. After that, whatever allure there might have been to having my own scale vanished. He kept it in my room anyway. He kept a big mirror in my closet, too, that he would pull out to cut lines for parties. I assumed they would take both of those things. I just hoped they wouldn't trash everything else. I was a particular kid, the kind who kept his room neat and organized, probably because it was one of the few things in my life I could control.

They finally finished, and the three of us were left to clean up another one of my father's messes. He was already in jail when the house was raided. He'd been picked up out on the street right before the warrant was executed. If he'd been any other Long Island drug dealer, he would have copped a plea, maybe rolled over on some low-level schmuck, and been nothing more than a brief footnote in the history of the war on drugs.

But my father wasn't any other Long Island drug dealer. He was connected. *That* word I'd heard, though it was only when I got older that I realized what it truly meant. When I was younger, it meant that he could get box seats to the World Series, that sometimes he had wads of cash to throw around and a closet full of Italian suits and boxes of watches and toasters and microwaves that my grandmother would sell to her friends the way other old women on Long Island had Tupperware parties.

I knew a lot of what he did wasn't really legal, but I always thought it fell into a gray area, not much worse than gambling. I certainly never thought of him as a Mafia guy—and, technically, I was correct, because as a half-Irish convert to Judaism, he could never be a made man in the Italian Mob. But for all intents and purposes, he was one of them. He grew up with wiseguys, went into business with them, became part of their families, and made their families part of ours. It turned out that my rotund Uncle Paulie was Paul Vario, a capo in the Lucchese mob. Uncle Jimmy was Jimmy "The Gent" Burke, a killer and borderline sociopath who masterminded the biggest cash robbery in U.S. history, $5.8 million from a Lufthansa warehouse at Kennedy Airport. Tommy DeSimone was a flat-out lunatic with crazy eyes and a boxer's build; my mother always said he was looking to start trouble. Billy Arico, from Valley Stream, was an exterminator by day and a hit man by night—bugs, vermin, people, he killed them all. There were dozens more, men with whom my father drank and stole and extorted. He had twenty-five years of history with those guys. He literally knew where the bodies were buried, and he'd even helped dig some of the graves.

And that was his leverage.

He was arrested that night on state charges. But then federal agents stepped in and grabbed him as a material witness in the Lufthansa theft, which was still unsolved partly because people connected to the heist kept turning up dead or simply disappearing. My father was only on the fringe of Lufthansa, but he was also on the short list of people expected to be killed next. So the feds explained his options to him: Go to prison and probably get killed. Go back on the street and definitely get killed. Or cooperate.

My father decided to cooperate. Less than a month after the house was raided, he agreed to be relocated by federal marshals running the Witness Security Program, which the feds call WitSec and everyone else calls witness protection. The rest of us, me and my sister and my mother, we didn't get a choice: He wouldn't go without us, and the feds told us we were in danger of getting killed too if we stayed behind, like live bait the wiseguys would use to draw out my father.

On May 20, 1980, our lives as we'd known them officially ended. Gregg and Gina Hill ceased to exist. Our names were erased. Our IDs were confiscated and shredded. Our friends were banished to memory. My grandmother and grandfather and aunts became people we used to know. We were sent far away, someplace we'd never been or even imagined, strangers in a strange place, to start over with nothing but fake names and everything to hide.

Like I said, I always thought the worst thing that could happen to my father was that he'd go back to prison or get killed.

I was wrong. This was much worse. And it was only beginning.

GINA: One of my earliest memories of my dad was my mom telling me he was going away. That's how she said it: "Daddy has to go away for a little while." It was late in the afternoon, and she was leaning down so her face was close to mine and I could smell her perfume. She was crying just a little. I'm sure she never used the word *prison*, and it wouldn't have mattered because I was only six years old and wouldn't have known what prison was.

We were living in the Fairview, a luxury high-rise right across the highway from Flushing Meadows, in Queens. There was a doorman at each of the three different sections of the complex and a big circular driveway out front, and we had a small terrace that overlooked the park. My dad owned a restaurant called The Suite, and he must have been doing pretty well because we could afford to live in a place like the Fairview.

We moved a lot when I was little. When my parents first got married, in 1965, they lived with my grandparents, my mom's parents, in Valley Stream, on Long Island. Gram was always tough on Dad. "That gangster," she'd say, only she'd spit out the words. She thought a nice Jewish girl like my mom should have married a doctor or a lawyer, not some hoodlum Catholic from Brooklyn that she'd met on a blind date. Dad had a union card, and the bricklayers supposedly paid him $135 a week, but he didn't even pretend to work a normal job. He went out every night dressed in sharp suits and stayed out until dawn if he came home at all, and he always had money to throw around, twenty for the doorman, fifty for the waiter. When I was older, my mom told me that that was part of what attracted her to my dad—the glitz, the way he could get them a front-row table at the Empire Club or the Copacabana, the way he seemed to know everyone and everyone knew him. One day she's a dental assistant from a middle-class family on Long Island, and the next she's sipping from a bottle of champagne that Sammy Davis Jr. sent to Dad's table at the Copa.

My dad had a dangerous side too, and I think

Mom liked that, the whole outlaw mystique. She once told me a story about how, after they'd been dating for a couple of months, this boy from her neighborhood, Ted, someone she'd known her whole life, took her for a ride in his Corvette one afternoon and made a pass at her. He started groping her in the front seat and my mom told him to stop but he didn't so she slapped him. He got mad and threw her out of the car, miles from home, and tore off so fast that the tires threw gravel in her face. My mom called my dad and he picked her up and drove her home, but instead of going into the house with her, he went across the street. He saw Ted in the driveway, grabbed him by the hair, pulled a gun out of his pocket, and pistol-whipped him. Pistol-whipped him! Then my dad came trotting back across the street, all sweaty and red, and gave my mom the gun and told her to hide it. Most girls would have been terrified, but my mom said she thought it was sexy.

That's how their life together started, night-clubs and pistol-whippings. They eloped not long after my dad beat up Ted, and moved in with my grandparents. They were so young, my dad twenty-two and my mom just nineteen. And she was already pregnant with my brother. For as much as Dad might have irritated my grandma, she wasn't one to throw her daughter into the street.

I think sometimes my grandparents liked my

dad in spite of themselves. He wasn't the kind of man they wanted their oldest daughter to end up with, but he could be awfully charming. That was my dad's greatest asset, his charm. And his connections. That's how he always explained it—*connections*. Like the time the pavers showed up with a truckload of asphalt to blacktop my grandma's driveway. "Don't worry about it," one of them told Gram. "Henry took care of it." Or when my dad and his friend Tommy DeSimone would back a truck up to the garage and unload boxes of microwaves or knit shirts or toaster ovens. He'd tell my grandma he did a guy a favor and bought a load of merchandise from him, stuff she could help sell to the neighbors. Gram probably knew it was stolen, but she never asked, so my dad never had to answer.

My dad tried to make my grandma happy. He even converted to Judaism, got circumcised and everything; my grandma made a little tent for the sheets when he was recuperating so his sore parts would be protected. But he didn't try hard enough. My grandma is strict to begin with, and my dad wasn't used to following rules. He had a hard enough time obeying the law, let alone my grandma. He would stay out all night, and then my mom and grandma would get into terrible arguments. "He's a married man!" Gram would scream. "That's no way for a married man to behave!" So my parents moved in and out, depending on how much money they had. My mom and dad got their own place for a while, a small apartment, then moved back right before my mom had me. Over the next couple of years, they moved six times—out to Kew Gardens, back in with my grandparents, out to Forest Hills, back to Valley Stream.

Of course, I don't actually remember a lot of that, and I didn't know most of those stories until years later. But I definitely remember the Fairview. We lived on the third floor, overlooking the pool, and I shared a bedroom with my brother. I was in first grade at P.S. 220, and maybe a little precocious. I had a friend in the building, and we'd go roaming around the hallways, knocking on doors. We'd tell people we were Girl Scouts and ask for cookies. We had it backwards, Girl Scouts asking for cookies, almost like a scam. But there would always be at least one nice old lady who'd say, "Oh, how cute," and give us cookies and milk. I guess I had my dad's charm.

I don't know how long we'd lived there before my mom told me Dad was leaving. But it was about the same time he'd bought me Baby Alive, this doll that you could feed pretend baby food and her mouth would move, like she was chewing. My dad was always buying me dolls. He'd say, "Whaddya want, Princess?" and I'd say, "Barbie's swimming pool!" or something like that, and the next day or the day after, he'd bring it home. That's who my dad was to me then, a wonderful man who brought me dolls and called me Princess.

And then my mom told me he was going away. She wiped the tears from her eyes and streaks of mascara from her cheeks. She didn't want me to know how upset she was.

"For how long?" I asked.

"Just a few years," she said, like a few years was a long weekend. That was my mom, trying to make something very big sound very small. "It's just temporary," she said. "Just a temporary situation." My mom used that expression for everything bad that happened. In time, I would grow to hate those words.

I was already used to my dad being away. He'd been locked up a few times since I'd been born, once for seventeen months; my mom took me to visit him in the Nassau County jail when I was about four. And if he wasn't in jail, it wasn't unusual for him to go out one night and come back three mornings later. Still, I knew it was different this time because my mom was crying.

She hugged me and then left me alone. My mom had a lot of things on her mind that day. I looked around the apartment. The sun had just gone down, and the kitchen was dark. I wanted to visit my dad right away. I wondered how long it would be before I could wrap my arms around his neck and feel the smooth leather of his blazer or smell his Paco

Rabanne cologne lingering in the apartment after he left to go to The Suite.

GREGG: We'd be up all night, I would be, anyway, riding in the front seat to help my mother stay awake. We'd leave at eleven o'clock, sometimes even later, and drive west into Pennsylvania. It was a long ride, five and a half hours, too long to feel comfortable in a car, especially with two dogs dozing in the backseat with my little sister. We'd bring pillows and blankets with us, which made me self-conscious when we pulled into a truck stop or the Perkins House of Pancakes because if anyone saw us they might think we were homeless. I hated being poor, which we were since my father had gone to prison, and I hated even looking like we were poor.

Then the prison would rise up through the windshield, climbing above the trees like a fortress in the woods. The federal penitentiary at Lewisburg was a big beige block with a tower in the center near the front where I could see a guard with a military rifle slung over his shoulder. There were twenty-two hundred men inside, some of the worst criminals in the federal system. My father was one of them.

Eight years old, and I had to get past an armed guard to see my father.

He'd been sentenced to ten years on

November 3, 1972, but his lawyer kept him out for almost two more years with a long string of appeals. I'm not sure exactly what my mother told me he'd been convicted of, but I know it wasn't the truth. Maybe it was because we were so young, but my mother always told us that my father wasn't a *real* criminal. She usually fell back on a gambling charge if she got specific at all. "Your father did some things he shouldn't have done," is how she'd put it. "But nobody got hurt, and those bastards just kept coming after him until they convicted him of something."

The truth was, as I found out later, somebody did get hurt. His name was John Ciaccio, and he owed a gambling debt to a friend of my father, a guy who ran one of the unions at Kennedy Airport. My father, Jimmy Burke, and the union guy flew to Tampa, where Ciaccio owned a nightclub and a liquor store, and beat the shit out of him; my father, by his account, smacked him in the face a few times with a .38 revolver. Apparently, he had a thing for pistol-whipping.

The state of Florida indicted them first for kidnapping and attempted murder. They were acquitted in that case. But then federal prosecutors indicted them for extortion, which they could do because my father had crossed state lines. My mother explained it to me in pretty blunt terms, considering how old I was. "They beat the state case,

and now the feds are going after him," she said.
"Those bastards." She made it sound like the government
was picking on him over something petty.

In the late sixties and early seventies, when he
had a wife and two young kids at home, my father
was a full-time criminal. He stole, fenced, boot-
legged, loan-sharked, and extorted. I'm probably
leaving out a few things too, like arson. My father
would do almost anything to make a score. Truck
hijackings were a favorite thing for him and Uncle
Jimmy, stealing a load of goods that they could
fence below wholesale, which was all pure profit
for them. They'd get a tip from one of the guys on
the loading docks at Kennedy Airport whenever a
good load was going out, and they'd follow the
driver until he stopped at a red light. Then one of
them would stick a gun in his face. Jimmy Burke
usually tucked a fifty in the guy's shirt pocket for
his trouble; that's where he got his nickname, The
Gent. Some of the other thefts were easier:
They'd just walk into a garage and steal the truck,
or they'd buy off the driver so he'd leave his keys
in the cab when he stopped for coffee.

Stealing was second nature to my father. He'd
been running with mobsters for more than half
his life, since he was eleven years old and started
cutting school to hang out at Uncle Paulie's
cabstand in the Brownsville East section of
Brooklyn. His father, Grandpa Hill, beat him with

a belt when he found out; he was an honest man, an Irish electrician with a Sicilian wife raising eight kids—my father and his five sisters and two younger brothers—in a walk-up. But that only pushed my father closer to the men at the cabstand. He told me once that the wiseguys were the only people who were nice to him. My father had a hard time in school because he was dyslexic—he didn't learn to read until he was sent to prison, and he still can't recite the alphabet without singing that song kindergarteners learn —and he had a harder time at home because of his troubles at school. "I got smacked at home, I got smacked at school," he said later. "The guys at the cabstand, they didn't smack me. They patted me on the back, they took me in, they gave me money." I'm not making excuses for him, only trying to explain it the way he explained it to me.

So he grew up to be a gangster. And like all gangsters, he acted like he owned the world. None of them ever did, but my father did his best to rip it off. He stole everything and from everyone. He ran up huge bogus tabs at his own restaurant, The Suite, on stolen credit cards. He torched a few buildings. He ran numbers and sold bootlegged cigarettes out of his car. His greatest success, the heist that made him a minor legend in the New York underworld, was burglarizing an Air France strong room at Kennedy Airport in

1967 and walking out with $480,000. I had a few fancy birthday parties after that one—clowns, magicians, ponies, the whole thing.

The details of my father's line of work were sketchy to me when I was eight. All I knew was that my father was in trouble, and I resented him for it. The day before he went to Lewisburg, the same day my mother was telling my little sister that he was going away for a while, he went out drinking with his friends. He stayed out all night, and in the morning he hired a limousine to take him to prison. He had a better ride through the Pennsylvania farmlands than I ever did.

Our trips to Lewisburg were always miserable. Visiting hours began at eight o'clock in the morning, so we'd either leave late the night before, around ten o'clock, or early in the morning, at about three. Uncle Paulie let us use his car once, a big cream-colored Lincoln Town Car that rode like it was on a cloud. Usually, though, we were in our beat-up Oldsmobile Toronado, the car we got after my father accidentally dropped a lit cigarette in the front seat of our 1969 Chrysler Newport, causing it to go up in flames. That was still better than the Plymouth Duster with the bald tires we had to rent one time from some low-budget lot. I knew it was a bad sign when we needed to be towed up the exit ramp of the parking lot at the Howard Johnson's Motor

Lodge. On the way home in a blinding snow-storm, the wheels slipped on a curve and threw the Duster into a spin, bouncing one side off the guardrail, then whipping around so the other side smashed it too.

If I had a headache, the drive was even more unbearable. When I was five, my mother made a left turn into a gas station in Island Park in front of a drunk driver who was speeding. We got hit pretty hard, and we all got hurt pretty badly— Gina was thrown through the windshield, and I was pinned under the dashboard. The scar on my mother's face never completely healed. Ever since, I'd suffered migraines, maybe once a week or so. They'd come on fast, this stabbing, throb-bing pain right behind my eyes that would spread through my whole head. Once a migraine started, I was done for the day. I'd have to stay in a dark room with a cold compress tied around my head. The pain was so bad I'd get nauseous, couldn't keep anything down, not even aspirin. So if I got a migraine in the car, sometimes I'd have to hang my head out the window to vomit. My head hurt so bad I didn't care how I looked to anyone driving by.

And then we'd get to the prison. There would be a guard at the main entrance, an enormous black steel gate, waiting with a massive key, just like in the old movies. Beyond that was a small courtyard that led to another gate, and another guard would open that one only after the first had been locked, so for a few seconds it was like we were trapped in a cage. Then we went up a set of wide stone steps into the building, where we got in line with everyone else who had a father or a brother or a son locked up in Lewisburg.

It always took a little while to get past the guards. My sister and I had to empty our pockets, and my mother had to hand over her purse to get searched. My mother always brought a big bag jammed with all kinds of stuff. The guards made her take everything out and then they searched the bag with a baton and a miniature flashlight. I could never understand why my mother always brought so much with her. Later on, my father used to brag that he'd bought off the guards so that my mother could smuggle things in, but it didn't seem like it at the time. They poked through everything with their batons, and they glared at us, like we were the criminals instead of the men inside.

We followed a long, wide hallway after that, passing through a series of gates in the same stutter-step—through one, wait for it to clank shut behind us, then on to the next one. After the final one, there was a short set of stairs that emptied into the visiting room. It was huge, bigger than a gymnasium, and it probably had looked fancy once.

Lewisburg was built when federal prison officials thought inmates should be rehabilitated instead of simply punished. So they designed a kind of classical hall with tall windows to let in the sunlight and mosaics and murals on the walls and ceiling. They were faded by the time my father was locked up, and the room smelled like ammonia, but it wasn't quite strong enough to get rid of the must.

It was usually fairly crowded on visiting day, a lot of women, a few kids, a handful of men, all of us waiting on plastic chairs next to long tables, like in a big cafeteria. The inmates came in later, through another gate at the far end, after their visitors had been cleared through security. We'd sit there, staring across the hall, waiting for my father, and then he'd come shambling out in his prison tans. He didn't wear stripes like convicts in the movies I'd seen. He wore beige trousers and a short-sleeved shirt that showed off the tattoo on his left arm. It was from the 82nd Airborne, my father's one stint in legitimate life, a stretch in the army. "They turn you into a motherfucking killing machine," he told me once. He was drunk and reveling in the memory. "They brainwash you, strip you down so you kill on command, shove a bayonet through some cocksucker on command." He never saw combat, though, and he never talked about patriotism or serving his country. Other than the basic training, the only thing he really talked about was how cool it was to jump out of an airplane. "Craziest fucking thing I ever did," he said. "I loved it."

GINA: I was always happy when we went to Lewisburg. We didn't go every week, but pretty often, maybe every other week, at least once a month. It was a long ride, but my mom always tried to make it as much fun as she could, like we were going off for a weekend adventure. She'd pack some toys and some games, and I'd get to play with Gregg, who I adored. At that age, he didn't want much to do with me, but when it was just the two of us in the car, he didn't have a choice. And we usually stayed at a Sheraton that had an indoor pool, and there would always be other kids there who we could run around with and play hide-and-seek and pinball.

I hated getting ready to leave, though. There was always an argument. My grandma would yell at my mom. "Why are you taking them to see that gangster?" she'd say. "That's no place for children. Children don't belong in a prison. Let him rot in hell."

Those were terrible words for a little girl to hear about her dad. As far as I was concerned, my grandma didn't understand him. My mom had built him up pretty well in my mind, probably more than she had to because when you're six years old it doesn't take much to believe your dad is the best man in the world. To me, he was smarter than everyone else, which meant that everyone else—the prison guards, the police, my grandma—was wrong. I knew he got in trouble for doing things he shouldn't be doing and that's why he had to go away, but I never thought of him as a criminal. Never in a million years could Dad hurt someone or steal or kill anyone. He had a weak stomach and loved everybody. In fact, my dad saved lives. I was sure of it, because I would make my mom tell me the story over and over.

"Tell me how Dad saved that little black boy at Jones Beach," I'd say to Mom, and every time she told it, it was like hearing it for the first time.

"Your dad and I were dating and we were laying on the beach," she'd begin, "and then Dad yelled, 'That kid is drowning in the undertow!' Dad was the only one around who noticed. And he got up and ran into the water with all his clothes on and he grabbed the little boy and carried him to safety."

"Was his mother happy Dad saved him?" I would ask. And Mom would answer really loudly, "Oh my God, was she happy. She hugged and kissed Dad to pieces!" That always made me laugh.

Anyway, my dad didn't seem too upset to be in prison. I can't imagine he liked it, but he always came into the visitors' hall with a big smile on his face. He'd say, "Hi, Princess!" and he'd pick me up and I'd get to hug him and kiss him, and he'd tell me how great things were going to be when he got out, how we'd get a big house and he'd buy me a horse. That was another thing Gram didn't understand, how generous he was, which in my eyes showed what a caring person he was. He always asked me what I wanted, even then when he was in prison.

We'd stay there all day, from eight in the morning until the guards made us leave in the afternoon. I don't remember being bored, though. We could get snacks from the vending machines at one end of the hall, and I had crayons and paper to keep me busy. I drew a lot of houses. That was my specialty. All kinds of houses, but mostly little Cape Cod-style ones, and incredibly detailed, down to the little tassels on the window shades. I never drew people inside the houses, but the lights were always on in the windows behind the bushes, and I could imagine that there was a family inside sitting down to dinner or watching TV together or playing with the dog.

A psychologist would probably have a field day with that detail, a little girl obsessively drawing cozy houses. But I never felt depressed—just the opposite; I was the bubbly one in the family. Looking back, though, I can see the symptoms, starting with those drawings. When my dad went to prison, our life became a lot more difficult. We were suddenly poor, so poor that we had to move out of the Fairview and go on welfare and buy our groceries with food stamps. My mom moved us back in with my grandparents for a little while, but she fought so much with her own mother that we got an apartment in Elmont, a run-down little town on Long Island. She tried so hard, my mom did. There were only two bedrooms, and instead of putting Gregg and me in one and taking the other for herself, she slept on the couch in the living room. She never wanted us to go without anything.

Whatever anyone tells you about the Mafia taking care of their own, don't believe it. Maybe Uncle Paulie gave Mom some money, but not enough to support her and two children. Even with the welfare, she needed to go to work. She learned how to groom dogs, and I used to ride around with her at night when she was dropping off pets she'd washed and combed and clipped. I think that's where my fascination with houses started. No matter what street we were on, even driving through the city streets, I'd look up into windows and see lights on and wonder what those people were doing. It was never anything bad. In my mind, it was always normal families having normal interactions, just people living their lives. Then we'd go into these lovely homes in manicured neighborhoods at eight, nine, ten o'clock at night and deliver the dogs she'd groomed, and I'd see these nice, quiet, serene living rooms—matching furniture, clean carpets, children in their pajamas welcoming their pets home. It was so bittersweet for me because I wanted to be one of those kids in one of those houses.

Then we'd drive back to Elmont. It wasn't such a bad neighborhood, and there were a lot of kids to play with. But I used to hate going to school. I wasn't doing very well, especially in math; my mom would do my homework for me, but that didn't help me understand the numbers any better. And sometimes on a school night I would get this awful pain in my neck, like a spasm or a pulled muscle. I don't know if it was psychosomatic, but it hurt so bad I couldn't turn my head.

Gregg and I were so different like that. He loved school. He was always the smart one, the one who brought home the grades, the one who did his homework without any trouble at all. My grandma decided when he was really little, barely into elementary school, that he would grow up to be a doctor because he was the smart one in the family. He wasn't geeky or anything like that, but just one of those kids who was hungry for knowledge and for whom learning just seemed to come naturally. During those years when my dad was in Lewisburg, Gregg was fascinated with sharks. He memorized fifty different species, how their fins were different and how big each one was and how sharks could smell through their skin—quirky facts like that. He'd announce them over dinner sometimes, which

I suppose was better than talking about Dad.

But I know those years were terribly hard on him. He was always serious to begin with, very reserved, especially when it came to our dad. Like when we went to visit him and Dad would ask us what we wanted, I always had something on my list, like Barbie's Dream House. Not Gregg. He didn't have a list and never asked for anything. He would just shrug his shoulders or shake his head.

There was such a deep sadness in my brother back then. And sometimes he couldn't even hold it in. He would be sitting in his fourth-grade class and just burst out sobbing. There was no trigger, like if a bully teased him or made some smart remark about his dad being in jail or his mom being on welfare. It would just happen, like there was an awful hurt that he buried way down deep where it would bubble and build and finally explode and come pouring out. It was so embarrassing for him. He went to counseling for a little while, and I think the school even put him in the slow-learner class for a time, which was even more humiliating considering he'd always gotten straight A's. It broke my heart, all of it, knowing how sad he was. I couldn't understand why he was like that, why he couldn't see any hope.

GREGG: I always hated those trips to Lewisburg. I can't say I ever missed my father, but it was still nice to see him, at least in those first few moments when he came out smiling. I'd hug him, and it was sincere. I mean, for as hard as things were for the rest of us, for my mother and my sister and me, he was still my father.

But that feeling was fleeting. The moment would pass, and I'd suddenly feel tired from the drive and I'd pull away and look around and remember I was in a prison because my father was a criminal. And the rest of the visit would be either uncomfortable or incredibly boring. We never had any serious talks, real father-and-son stuff. It was all superficial. "Hey, I hear you're doing well in school," he'd say, which was meaningless because I'd always done well in school. Or he'd joke around a little. "Do I have to come out and toughen you up?" he'd say, things like that. And then he'd try to buy me off. That's how I used to hear it. "Whaddya want? Whaddya want?"

That always drove me nuts, triggered a quiet rage. We're living on welfare, my mother's working herself to the bone grooming dogs, we drive half the night to a prison to see my father, and all he wants to know is what toy he can get me, like one big gift is going to make it all better. And it's not. Nothing's going to make it all better. What I really wanted was a father. Or maybe I wanted my mother to leave him, to stop visiting him in prison so we could move on with our lives. It was his mistake, his fuckup, that created all these problems, that made her work so hard, that made us rely on food stamps to eat, that got the electricity shut off because there wasn't enough money to pay the bill. I didn't know how to say that then, but I knew having a normal father would have been better than any present.

(Okay, one time I asked for something. He was so damned persistent about it—"C'mon, I'll get you something fun"—that I broke down and told him I wanted a minibike. We were spending a lot of time at my grandparents' house, and a kid in their neighborhood had one. It was a sort of kid's motorcycle, short and squat with fat tires and a two-stroke engine, like a lawn mower engine. I never got it. I never asked for anything else.)

There wasn't much to do after that. Sometimes he would introduce us to other inmates, guys with names like John the Beetle. Usually there'd be someone there selling Polaroid portraits, and we might pose for one of those. My mother would have us dressed in nice clothes, and we'd smile into the flash, but it's not like I could show them to my friends. ("Where was *that* picture taken? Why is your dad dressed like that?") If I got hungry, there were some vending machines along one wall that sold crappy sandwiches, slimy ham and stiff cheese on stale white bread, and pop-top cans of Chef Boyardee that you could eat cold. Mostly, though, I just sat there. Silently.

I guess my father *had* bought off the guards because I know my mother was smuggling things into the prison. For the first year or so, she'd stop at a Perkins pancake house on the way to Lewisburg and go off into the bathroom and stuff her poncho with meats and olive oil and liquor that the guards must have overlooked on purpose. After my father had been locked up for a while, he got transferred to the minimum-security farm next door and my mother got into serious smuggling. At the end of the first day of our visit, once we'd left the visiting hall, my mother would go back to the hotel to pick up duffel bags full of meats and cheeses and booze— Scotch, vodka, gin—and God knows what else that we'd brought with us. Then she'd drive out to an empty country road at nightfall and pull up next to what looked like an abandoned school at the bottom of a small hill. We'd wait for a few minutes. Then my father and a couple of other guys would come running down the hill. They were wearing dark sweat suits, like tennis suits; it reminded me of the opening sequence to *S.W.A.T.,* this television show I used to watch. They'd get to the car, my father would kiss my mother and me, they'd grab the bags, and then hustle back up the hill.

I was always uncomfortable, which I suppose a ten-year-old boy should be when his mother is smuggling contraband into a federal penal institution. My mother and father, though, they acted like it was the most normal thing in the world, not much different from picking up the dry cleaning. Worse, much worse for me, was when my mother snuck booze into the visiting hall. During one of those visits, she pulled a small plastic flask out from somewhere, and I saw my father pour a crystal-clear liquid into a cup. My stomach knotted up. I knew it was vodka, and I knew he was going to get drunk, and probably pretty quickly. And then there was no telling what he'd do.

My father was a big drinker with a ridiculously low tolerance and, more often than not, a nasty drunk. By the time I was eight, I'd been embarrassed by him in public more times than I could count. If we went out to dinner, he'd start drinking right away, and the drunker he got, the louder he got, and the louder he got, the more rude and offensive he got. It wasn't just dinner, either. No place was safe if my father got hold of some Smirnoff. And the worst thing anyone could do was tell him to slow down or keep quiet. Then he just got mean.

I knew he was going to get mean in the visiting room. I could sense it, see it coming as clearly as I saw him holding his cup. That was another part of the frustration: My father never seemed to realize that he was locked up, that he was being punished for breaking the law, that he was making life miserable for my mother and Gina and me. He was partying, laughing and making promises he wouldn't keep and getting drunk on smuggled liquor. If my mother ever challenged him on it, if she even hinted that she was having trouble paying the bills or was worn out from working so hard, he'd get self-righteous, jump all over her. "Quit breaking my fucking balls," I heard him snap at her once. "I'm the one who's in fucking prison."

Maybe he was drunk then too. All those times blur together. They were sitting at one of the long tables, my mother and father, talking in low, hushed voices, my father knocking back the vodka. I couldn't hear what they were saying, but I noticed my father's voice getting louder, more belligerent. A few minutes would pass and I'd hear it again, a surly word, an extra curse, the volume notching up a couple degrees.

"Henry, keep it down," my mother said. It was a stage whisper, a bit stern, as if she was trying to get his attention and shut him up at the same time. "Not so loud."

He looked at her for a moment, like he was surprised. He knocked back the last of his vodka and slammed the cup on the table. It made a hollow, plastic, plinking sound. He drew a breath, gathered steam. Then he let it out.

"I am a man!" he hollered.

The visiting hall at Lewisburg was a fairly loud place, voices echoing off stone walls and steel bars. But at that moment it got quiet, everyone else suddenly lowering their voices. My father popped off again.

"I'm a motherfucking man," he yelled again. "You got that? A motherfucking *man*."

It takes a lot to embarrass a kid in prison. Every other adult there was either a criminal, related to a criminal, or friendly enough with a criminal to drive to rural Pennsylvania to see him. The threshold for humiliation in Lewisburg was set pretty high. Yet my father met it. He crossed it, leapt clear over it with room to spare. And that was early on. For four years we drove back and forth to Lewisburg, my mother promising the whole time that it was just temporary, that we'd get through it and that everything would be fine. It never was, though.

GINA: Somehow or another my dad convinced the prison officials that he was a model inmate. Despite all the rules he was breaking, he was moved to the minimum-security farm next to Lewisburg only about a year after he was locked up, and then he was transferred to Allenwood, a federal prison where he was able to get all kinds of furloughs, and then, in the summer of 1978, to a halfway house in Manhattan. Maybe he did bribe all the guards.

I wouldn't have cared if he did. He was almost all the way home, almost back with us. "Oh my gosh," my mother used to tell me, "things are going to be so wonderful when Daddy comes home." We were going to get a house, and the four of us would live there together and maybe we would even dress up for dinner sometimes, like a normal family.

Dad started moving and shaking as soon as he moved into the halfway house. That's what we called it, moving and shaking, my dad making deals, concocting schemes, wangling. He got paroled on July 12, 1978, partly because Uncle Paulie arranged for him to have a job managing a nightclub for $225 a week. He didn't work at it, though, just like he was never a bricklayer. It was a no-show thing, kind of like the club owner doing a favor for Uncle Paulie and my dad. That made it look like he had a legitimate job so he could go to work making money his way.

Two days after he was released, my dad bribed a staffer at the halfway house and flew to Pittsburgh —a violation of his parole right there—to see a man named Paul Mazzei who owed him some money. Only Mazzei didn't have the money, so he gave my dad two suitcases full of marijuana instead. He was afraid to fly home with it, so my dad took a bus all the way from Pittsburgh, getting off at every stop to watch the luggage compartment and make sure no one walked off with his bags.

That's how my dad got into the drug business. After he sold the pot, he got some more, and then he started dealing cocaine too. "I needed some operating money," he said later, "and I didn't want to get a gun, so that seemed like the easiest way."

I didn't know any of that, of course. All I cared

about was that he was home and we had money again. Mom and Dad found a house for us right away in Rockville Centre. It wasn't in the best part of town, more of a working-class neighborhood, but Dad had it fixed up so it was the nicest house on the street. I always thought so, anyway. He had the front refaced with new bricks and he put an above-ground swimming pool in the backyard and he replaced all the musty old carpets inside with new shag and took down the crucifixes that the last old lady who lived there had hung in every room and gave the whole place a new coat of paint.

My room was in the front. It was small, but it was everything I wanted. The brown paneling on the walls was painted white to match the furniture, which was French provincial. There was a desk in one corner and a dresser and a bookcase and, my favorite, a four-poster bed with an apple-green canopy. It was beautiful furniture to begin with, but I loved it even more because I inherited it from my Aunt Ellen, who's my mother's youngest sister. I adored Ellen. She was still a teenager, so it was almost like she was my older sister instead of an aunt. I'd always thought of myself as a grown-up girl, and Ellen treated me like one. She'd give me advice about fashion—Ellen was very stylish—and she'd show me how to put on makeup and then let me wear it for a while instead of making me wipe it all off right away.

Of course, I had all my little-girl things too, my dolls and stuffed Snoopys and all the Ziggy and Muppet things I collected. On one shelf was a one-of-a-kind baby doll from France that came in her own handwoven basket. I'd named her Kimberly, though I have no idea why, and she cost $107 at FAO Schwartz. My dad bought her for me on my tenth birthday, in 1978, which I remember so vividly because it was wonderful and terrible at the same time.

He was still in the halfway house then, but he was determined to make my birthday special, probably because it was the first one he'd been around for since I was six. Weeks before, he promised he'd take me to the big FAO Schwartz store in New York City, where I could pick out anything, anything at all, and he'd buy it for me. He said I could bring my friend Carol Ann, and, after the toy store, he'd take us all out to dinner in Manhattan. As I counted the days, I built it up in my head as this amazing adventure where I'd be treated like the princess my dad always said I was.

When my birthday finally came, I put on my nicest dress and got in the car with my father and mother and Carol Ann. I'd forgotten how uncomfortable my dad's driving made me, even as a little girl. He liked to hold a beer and a cigarette in his left hand, both of them, so if he did anything else, like light another cigarette or fiddle with the radio, he'd have to use his right hand, which meant he would steer with his knee. If he was a normal driver, that might not have been too bad. But he wasn't. My dad was very impatient, always rushed, like there was always something he was late for. He sped through residential streets and would weave through traffic, and if I got scared, if I said, "Dad, slow down," he'd laugh and speed up instead.

He was still in a hurry when we got to FAO Schwartz. He double-parked on Madison Avenue, told my mother to wait in the car, and led me and Carol Ann into the store.

"Okay, Princess," he said. "Pick out anything you want."

I looked one way. I looked another way, then another. The shelves climbed all the way to the ceiling. I was overwhelmed. You have to understand, to a little girl from Long Island on her tenth birthday, that place was like the Emerald City, some fabled, fantastical wonderland. There were three whole floors of toys, every toy you could imagine, giant stuffed elephants and camels and St. Bernards, cities built out of Lego, board games and roller skates, shelf after shelf after shelf of dolls. There were pinks and blues and creams and bright silvers, soft things and shiny things and furry things, and that silly song—*welcome to our world, welcome to our world, welcome to our world of toys*—tinkling in the background. It took a few minutes for all my senses to adjust, like when your eyes need a moment or two to get used to a sudden light, and only then could I really start to explore. I could have spent my whole birthday wandering around in there, and maybe the next day too.

"C'mon," Dad said. "Pick something. Do you want a doll? You like dolls, right?"

I nodded. I was speechless, and I was also partially paralyzed. I didn't know where to start, which wall or aisle or even floor to begin my search. Carol Ann was standing next to me staring at her shoes, not saying anything. She was a timid little girl to begin with, very quiet and shy. I always felt bad for her because her mother was an alcoholic hooker with bleached hair and gold lamé outfits and a round bed in her apartment. Carol Ann's mom had her good side—we lived with her for a summer when my father was in Lewisburg, which is how I know so much about her—but when she got drunk, she would practically terrorize poor Carol Ann. And now my dad's impatience was making her nervous.

"Princess, let's go," he said. "C'mon, what do you want? Pick something."

I saw a giant dollhouse, one so big that I could play in it. It was beautiful and incredibly expensive, a couple thousand dollars. My dad immediately shook his head. I looked around some more until I found a miniature car, one of those battery-operated ones that kids can drive. I loved driving. When I went out with my mom, she would let me steer. I'd kneel on the seat next to her and she'd wrap her right arm around me to hold me in place and I'd take the wheel. Her hands were close enough that she could grab it back if something happened, but she never had to; I was a good steerer.

Dad shook his head again. "No, not that," he said. "C'mon, don't you want a doll?"

I bobbed my chin up and down again. Now I was getting uneasy too.

"Princess, I've got things to do. Just pick something."

I knew I was going to cry. I could feel my stomach churning and my face was hot and I couldn't swallow the lump in my throat. My dad's face got blurry through the tears in my eyes.

I ran outside, embarrassed and frustrated and sobbing. Mom saw me coming. She flung open the car door and leapt onto the sidewalk, waiting for her daughter crying on her birthday. I thought she'd hug me. She grabbed my arm instead, though not hard. "C'mon, Gina, go back inside," she said. By now a police officer had noticed the double-parked car and was waving her along. It seemed like every time I went anywhere with my parents we were double-parked and rushed. "C'mon, I've got to go. They want me to move the car now. I'll circle the block," she said. "Now go inside. Your dad went to

a lot of trouble for this, so you get back in there and
pick something out."

I think I was too stunned to keep crying. I wiped
my cheeks and trudged back into the store. My dad
was waiting next to a shelf full of dolls. Carol Ann
had already picked out a Barbie, and I pointed at
one on the top shelf, Kimberly. The saleswoman
took it down and handed it to me.

"Do you like it?" Dad said.

I could have been holding a cantaloupe at that
point and I would have said I liked it. But I really did
love that doll.

GREGG: I didn't like Gina very much when we
were kids. I thought she was selfish and spoiled.
She'd cut corners, she'd have my mother do her
homework. Sure, she had more faith in our family
unit, such as it was, but she also had to be at the
center of everything. When we were very young,
when she was still a toddler, Jimmy Burke used to
put an unlit cigarette in her mouth. He thought it
was funny, a tiny girl with a smoke. Then the
adults, whoever was there, would start laughing
and saying how cute she was, and Gina would
giggle and sort of wiggle, like she was dancing. A
few years later, she was doing the same kind of
things. When Uncle Jimmy got mad, his eyes
would twitch into a half squint and turn to ice,
hard and cold. My sister used to imitate him. "Do

your crazy Jimmy eyes," one of my father's friends would say, and Gina would twist her face up until her eyes got weird and all the grown-ups would laugh.

I was much more serious, much more independent. I don't know where I learned that, or if it was even learned behavior. It came naturally. Sometimes I think it was almost instinct, like my psyche was programmed to react to my father's craziness by creating my own stability. All I ever wanted was a normal, reliable family, one where the father went to work every day and paid the bills and came to my track meets and tennis matches—basically, a father I could depend on. I never had that, and I knew never to expect it. The only lesson my father ever taught me, the only one that really mattered, even when I was just a boy, was not to depend on anyone else.

It wasn't because he spent so much time locked up, either. In a strange way, his being in prison was easier to reconcile: When I didn't see him in the bleachers, at least I knew it was because he was doing ten years in Lewisburg. If he wasn't in jail, I never knew where he was—only that he wasn't with me.

When I was seven years old, he took me to get a haircut at a salon called For Men Only on Queens Boulevard, right next to The Suite. His friend Marty Krugman, an animated, bug-eyed man with thick glasses and a bad wig, owned it. Like my father, Marty was connected: He took bets in the back room, and he was a regular at The Suite, where my father's criminal friends hung out. I know my father liked him a lot because every time we went over to the Krugmans' house, he would give Marty a big hug. I guess I liked him all right too.

My father pulled to the curb in a red Triumph TR6 he was wheeling around in that week. As I got out of the car, he said to me, "I'll be back in a half hour. Go inside, have one of the girls give you a haircut, and meet me back here in a half hour. Got that?"

"Got it," I said. It wasn't a difficult set of instructions: Get a haircut, come outside, get back in the car.

Thirty minutes later I was back on the curb, right where I was supposed to be. Queens Boulevard is ten lanes wide, more like a highway with traffic lights than a city street, and both sides are lined with buildings five and six stories tall. I wasn't a skittish kid, but that could still be an intimidating stretch of the borough, especially at rush hour in the early winter when the air is cold and the wind is blowing and your neck itches from a fresh haircut.

My father wasn't there. I looked up the block. No red Triumph. I looked down the block.

Nothing. An hour passed, then another. The street-lights came on. I knew he wasn't coming. I could have walked home. I could have gone into The Suite to get warm, maybe even pull him off a bar stool. I didn't want to let the bastard off the hook.

So I waited there, just like he'd told me to, scuffing my feet on the sidewalk, rattling the parking meters, shivering in the cold. Fathers and sons are supposed to have a protocol: The father tells the son what to do, the son obeys the rules, the father follows through. Parenthood 101. I wasn't giving him a free pass. He was going to pick me up, or I'd die waiting, just to spite him.

Long shadows spread across the pavement. The cars, barely more than pairs of headlights, seemed to move faster against the night background. Another hour. The temperature must have dropped ten degrees. I shivered, wiped my nose, cursed my father.

Four hours, then five. From the corner of my eye, I could see regulars at The Suite stopping at the door and giving me a curious look before they went in. Every so often, a head would pop up in the window and twist, checking to see if I was still there. Finally, after almost six hours on windswept Queens Boulevard, one of the guys who hung out there—I can't remember his name, but I knew his face—came out.

"Hey," he said. "You're Henry's kid, ain'tcha?"

I glared at him, mostly because my cheeks were too numb to smile, and nodded.

"C'mon, kid," he said. "I'll give you a ride home."

I thought about it for an instant, weighing the satisfaction of holding my father accountable against how goddamned cold I was. The cold won. I knew that even if I'd stayed there all night, if I'd curled up and died and they found me in the morning like a prepubescent Popsicle, my father would shrug. "What is he, a fuckin' moron?" he'd say. "He didn't know enough to get out of the fucking cold? What an asshole." He wasn't a man who felt a lot of guilt about anything.

What's astonishing about that memory is how typical it was. I don't think he remembered, and I never mentioned it to him. It almost would have seemed petty because the odds of my father being where he said he'd be were, on a good day, less than fifty-fifty. That afternoon when we got hit by the drunk driver and an ambulance had to haul us all to the hospital, the nurses couldn't find my father, either. His whole family was nearly killed— in fact, my grandmother came to the hospital expecting to find us all dead from the description the police had given her—and he didn't show up for two days. My mother told me later that he was squirreled away in a hotel room with some floozy. She used words like that, *floozy*.

Having him around wasn't much better anyway. My father is the single most irresponsible and uncaring person I've ever known. Everything was a scam to him, everything a racket. Nothing was paid for with honest money, if it was paid for at all, and nothing was done by the rules. The Triumph he was driving that day was one in a long line of temporary rides, none of which he ever owned. "Some guy owes me money," he told me the first time he took me for a ride in it. "So this is, you know, like a down payment. Usually, when I take their car, they find a way to pay me." He once had a boat, a red cabin cruiser that lasted about a week. We went out on it one afternoon, me figuring I'd learn how to operate it so I could take it out fishing when I got a little older. My father had a beer and a cigarette in his left hand, gunned the throttle with his right, and slashed through Long Island Sound like a bootlegger. He crossed wakes, he swamped other boats, he ignored the channel buoys, and if anyone complained, he screamed, "Fuck you" and laughed. He raced around until there was this awful, scraping shudder just off the shore. He'd run it aground, hard, and we had to wait until the tide came in and lifted us clear. A few days later he came in the kitchen door shaking his head. "Fucking boat sank," he said. "Right at the dock. What a piece of shit." He seemed surprised.

That was his attitude toward everything and

everyone. He didn't give a shit. He went through life without a care, which sounds like a great way to live, and maybe it is—unless you're related to him. I mean, I wore braces for five years because my father kept stiffing the orthodontists, three of them, one after the other. I had to start over with each one. I never understood why we couldn't just pay the bill and be done with it.

By the time he came home from Lewisburg, I knew the only stability I would have would be what I created for myself. I was pretty adept at it already. From the outside, I probably looked like a normal kid: I played stickball and roller hockey with my friends, I had clean clothes and enough to eat, I did well in school, I kept my room neat and organized. But it felt like I was raising myself most of the time, that I was the adult. My grandmother was pretty strict with me, and one of my aunt's boyfriends, a muscle-bound guy named John who worked as a bouncer to put himself through college at Stony Brook, was like a big brother to me. Other than that, though, I was on my own. Given my options, I preferred it that way.

So that's why I never asked for anything all those times my father tried to buy me off. If he brought something home, unsolicited, it was always bittersweet. Finding a new fishing rod in my room was a great thing, but it made it hard to resent my father for that particular day, almost like it was delaying the inevitable.

If I really wanted something, I'd save my money and buy it myself. I'd always worked, starting when I was seven years old busing tables at The Suite. Because I was Henry's kid—no one in there called me Gregg; I was always "Henry's Kid"—I made some decent tips from the wiseguys, crisp twenties, sometimes even a fifty. They'd stick them in my shirt pocket. On a good weekend, I could walk out with $150, maybe $200 in cash, money I'd earned myself.

Yet even that wasn't safe. Every couple of weeks my father would grab me at home in the morning. "How much ya got?" he'd say. I was a fool most of the time and told him the truth. And he'd always say the same thing: "Great. Give it to me and I'll take care of you later."

He never once paid me back, and he would have gotten indignant if I'd asked. Eventually, I just tried to avoid him the morning after a good night.

GINA: I guess we were never what other people would call a normal family, but I convinced myself that we at least looked like one. I took skating lessons and Gregg took tennis lessons and we both went to Hebrew school and Gregg got ready for his bar mitzvah. My dad had started his own company, a legitimate silk-screening business that he ran out of the garage with one of my aunts and a pretty blonde named Amy Mulry. She was the artist of the company, and I used to watch her draw the designs that would be screened onto the shirts. I thought she was really talented. I didn't know then that she was sleeping with half of New York, including my dad, or that she was my dad's drug courier.

If we were different in any obvious way it was because we seemed to have more material things than most of the other kids we knew. There was the pool, an above-ground one but a pool nonetheless, in the backyard. In the living room a new Betamax sat next to a big color television, and my dad would bring home tapes of movies that were still playing in the theaters. (It didn't last, though: My parents put a lit candle on top of it one night and the wax melted and dripped inside the machine and ruined it.) I always had a few dollars to take to the corner store, and any toy I wanted I usually got. One afternoon, Dad bought roller skates for every kid on the block who wanted them.

It was just like my mother had promised during all those years of living in low-rent apartments and eating dinners bought with food stamps. She'd been right all along, just like I knew she'd be because she was my mother and I trusted her. My dad was home, and in my resilient ten-year-old mind, it *was* wonderful. And all the parts that weren't, all the times that were uncomfortable or scary, those were just temporary situations, things that I just had to get through before life would be normal again.

There were a lot of those times too. My dad would come home beaten up sometimes after he'd gotten into a bar brawl. And my mom and dad used to have terrible fights, really awful, violent battles. One time my mom thought she'd lost a ring my father had given her—a twenty-carat Burma ruby surrounded by quarter-carat diamonds. We hunted all over the house for it. A friend of the family, this gay hairdresser named Scott, helped us look for it, but we never found it. A few days later Dad found out—or just assumed, because I don't know if it was true—that Scott had actually stolen the ring and broken it up and sold the stones. So when Dad came home one afternoon, probably a little drunk, and found Scott in the kitchen with my mom, he exploded. He screamed at Scott, called him a faggot and cocksucker and motherfucking thief, and started pushing and slapping him. Then he took off one of his shoes and started beating Scott with it.

First I was horrified that my father could do that to another person, and then I was horrified that Scott wasn't fighting back. He was just taking it and crying like a little girl. My mother was trying to defend him, yelling at my dad to stop, but that didn't help. Dad just got mad at her. He grabbed this antique phone off the counter and bashed my mom in the head with it. Then he chased Scott into the bedroom and beat him some more.

Mom was bleeding and screaming, Scott was squealing and whimpering, Dad was yelling all sorts of obscenities—I was terrified. I did the only thing I could think of, which was call my grandmother. I knew that would create even more problems because Gram didn't like my father. But I didn't know what else to do. I was crying hysterically and begged my grandma to call the police. She did, and a squad car pulled up to the house a few minutes later. By then, though, my dad was finished beating Scott, and my mother had stopped crying. She sent the police away. And then everything went back to normal, almost like nothing strange had ever happened.

More than the fighting, though, I remember the parties. There were always people at our house drinking and getting high and having sex. Everything was out in the open. My dad had a friend named Paul Stephens who produced porno movies, and he came over one summer day with his wife and a couple of his starlets for a pool party. It was a Saturday afternoon, and it began like any other normal party with music and dancing and drinking and drugs. But then one of the actresses— is that what you call a woman in a porno movie?— took off her top. It was like she'd broken the ice, because then the other women dropped their tops, first the actresses and then friends of my dad and friends of Ellen, people I knew. "Hey, Paul," they were saying, "what do you think of these?" Almost like they were auditioning. They were splashing in the pool and prancing around the kitchen and flopping down the hall to the bathroom. It was like a battlefield—everywhere I turned there were tits flying up in my face.

That wasn't unusual at all. Weekends were two-day parties at our house. People had orgies in my parents' pink bedroom, and couples would have sex on the foldout couch, right in the living room. My baby-sitters would be there having sex with men they'd just met. One time I was in the kitchen and I overheard two women talking about how big John's cock was. John was Ellen's boyfriend—how would they know how big his cock was? I was blushing, so embarrassed, but I couldn't stop listening. They finally stopped when they saw me, and I retreated to my bedroom. I think they were embarrassed too because they followed me a little while later and started asking me about my Barbies, like they'd remembered I was only ten years old and shouldn't be hearing about cocks.

I'd try to get away, either go play outside or in my room. But there was no escaping it. The parties went on all day and all night. If I woke up in the middle of the night and had to go to the bathroom, I would walk past the living room and see people smoking joints and snorting lines of cocaine. Farther down the hall, I'd pass my parents' bedroom and I'd hear people inside having sex, and if they happened to open the door when I was nearby, a giant cloud of sweet smoke would come rushing out. Some mornings my Miss Piggy mirror would be missing from the wall above my dresser. I'd usually find it on the table in the living room with traces of white dust on it. I never said anything about it, and eventually it would go back up on my wall.

And that, I guess, is how I coped with things: I simply waited for the mirror to go back on the wall, so to speak. A lot of things that went on in our house made me uneasy—I always had an innate sense that I should never bring my friends over, even though no one ever told me I couldn't—but I knew the uneasiness would pass. I would say to myself, "Okay, this is making me uncomfortable, so I'm going to do something that makes me comfortable. And in the morning it will all go back to normal. I'll be able to do what I want and my mother won't act like that and my father won't be that way."

GREGG: I was never afraid of my father's friends. If anyone ever scared me, it was my father—not because I thought he'd do anything intentionally to hurt me, but that his belligerence would get us into some kind of trouble. Like if we'd be driving to visit Stacks Edwards in Harlem on a summer day with the windows rolled down. Stacks was a big black man who hung out at The Suite, a really nice guy whom I liked a lot. But on the way, my father would start talking loudly about "these fuckin' niggers." I'd say, "Dad, shut up." He'd just laugh. "Are you fucking out of your mind?" he'd say. "These fucking niggers aren't going to touch us." Then if some black guys looked over, he would slow down and stare back at them. "Daaaad! Just go," I'd say.

It was weird because, for all his many flaws, my father wasn't a racist. He was just crazy. I'd sit on the edge of my seat hoping no one close to the car could hear him. But he didn't give a shit. He didn't give a shit about anything. Like the time we were out with one of his drug-dealing friends, Paul Mazzei, walking down Central Park South after dinner at a fancy restaurant. He stopped in front of the St. Moritz, unzipped his fly, and started peeing. He didn't go down an alley or anything—he just pissed right on the building. The bellman started yelling at him and tried to push him away, but Mazzei got to him before he reached my father. "C'mon, Dad, hurry up," I yelled at him, but he just kept going, splashing on the building. It was humiliating, even if he didn't get arrested.

As for his friends, though, most of them were

real nice guys, at least to my sister and me. I never knew them as criminals, not really. They were the guys who gave me the fat tips at The Suite, the sharply dressed men who always took a minute to say hello to Henry's Kid. One guy, a big, burly man who I found out later was a hit man, went out of his way to give me pointers about lifting weights. They could even be caring, or seem to be. When my sister joined Weight Watchers—she was chubby when she was little—Uncle Jimmy gave her a very solemn nod. "That's good," he told her. "You stay with it. Losing weight's hard."

I wasn't naive, though. I realized these were, on some level, bad guys. I didn't know the extent of their criminality—I was surprised when I found out years later that Billy Arico, the bug exterminator from Valley Stream, was a hit man—but I knew they were on the fringes, making deals that weren't quite legitimate. And I knew that some of them wouldn't hesitate to use violence, or the threat of it, to get what they wanted. I learned early that my father and his friends were not to be messed with, when I was maybe six years old and we went to Miami Beach with Uncle Jimmy and his family for a short vacation. We were staying at the Castaway Hotel, a resort with a Polynesian theme, and on one of the first nights Jimmy made a seven o'clock dinner reservation for all ten of us—our family, Jimmy, his wife Mickey, his two girls, and his sons, Frank and Jesse, whom he named after the James Gang outlaws.

At seven on the dot, we went into the restaurant. "Roberts, party of ten," Uncle Jimmy told the maître d'. Roberts was one of the lounges where my father and his wiseguy friends hung out. Jimmy liked using the name when he traveled.

"Yes, sir," the maître d' said. He was in a tuxedo, standing behind a small podium. He ran his finger down a page in his book. "That'll be about ten to fifteen minutes."

"No," Jimmy said. "I reserved for seven o'clock. It's seven o'clock."

"Yes, sir." He gave Jimmy one of those patronizing smiles. "Just a few minutes."

"No minutes. We want to sit down now."

"Yes, if you'll—"

Uncle Jimmy cut him off. "That the phone I called you on?" He nodded at the podium. He didn't wait for the guy to answer. In one quick motion, he grabbed the handset with his right hand and the guy's head with his left. Then he wrapped the cord around the maître d's neck, tugged it tight, gave it an extra twist. "I said now, you cocksucker." Uncle Jimmy didn't yell; his voice was almost calm. "You got that? I said now."

The maître d' nodded up at Jimmy. He let him go as quickly as he'd grabbed him. No one screamed; no one called security. Except for the maître d', who was a bit pale, no one even seemed to have noticed that anything odd had happened. And the guy did exactly what Jimmy wanted: He led us to our table as soon as the phone was back on the hook.

I took my cues from everyone else. If I felt any discomfort, it dissipated as soon as we sat down and Uncle Jimmy cracked a joke and everyone was laughing again and having a good time, like any two families on a Florida vacation. If that moment taught me anything, it was that my father and his friends could get what they wanted, when they wanted it.

There were undeniable perks to my father's lifestyle, especially for a teenaged boy. I'd be lying if I said I didn't enjoy some of the benefits of growing up the son of a wiseguy. My Aunt Ellen's boyfriend, John, would take me to this nightclub called Detroit where he worked the door, and I'd sit at the bar drinking screwdrivers and listening to a Led Zeppelin cover band. How many thirteen-year-olds get away with that? And everyone at the club knew who I was, who my father was, who his friends were; reflected power, even dimly reflected onto a tipsy boy, is still intoxicating.

There were other things too, always brief and fleeting, but cool anyway. I saw the Yankees play the Dodgers in the 1978 World Series from box seats, all three home games. I got cartons of fireworks. I fired an Ingram Mac-10 submachine gun in our basement in Rockville Centre, which was awesome because I was a gun nut. I'm not sure where that fascination started, but after I'd memorized all those species of shark, I moved on to firearms. I told my mother the only thing I wanted for my twelfth birthday was *Small Arms of the World*, a nine-hundred-page encyclopedia of pistols and rifles and machine guns, and I was probably the only adolescent subscriber to *Guns & Ammo*. I knew makes and models and calibers the way other kids knew ERAs and RBIs.

My father would bring home guns every now and again, usually pistols still new in the box and usually stolen and waiting to be sold, and I'd poke through them, pick out the ones I recognized, hold them just to feel the weight. We would sit in the living room together, me and my father, ogling guns. There were always a lot of Smith & Wesson revolvers and nine millimeter semi-automatics and, in one shipment, a .44 Magnum Model 29, the one Clint Eastwood carried in the Dirty Harry movies, a huge, heavy gun. More like a cannon.

The Ingram submachine gun was in the same shipment. It was in my *Small Arms of the World*, so I recognized it instantly. This one was a .45 caliber. There was a silencer with it too, about a foot and a half long and two inches in diameter, and several twenty-round clips. An impressive weapon. "We'll shoot it sometime," my father promised me.

I figured we'd take it out to a farm or go somewhere upstate. But a few days later, right around dinnertime, he cranked up the stereo in the living room and carried the Ingram through the kitchen. "C'mon," he said. "Let's go downstairs."

I followed him to the basement, which was finished into a rec room. He stacked a half-dozen phone books on the floor. He raised the gun, pointed it straight down into the books, and squeezed the trigger.

It was loud. Even with a silencer, it was like a firecracker going off, much louder than the *pffft* I'd heard in the movies. My ears were still ringing when he handed it to me. I checked to make sure it wasn't switched to fully automatic (which would have sent a stream of bullets out of the barrel with a single pull on the trigger, instead of semi-auto, which fired a single shot) and aimed the same way, directly into the books. I squeezed the trigger and fired one shot. Another bang. There was almost no kick; firing it downward masked the recoil. I fired another round. "This," I told myself, "is *really* cool."

My mother came barreling down the stairs before we could get another round off. She was screaming. "Henry! Henry? Are you shooting a gun? Not in the house! What the hell is the matter with you? Are you insane?" I suppose we were, shooting a submachine gun inside a house a block and a half from the police station. But I dug the slugs out of the phone books as a souvenir.

Yet I was never drawn to the wiseguy life. It just wasn't in my gut. I always thought I'd be a doctor or a marine biologist, but I rationalized that I would have the best of both worlds: a normal, stable life that I would build for myself and then another side where I would have connections. No one would fuck with me, and I would get things that other people never could all because I was Henry's Kid. If I had to do an occasional favor for someone, well, that wouldn't be so bad. After all, we were all like family. In the fantasy, if you can call it that, I would be the honest one they would turn to, someone they respected. But I could never be one of them. I cared too much about everything, especially my freedom.

A part of me knew that scenario was a long shot, though, a fool's dream. For one thing, I'd figured out that what my father did wasn't particularly smart. All those guys went to prison; literally all of my father's friends, at one point or another, got locked up. And whatever romance there might be in the Mob life fades as soon as your father goes to prison and your mother starts grooming other people's pets and collecting welfare and food stamps to feed her kids. Any illusions I ever might have had of becoming a wiseguy were shattered by those years my father spent in Lewisburg.

GINA: Uncle Jimmy never came to the parties. In fact, by early 1979, Jimmy stopped coming to our house at all, and we didn't go to his either. When we were younger, I loved going over there. His youngest son, Jesse, had a mountain of toys in the finished basement, every kind of toy anyone could think of, boys' toys and girls' toys too. While the adults were upstairs, Gregg and I would tromp down to the basement with Jesse to raid his toy pile. He was a funny little kid. He swore like a sailor, just like his father and my father, but he had a bad lisp so his curses sounded silly. *Muthafucking cockthucking ath-hole!*

I asked my mother why Jimmy didn't come over anymore. "Oh, it's not good for him to come over here," she told me. "It's too dangerous. It's not good for your dad and Uncle Jimmy to be seen together." She said it matter-of-factly, the same way she would tell me what was for dinner. And I just accepted that answer, like I knew what she was talking about.

I didn't, though. I didn't know that a felon on parole like my dad couldn't associate with another felon, which would have been reason enough for him to stay away from Jimmy. But there were other things happening too, horrible and terrifying things that I would have been too young to understand. Even now, the truth of it scares me, knowing just how dangerous our world had become.

Early on the morning of December 11, 1978, six or seven masked men—the witnesses were never sure—broke into the Lufthansa cargo building at Kennedy International Airport. They had shotguns and pistols, and they tied up the guards. Then they cleaned the place out, $5 million in cash and $800,000 in jewelry, which they loaded into a black Ford van. It was the largest robbery in U.S. history, and they got away clean.

The case would never be solved, but FBI agents and police detectives, who all had snitches on the street, had a pretty good idea who was behind it almost immediately. My dad knew for sure: Uncle Jimmy.

It started with a cargo agent at Lufthansa named Lou Werner, who was a big gambler. He got a tip that the warehouse would be easy to rob, so he told his bookie, who in turn introduced Werner to my dad's friend Marty Krugman. Marty told my dad about the idea and said he wanted to talk to Jimmy about it. My dad didn't think that was a good idea. He knew Jimmy didn't like Marty because Marty never shared any of the money he made as a bookie, like as a tribute or a fee for protection. "I'm not giving any money to that fucking Irish prick," Marty told him once, meaning Jimmy. One time Marty even threatened to go to the district attorney when Jimmy tried to shake him down.

But Marty kept going on about how Lufthansa would be "the score of a lifetime," and eventually my father told Jimmy about it. Jimmy finally agreed to meet with Marty to get all of the details, and then he organized the robbery with Tommy DeSimone and some of the regulars at Roberts Lounge. And it *was* the score of a lifetime, an almost perfect crime.

Except no one knew that morning how greedy Uncle Jimmy was, or how vicious. Within days, people connected to the robbery started dying or disappearing. The first was Stacks Edwards. He stole the black van that was used to haul away the loot, and he was supposed to get rid of it right after. But he didn't. The police found it two days later in a no parking zone, and they lifted fingerprints that could eventually lead to the robbers. So Jimmy had him killed. Tommy DeSimone went to Stacks's apartment in Ozone Park a little more than a week after the robbery and shot him six times in the head. Stacks probably never saw it coming because he let Tommy into his apartment. My dad spent Christmas Day at the funeral parlor.

Marty was next. "Jimmy wanted to kill him the day of the robbery," my dad told us later. "He wanted me to drive Marty to the Riviera Hotel, pull in the back, and then get out so Tommy and Angelo Sepe could whack him. But I figured I might get whacked too. I mean, why not? I would be there. But I talked him out of it. I told him that Marty tells his wife everything, and that if anything happened to him she'd blow the whistle."

It was only a short reprieve. "I told Marty to stop breaking balls," my dad eventually told us. "Every day he'd go to Roberts and break Jimmy's balls. 'Where's my money? Gimme my money.' He wouldn't listen." About a month after the robbery, in January 1979, Marty just disappeared. He probably didn't suspect Jimmy would kill him either. "The Sunday before they whacked him, Marty had dinner at Jimmy's house," my dad said. "Then Jimmy calls me one morning at five o'clock and tells me to meet him somewhere. I go, and he tells me to go to Marty's house and tell Fran, his wife, that Marty must have gone to Majorca, left with one of his girlfriends. The thing about Marty was, he always went home. Even if it was dawn, he went home. He always checked in with Fran. So I go home to get Karen—I was going to take her with me—but she already knew because Fran had called the house."

I remember that part. I was too young to connect all the dots, but the part I heard was awful. I was in the kitchen when my dad came home. My mom was so upset she didn't notice I was there listening.

"What am I supposed to tell her, Henry?"

"Tell her you don't know."

"But *she* knows," Mom said. "She keeps asking me if I think he's dead. She's saying, 'I know he's dead, I know they killed him, I know he's dead.' What am I supposed to say to that?"

"Tell her you don't fucking know," my dad said. "Look, they're never gonna find him. They cut him up in a million little pieces."

I felt sick. *Cut up in a million pieces?* I tried to imagine that, a body all diced up. It didn't make any sense. Why would someone do that? And who were "they"? I didn't know, and I didn't ask. I never would have suspected Uncle Jimmy, though. In less than a month, two men I liked a lot, two of my dad's friends, were dead. And it was only beginning.

Tommy DeSimone disappeared about the same time as Marty, but not because of Lufthansa. My dad said he was executed by some other gangsters because Tommy had killed a made man in the Mafia named Billy Batts. They lured him to a house, telling him he was going to be inducted into the Mafia, and shot him in the head just out of revenge.

A month later, on February 18, the police found a man named Richard Eaton curled up in the back of a freezer truck, his neck broken and his hands and feet tied. He had Uncle Jimmy's name in an address book the police found on his body. The FBI thought he had tried to launder some of the money from the Lufthansa robbery, but my dad later said he was killed because he ripped off Jimmy in a quarter-million-dollar drug deal.

Six more people got killed, or disappeared, in the spring of 1979, all of whom could connect Jimmy to the Lufthansa case. In March, Fat Louis Cafora, who was one of the robbers, disappeared with his wife, Joanna. On May 16, the police found Joe Manri, who everyone called Joe Buddha, and Robert "Frenchy" McMahon in the front seat of a Buick in a desolate part of Brooklyn. They'd both been shot in the head, most likely by someone they knew who was sitting in the backseat behind them. Two days later a torso washed up on the New Jersey shore. It was what was left of Theresa Ferrara, a twenty-seven-year-old woman who used to date Tommy, which means Tommy might have told her something. A month after that, on June 13, Paolo LiCastri was shot to death and dumped half-naked on a garbage pile on Flatlands Avenue. The FBI agents working on Lufthansa believed that LiCastri had been hired to kill Manri and McMahon. Once that job was done, he became a liability, someone else who knew too much. So he got killed too.

One by one, Jimmy was eliminating every connection between him and Lufthansa. My dad wasn't scared, though, at least not in 1979.

"Believe it or not, I felt half-assed safe because of Paulie," he said later, when I was old enough to understand everything that was happening then. Uncle Paulie was his mentor and his protector; he would have never given Jimmy permission to kill my dad.

A year later, in 1980, though, even Dad was uncomfortable around Jimmy, but for a whole different set of reasons. "Jimmy was into everything then," my dad said. "He was taking liquid speed, drinking like a fish, paranoid. And he went into the heroin business with Paulie's son. He called me down one day and threw a package in my lap, a quarter pound of heroin, and says, 'Can you move this?'

"I said, 'What the fuck?' I'd never seen heroin before. But they knew I was messing around with pot and coke, so they asked again: Could I move it? I had my connection with Mazzei, I knew a couple of black guys in Harlem. I said, 'I don't know. Probably. I'll give it a shot.'

"I'm driving back to Long Island, and I'm thinking, this is the beginning of the end. You mess with this stuff, you wind up dead, you end up doing life, or you become an informant. But it was an insane amount of money. They were paying a quarter million for a kilo, and on the street you can hit that thirty-two, thirty-four times. Do the math. The money was addictive. But I'm still thinking, 'This is the end.'"

He was right. The FBI had been bugging Jimmy and a bunch of other guys for more than a year, trying to gather evidence about Lufthansa. The only person they'd ever been able to charge was Lou Werner, the cargo agent who gave Marty the idea, but he wouldn't testify against anyone else, even when he was sentenced to sixteen years in prison. That's how scared everyone was—even prison couldn't make them talk. But the investigation eventually led to my father, just because he was an associate of Jimmy's. That's how an investigation like that works: The agents on the case get a tip or a name, and even if they can't prove anything they figure out a reason to harass him. With my father, it was drugs. In the spring of 1980, the FBI got a warrant to search our house in Rockville Centre. They waited until Gregg and I went to school, and my mom says she was really polite. She wasn't worried because she knew there wasn't anything in the house that day.

But Jimmy found out about it—wiseguys found out about everything—and that made him even more paranoid. He also knew my dad was doing a lot of drugs, even heroin, which made him even more of a risk. One day when they had a meeting at this restaurant in a strip mall they used for an office, Jimmy pushed my father into a bathroom stall and started tearing his clothes off, looking to see if he was wearing a wire.

That's how bad it got, my dad's lifelong partner in crime not even trusting him. It *was* the beginning of the end. Only I had no idea it was coming.

GINA: There was a parking lot behind our house and, on the other side of it, some small apartments that were behind storefronts that faced out the other way, out onto the sidewalk the next block over. In one of those apartments was a man who had a dog, some kind of shepherd mutt, and a litter of puppies. I liked dogs—I had two Chihuahuas and an Irish setter, and what little girl doesn't like puppies?—so we got to be friendly. He was in his thirties and very nice but poor, almost like a homeless person except he had a roof over his head, so sometimes, if I had extra money, I would buy dog food at the deli and bring it over.

"Gina," he said one day, "there's some guys watching your house from the apartment next door."

"Huh?" Why would anyone want to watch our house? Except for the porno starlets splashing around naked in our pool, I didn't think there was much to see in the Hill household.

"Really," he said. "A bunch of guys in suits. They've got cameras and everything. They've been taking pictures."

I gave him a quizzical look, like I didn't understand, which I didn't. But I knew it wasn't good. I had a sinking feeling in my stomach, and I might have blushed because I was embarrassed. Whatever reason a man in a suit had for wanting to take a picture of our house, it couldn't be good. "Okay," I said to him. Then I said to myself, "I think I need to talk to my parents about this."

Later that night I told my dad what the man with the dogs had told me. He didn't seem embarrassed or even surprised.

"Yeah?" he said. "So what. Don't worry about it, Princess. Let 'em take all the pictures they want." He gave a dismissive wave, as if someone photographing the house was no more unusual than the electric company checking the meter. "You know," he said, almost as an afterthought, "they listen to the phone conversations too."

They listen to the phone conversations? I was mortified. Whose conversations? All of them? *My* conversations? The ones where I giggled with my eleven-year-old friends about who liked who and which boys were cute and who was kissing who and who was wearing a bra and who got her period? *Those* conversations? And who was listening, anyway? No one was supposed to hear those conversations—or any of my conversations— let alone a bunch of old men in suits.

This was terrible, maybe the worst thing I could imagine happening to me, my pubescent privacy invaded. And it made no sense. What could my dad have to say that was so interesting? He was a businessman—he silk-screened pictures onto T-shirts. Whenever my friends had a birthday party, I gave them T-shirts my father made in the garage, and when the pope came to Yankee Stadium in the fall of 1979, my father gave all my Catholic friends' mothers shirts with John Paul II on the front. Maybe there were bad things happening, like Marty and Stacks disappearing, but my father wasn't involved in any of that.

GREGG: The guys watching the house and tapping the phones were Nassau County narcotics detectives. They'd been on to my father for a few months, after a high school dropout got arrested for selling quaaludes and, in order to get himself out of trouble, snitched on my father. That's the way a lot of law enforcement works: The police arrest a little fish who gives up a bigger fish who gives up a bigger fish and on and on. The irony?

The dropout who started the case against my father was Jerry Peters Jr., the son of one of my father's main drug partners, Gerald Peters. If it is true that there is no honor among thieves—and it is—then there is outright backstabbing among drug dealers.

The case that Nassau County put together against my father, I learned later, was extremely solid. He'd been right about the phones: The detectives had miles of incriminating audiotape. By the time they were finished listening, they had the names and addresses of a dozen of my father's cohorts, including Sandra Cooper, a girlfriend whose apartment he used to cut and package most of the drugs; Amy Mulry, his drug courier; and Gerald Peters.

But all those months my father thought it was the feds chasing him, maybe agents from the Drug Enforcement Administration but probably FBI guys just listening in to see if he'd give up something about Lufthansa. They'd already tried to squeeze him, telling him he could be the next one to get killed. They didn't know how much he knew about the robbery, but simple hoodlum algebra suggested he knew something. The basic facts were that he was a thirty-seven-year-old ex-con known to have committed crimes with Jimmy Burke, the number one suspect in the Lufthansa case. They never got anything out of him, though.

Not because he was a stand-up guy, necessarily, but because he was such a mess.

In March they'd subpoenaed him to testify in front of a federal grand jury. Edward McDonald, who was an assistant U.S. attorney running the Lufthansa investigation, would remember my father showing up in his office one morning after he got the subpoena. "He looked like a character out of *Guys & Dolls*," McDonald said later. "He had a big plaid checkered jacket on, and he was high. . . . He was sort of blithering. Not completely blithering, but not really coherent either." McDonald had two FBI agents with him, but my father was alone; he didn't think to bring his lawyer.

McDonald remembers telling my father, "Get out of here. And next time we bring you in, you're going to have to get a lawyer. We're not going to take advantage of you now." Said McDonald, "We figured we'd gain some points with him by doing that. I don't know whether he even remembered it because he was pretty high. My experience with the agents was, this guy's a complete waste. You know, what are we going to do with this guy?"

As it turned out, nothing, at least not right away. My father got arrested by the county before he had a chance to go back.

GINA: I'd been out shopping with my Aunt Ellen. It was a Sunday, and she took me to one of the malls, either Green Acres or Roosevelt Field, where there was a Bloomingdale's, to buy my first bra. I don't know if I really needed one yet—I was only eleven—but my friends were starting to wear them, so I wanted one too.

We got home right about when the sun was going down. My grandmother was there, and she was in my bedroom complaining about how messy it was. I didn't think it was so bad. Even if I did, I wouldn't admit it; I had my mother's stubborn streak. So there we were, my grandmother lecturing me about the mess and me trying to defend myself, feeling all grown up because I had a Bloomingdale's bag with a bra in it.

And then there were lights everywhere. It happened so suddenly, like someone flipped a switch. There was a bright white light right outside my window, in front of the house, and then flashing red and blue splotches swirling across the walls. I knew they were police lights, but I'd never seen so many of them and so close, almost like they were inside the house.

I heard a loud noise—*boom! boom! boom! boom!*—from the front door, and I peeked around the corner to watch. There were a few men in suits and behind them, officers in uniform, all of them marching through the entranceway until they filled the hallway and spilled into the living room. One of the detectives—I assumed he was a detective because he was wearing a suit—was talking to my mom, but it sounded more like he was giving her orders.

"Karen, we have a warrant. . ."

"But there's nothing in the house," Mom told him. "We don't have anything you're looking for." She sounded more annoyed than angry.

"Look, just take the kids and go sit in the living room," the detective snapped at her.

Mom took my hand. I'd never seen anyone boss her around like that, complete strangers telling her what to do in her own house. When it came to my parents, especially my mother, she was all-knowing. I looked to her for all the answers, and she would give them to me even if they weren't true. Now she was taking orders. I had that sinking feeling in my stomach again, and my face felt flushed like it did when my friend with the dogs told me the house was being watched. Only this feeling was worse. I didn't know the word *humiliation* when I was eleven, but that's what it was.

"Mom, what's happening?" I whispered.

"We'll get through this," she said. "It'll all be okay. Let's just get through this."

GREGG: The police were there for hours, ripping up the house. They tore everything apart—flipped over mattresses, emptied out the kitchen cabinets, dumped the drawers, pulled down the tiles from the ceiling in the basement. They were gentle with mine and Gina's rooms by comparison—in fact, they didn't take anything from her room, not even the Miss Piggy mirror that probably still had some residue on it—but the rest of the house was a mess.

My sister and I sat in front of the television, which the cops had turned off, staring at the blank screen as if we were watching a program. But we were watching the cops from the corners of our eyes. And listening. My nerves started to twitch when I heard them working in my room. There were at least two of them, shoving my closet door back on its slider, slamming it against the door jamb, tossing my *Encyclopedia Britannica* from the shelves onto the floor. It was hard to keep track of all the destructive sounds. After about a half hour, two cops came out of my room with the triple-beam balance and the mirror my father kept in my closet. They'd also taken the .45 slugs from the Ingram and the spent shell casings on my desk.

How was I supposed to explain those? I wondered what I would say if they started asking me questions. I wasn't prepared for that. I tried hard not to move so I wouldn't draw attention to myself. I sat on the couch cursing my father and cursing the cops and then, after an hour or so, cursing myself for not going to the bathroom before the police showed up. When I couldn't hold it any longer, I stood up and told one of the detectives I had to use the bathroom.

He nodded at me and then motioned to one of the uniformed guys. "Go with him," he said.

The officer followed me through the dining room, through the kitchen, and into the bathroom. I started to close the door, but he put his hand up, pushed it open, and followed me inside. It made sense, I suppose, the police making sure I wasn't flushing anything, but it was weird standing in the bathroom with a cop. He was big and tall, like a football player, and he might have been more intimidating if he hadn't been so young. He had a round, friendly face, the kind you could never mistake for a tough guy. My father knew plenty of tough guys who weren't nearly as big, but their faces and expressions, just the way they carried themselves, said, *Don't fuck with me or I'll bury you.* I knew the difference.

The cop discreetly stared at the wall while I unzipped. They'd already tossed the bathroom; the shower curtain was flipped up over the rod, the towels were on the floor, and the bottles and tubes from the medicine cabinet were spread over the vanity. I started to pee, the two of us standing in silence until he broke it. "You know," he said, "you could make this a lot easier on everyone if you'd just tell us where it is. You know what we're looking for."

I stared at the top of the toilet tank. My cheeks were burning. I hoped it didn't show. I thought of the things I could say. *Did you look under the stairs in my parents' room? I saw a big bag of cocaine there not too long ago. Oh, and did you check the ceiling in the basement? My dad likes to hide stolen guns up there. What, you didn't find any drugs? Well then I guess he must've sold the last shipment.*

But I didn't. "Sorry," I said without any hesitation, almost like a reflex. "Can't help you."

I never approved of what my father did, and I wasn't trying to protect him, not consciously anyway. And I certainly didn't have anything to hide. For years I'd managed to live in parallel worlds, separate and distinct, the two of them occasionally twirling around each other but never tangling or intersecting. My father had his life—reckless, dangerous, irresponsible—and I had mine—ordered, legitimate, self-sufficient. Even if I enjoyed the occasional perks of the gangster world, I never wanted to be fully a part of it. And maintaining that wall, keeping the distance between the two, included, curiously, not being a snitch. To tell the police where to find the drugs, to tell them about the compartment in the step leading up to the bed and how they would have to reach in and back and then up to grab anything, would have been to acknowledge that those two worlds had collided, that I had been dragged down into my father's world.

I finished, zipped, and went back to the couch. The police continued wrecking the house. After another hour or so, they left us to clean up the mess. My mother's cheeks were streaked with mascara and her eyes were red and wet, and Gina was trembling, but we got most of everything put away before midnight. Then we tried to pretend life was normal again. My father wasn't home because he'd been arrested, but even that wasn't particularly strange, his not being around. Monday morning I got up and went to school and tried to forget about it.

That lasted exactly one day. On Tuesday, the second morning after the raid, my father's arrest made the papers. It was at the top of the Region section in *Newsday*, the paper everyone on Long Island read.

5 Arrested; Cops Say Drug Ring Broken

MINEOLA—Police say they have broken up a $1.5-million-a-year drug operation with the arrests yesterday and Sunday of five persons — one of them a holdup man from Commack— and expect to make more arrests.

Most of the story was about Gerald Peters, the holdup man. He'd been indicted a few months before for trying to rob a Manhattan jewelry store with four other men, who handcuffed and taped up the mouths and eyes of seventeen people who walked in on them. When the Nassau County police picked him up Sunday night, shortly before they grabbed my father, they found "four ounces of cocaine valued at $10,000, $20,000 in cash, an assortment of amphetamines, quaaludes and valium, five handguns, and a sawed-off shotgun." At least my father didn't get top billing.

He was in the next paragraph, along with Amy Mulry and Sandra Cooper, his girlfriend. The paper printed his whole name, his age, his exact address—everything except "Gregg's father." It said that he and Amy were charged with "conspiracy and criminal possession of a controlled substance." I knew—anyone who read it would know—that that was just a fancy way of saying *drug dealer*.

Strange as it sounds, I never thought of my father that way. I knew he used drugs and that his friends did too, and I knew he sold drugs. Yet it seemed more benign than my image of a dealer. When I thought of drug dealers, I thought of heroin and Colombian cartels and seedy guys on street corners and junkies with needles. I never associated that image with my father. But there it was in black and white for everyone to see. Henry Hill, drug dealer.

I was in school by 7:30 that morning, but word was already out. I was a pretty sociable kid, the kind who got along with everyone, the brains and the jocks and even some of the delinquents. That day, though, I was alone. In the hallway, kids parted in front of me, like the Red Sea opening up for Moses's bad seed brother. I could feel eyes on me, and I could hear a low murmur, like a white noise of whispers. *Hey, that's him. That's the kid whose dad got busted.* I was a pariah, the circus freak of South Side Middle School, except among the biggest thugs in school, the ones who got high in the parking lot. They all gave me a knowing nod, like they were impressed.

My friend Tim, one of the guys I used to play roller hockey with, was one of the only people to actually speak to me that day. He came up to me in the hall fairly early in the morning with a sheepish look on his face.

"My mom heard about your dad getting arrested," he said. He was staring at the floor. "And, well, I can't go over your house anymore. We can't hang out anymore."

It was like he'd kicked me in the stomach. I was stunned and more than a little devastated. He might as well have said, "You're a despicable human being, so fuck you." He used different words, but that's what I heard.

I didn't fight him on it, though. I was still shell-shocked from Sunday night and the morning paper. I knew my father was looking at another long stretch in prison, and I knew his friends were disappearing. I wondered if he'd be next. I was afraid we'd have to move again and that we'd be poor again and that my mother would work herself half to death trying to keep everything together. Tim's telling me he couldn't be my friend anymore was just another drop in an already overflowing bucket. I looked him in the eye and shrugged. "Okay," was all I said, and I walked away.

My guidance counselor spotted me next and called me into his office. I knew him pretty well because he was also my cross-country coach. He was a nice guy, easygoing, the sort who would put up with pranks adolescent boys would play, like mooning people from the bus on the way to a meet or the time a few of the runners taped *Playboy* centerfolds across the rear window of his Datsun. He was also one of the only adults who looked out for me in those first few days. He was probably in over his head, though, since not many Long Island middle school counselors are prepared to talk a kid through his father's being arrested as a drug kingpin.

"You going to be okay?" he asked.

"Yeah."

"Anything I can do?"

"No."

"Things okay here?"

"Yeah."

I think he realized he wasn't going to get much more out of me. At least he tried. We stared at each other in silence for a moment or two. Then I got up and went to class.

GINA: I was so embarrassed, so mortified, when my dad got arrested. Up until that point, the other kids on our street sort of looked up to us. We had the swimming pool and the Betamax, and Gregg and I were both pretty popular. And now everyone knew that the police thought my dad was a bad man.

And I mean *everyone*. Even Mrs. Nastry who lived next door. She was old and hunched and she usually growled at us kids, so we called her Mrs. Nasty behind her back. She always had a string of rosary beads with her, which, as a Jew, I thought were really scary because I'd only seen them in movies like *The Exorcist*. I'd watch those horror movies with Gregg and get so scared that I would crawl into his room after he went to sleep and lie on the floor with one arm flopped up on his bed just so I could touch him. I knew he'd throw me out if I woke him up.

Anyway, the day it was in the paper, Mrs. Nasty saw me on the sidewalk and came out of her house, not running exactly but moving fast for an old lady. She grabbed me and hugged me and started kissing her beads. "I'm so sorry for you," she kept saying. "I'm so sorry." I know she was trying to be nice, but it was embarrassing having this decrepit woman hanging on me.

I wanted my mom to tell everyone that the newspaper was wrong, that Dad hadn't been arrested at all. I made up a story that he'd started a new business in Manhattan and had to leave early in the morning and work until late at night and that's why he wasn't around. To me, it seemed completely believable. I begged my mom to tell that story to Alice's mom and Debbie's mom and all the parents of my friends who weren't allowed to come over anymore, but she wouldn't do it. "I don't want to talk to anyone," she said.

I was so frustrated that she wasn't standing up for my dad and defending our good name. So I had to do it. I told everyone on the street that my dad was very busy with his new company. Nobody challenged me on it, but I don't think anyone believed me either. Not even my friend Alice. We used to play backgammon on the enclosed porch at her house down the block—my grandmother taught me how to play, and I was obsessed with the game—and even after my father was arrested and Alice's parents said she couldn't come to my house anymore, she still snuck over. We'd play in the vestibule of our house so her parents couldn't see her but we could hear if they called her to come home. I was probably more worried about getting caught than Alice, even though I wouldn't be the one who got in trouble. Alice told me once that I worried about everything.

It's funny, because I never thought of myself as a worrier. But looking back, she was right. Making up a story like that and being afraid of what other people thought—I must have worried myself sick. I just felt such a need to set everyone straight even if it was with such a big lie. My family used to say, and to this day they still joke about it, that I was very self-centered as a little girl, just like my dad.

I stuck to my story the whole time my dad was in jail. Finally, after almost three weeks, my grand-ma gave Mom the money to post his bail, and they picked him up on a Friday night. My parents had a horrible fight that night. I found out much later what it was about. The police, when they searched the house, had missed a pound of heroin hidden in the secret compartment in the bedroom, and after they left, my mom flushed it down the toilet. She thought she was helping by getting rid of any evidence the police could use against him, but my dad was mad that she'd flushed away so much money, something like eighteen thousand dollars' worth of drugs.

The screaming was terrible, yet I was still happy Dad was home again. When he got up in the morning, I begged him to set up the sprinkler on the front lawn or do something, anything, in front of the house so the kids on the street would see him. He smiled at me. "Sure thing, Princess."

That felt so good. When he walked outside, it was like, "See, I was telling the truth all along." Then I made up another story to go with the first one: It was his day off. He'd worked hard all week, and now he was home taking care of the yard. We were just like a normal family.

GREGG: My father was free on bail for less than seventy-two hours, from Friday night until Monday afternoon when federal agents arrested him again. I saw him only briefly that weekend, and he was in no mood to talk or explain what had happened. He spent most of that time out on the street trying to collect old debts and hustle up some new cash. I didn't care how dire his circumstances were. I just wanted answers, and they came from my mother in short, compact facts: Nassau County wanted to put him in prison for life, Uncle Jimmy wanted to kill him, and Uncle Paulie had written him off as a liability. Like I said at the beginning, I always thought the worst thing that could happen to my father was that he'd go back to prison or get killed. For three weeks in the spring of 1980, I was certain one of those things, or both, would happen.

So were Ed McDonald and the FBI agents working the Lufthansa case. The tapes from the telephone taps had convinced them that my father, while not the toughest gangster around, ran with some serious guys. For instance, McDonald figured that "The Big Irishman" my father referred to a couple of times had to be Jimmy Burke. "Jesus," McDonald thought, "this guy could be the key to unlocking the whole Lufthansa case." And now they had real leverage to use against him. Even if my father didn't believe he'd get killed, he knew the Nassau County charges could put him away for life. For a gangster, dying in prison is a bigger motivator than the threat of dying on the street: The former is guaranteed, and the latter only a possibility.

The morning after he was arrested, my father called Jimmy Fox, who was his federal probation officer. He was required to let Fox know if he got locked up. On the phone he told Fox that he knew his options were limited, that he knew he was facing a life sentence, and that he was thinking about cooperating.

"The next thing that happened," McDonald would say later, "was a real blunder." Fox told the FBI that my father might be willing to cooperate, and two agents went to see him at the Nassau County jail, where all the other inmates could see them walk to his cell. "It was a stupid move for the agents to go out and talk to him," McDonald said. "Fox had to go out there because he was his probation officer. He *had* to go and talk to him. But there was no reason for FBI agents to go to visit him except to try to turn him.

"Henry freaked out and refused at that point to cooperate. When Fox went back to talk to him, Henry said, 'That's it, I'm not gonna cooperate. You blew my cover. This is terrible.'"

But in a way, that also raised the ante: If his cover was blown, he was already a dead man. So the feds kept working on him, explaining how vulnerable he was. Then they started pressuring my mother too. A pair of FBI agents stopped her in a shopping center, right outside Genovese Drugstore. "Mrs. Hill?" one of them said. He flashed his badge, but she already knew who they were. "We just need a minute of your time."

The other agent had a file folder tucked under his arm. He opened it and showed her a photograph, a black-and-white eight-by-ten of a man hog-tied in the back of a trailer. "Richard Eaton," the agent said. "Your husband knew him."

He flipped to the next one, Frenchy McMahon and Joe Manri in the Buick with the backs of their heads blown off. Then a third, only a bleached and bloated torso. "Theresa Ferrara," he said. "You knew her, didn't you?"

She had. Not well, but she'd gone to school with her, and she knew that Tommy DeSimone had dated her for a while. She knew all the bodies in all the pictures. "Why are you showing me this?" she asked them.

"Because," one of the agents told her, "this could happen to your husband or you or your kids. We don't want that to happen. Do you want that to happen?"

They stopped her three or four times while my father was being held by Nassau County. Each time, they left her with a business card and asked her to call or come down to the office. Each time, she told them she didn't know anything, that there wasn't any reason anyone would want to butcher her or her children. She was badly rattled by the photos, of course, but she never let on to me and Gina. In fact, even though my parents understood how limited my father's options were, they both believed my father could wangle his way out of this jam too, that he could somehow keep Uncle Jimmy at bay long enough to smooth things over with Uncle Paulie.

The feds didn't have that same faith in my father. On Monday, as soon as McDonald found out my father had made bail and slipped out of jail two nights earlier, he got a judge to sign a warrant to have him locked up as a material witness. Four FBI agents grabbed him in the driveway late that afternoon, and he was gone again.

GINA: My grandparents were at our house when the FBI agents arrested Dad. They let him come inside before they took him away so he could tell my mom what was happening and change his shirt. She took it pretty well—she'd gotten used to my dad's being arrested, I suppose—but Gram was livid. She started screaming as soon as Dad came in the house with the FBI agents. "I told you he was no good! That dumb bastard! He's a bum, a gangster lowlife!" She wouldn't stop. That's one of the things the agents would remember, how loud my grandma was.

Gram might have known how grave the situation was and that this arrest was much more serious than even the last one. I didn't understand what was going on, though, other than that Dad was going away again. For a little while or for a long while, I hadn't a clue. It wasn't until later that night, after I'd gone to bed, that my mom tried to explain what it all meant.

She came into my room and sat on the edge of my bed. She was upset, but, like she always did, she tried not to show it. "I think we might have to move soon," she said.

"Why?"

"Well. . ." She was searching for the right words. "With Dad and Uncle Jimmy, something very serious happened. I'm not sure what, but Uncle Jimmy is very angry, and that's why we have to leave."

That didn't make any sense to me. "Uncle Jimmy's angry?" I asked.

"Yes. He's very angry."

"But why do we have to move?"

"Because he's very angry and . . ." She hesitated, but only for a moment. "And he might want to hurt us."

"Uncle Jimmy wants to hurt us?" I couldn't imagine Uncle Jimmy would hurt my dad, let alone me.

"Yes."

"Why?"

"Because Dad and Uncle Jimmy had a fight, and he's not our friend anymore."

"About what?" I wasn't afraid, which I realize sounds strange. But my mother was very good at masking her anxiety, and if she wasn't scared I wasn't going to be either.

"I don't really know," she said. There were, after all, limits to what my parents thought their eleven-year-old daughter should be told.

"But Uncle Jimmy wants to hurt us?"

"Yes, I think so."

"Why?" I wouldn't let up. I was genuinely curious, and I kept asking questions until I got the answers.

"Oh, Gina," my mom said, "people are disappearing, people are getting killed . . ."

"Uncle Jimmy wants to *kill* us?" I couldn't imagine such a thing. I knew people died; I'd overheard the conversations about Marty's being cut up and Stacks's being dead. But Uncle Jimmy's name had never come up.

"Yes," she said. "Yes, Uncle Jimmy might want to kill us. But don't worry. We're going to move away to someplace safe, and everything will be fine. Okay?"

She smiled at me. It sounds surreal, I know, my mom managing a smile when she knew how much danger we were in. But it was comforting. I knew I should be scared, that I should be whimpering with fear even if I didn't understand and really couldn't believe what I was being told. But my mom's tone, her face, her confidence made me feel strangely secure.

I nodded at her and said, "Okay," and she kissed me on the forehead and left me alone in the dark.

GREGG: I found out about going into hiding the next day, Tuesday. My father and mother were down at the federal courthouse in Brooklyn listening to Ed McDonald explain the program to them. My father, though, was resistant to the end. The night before, when the FBI agents brought him in, he told McDonald that he wanted to work undercover for them. "I'll be your man on the street," he said. "I can record conversations. I could really make cases for you."

"Henry," McDonald told him, "if you go back out on the street, you're going to get killed. We can't risk it. We're going to keep you locked up until you testify."

They went round and round for two hours that night, my father insisting he could get mobsters on tape, McDonald believing he'd be dead as soon as he got within shooting range. Finally, my father wore down. "All right," he said. "Let me get my wife. I'll get my wife in here tomorrow and we'll talk about it."

My mother went down the next day with my grandparents. My grandmother was still screaming; McDonald would joke later that he could hear her coming all the way from Queens. He separated them, put my grandparents in a conference room down the hall and took my parents into his office where they could talk in private. Every few minutes, though, the door to the conference room would open and he'd hear my grandmother crying and screaming, "That no good bastard! He's a bum!"

Late in the afternoon, after hours of talking to

McDonald, my mother called her sister, my Aunt Cheryl, and asked her to bring us to Brooklyn. An FBI agent picked us up and led us into the federal building. We weren't told exactly why we were being brought in, but I assumed we'd just get an update on my father's case. It never occurred to me that we—my mother and Gina and I—were in any danger. My father's friends were like family— there was no way they'd hurt us. I thought we'd ride this one out too, just as we had in the past.

I remember walking into the U.S. attorney's office and seeing a wall with a giant seal of the Justice Department's Strike Force on Organized Crime painted on it, and then watching the wall part, the seal splitting in two, each side retracting and opening into a suite of offices. To me it was like something out of *Get Smart* or James Bond, secret rooms hidden behind solid walls. I was already nervous, and that didn't help.

Gina and my aunt and I were ushered into McDonald's office. My father was slouched in a chair looking a little bored, but he flashed a smile when we walked in. My mother was on the edge of her seat, tense. I could always tell when she was agitated because her sentences got short and clipped, direct and to the point. She spoke first.

"We're going to need protection," she said.

I didn't know what that meant. I didn't say anything, and neither did Gina. I looked at

McDonald. He was tall with a boy's regular haircut, conservative and clean-cut and straitlaced, which meant there was nothing familiar about him or his demeanor, nothing that reminded me of anyone my father had ever associated with. That fact alone gave him an air of serious authority.

"We're going to put you in the witness protection program," he said.

I stared at him. I'd never heard of witness protection. At that time, hardly anyone had because it was still relatively new. There hadn't been any movies filmed or books written about mobsters being shipped off to some small town with a new name, their past blotted out, the slate wiped clean in exchange for information. I had no idea what witness protection entailed.

"Look," McDonald said to my mother, "you guys are unsafe. You and your kids are in jeopardy."

My mother interrupted him. "Why can't he go"—she nodded toward my father—"and I'll stay here with the kids?"

"That's not possible," McDonald said. "They'll get to you to get to him."

My father chimed in. "I'm not going if they don't go."

I didn't say a word. My jaw was clenched too tightly to speak anyway, and no one was asking me any questions. But my mind raced. McDonald's last words echoed in my head. For almost a month, since the Nassau County raid made the papers, I'd braced myself for the worst. I was so angry with my father for humiliating us again that I almost didn't care what happened to him. He'd go away, behind bars or dead somewhere, and we'd move on with our lives. I'd get over it. But this? *They'll get to you to get to him.* A federal prosecutor was telling me that I could be killed, my sister and my mother could be killed, maybe even my grandparents. At thirteen I was supposed to protect myself? And my family? I should have been terrified, and maybe I was. But all I felt was fury.

McDonald kept talking. My mind was racing so I heard only bits and pieces, key phrases. *No contact with family or friends. Leave everything. Take nothing that will identify you.*

I could feel the rage building. My gut told me that the safest place to be was as far away from my father as possible. Joining him would make us a target; avoiding him would not. Maybe I'd watched too many movies, but I thought this was the point where my father would stand up, stick his chest out, and tell McDonald no. "It's too dangerous," he was supposed to say. "I'll go. But promise me you'll protect my wife and children."

Instead he said the opposite: He wouldn't go without his family. My blood was boiling. His family? Since when was Henry Hill a family man? I could count on one hand with fingers left over the number of memorable father-son things we'd done. In my thirteen years he'd spent more time in prison or jail than on the outside. He was an abusive drunk who cheated on my mother. He was a selfish piece of shit, and this was his ultimate selfish act.

My fingers dug into the arms of the chair. Did he think I was a moron? He wasn't thinking about us or our safety—he was trying to keep himself out of prison. I wanted to kill him. I wanted to stand up and tell him to go fuck himself. I wanted to tell McDonald to fuck himself too. I wanted to scream at my mother for putting up with everything all those years. I wanted to tell my grandmother to shut up, to just stop her screaming. I wanted to get up and run, get as far away from all of them as possible. I'd done it before, bolted out of restaurants when my father made a scene. But I was surrounded by FBI agents and U.S. marshals and federal prosecutors in a fortified building in Brooklyn. If anyone had bothered to notice me in my chair, they would have seen a boy on the verge of exploding. But no one noticed. And I was too angry to say anything at all.

I'd built a nice little life for myself, as normal as I could hope for. It was funny, but in my own way I had it all. I did well in school and was popular among all sorts of kids. I was playing in tennis tournaments, and my game was getting stronger. I had a weekend job at The Spice of Life, a restaurant in Cedarhurst run by one of my father's friends, and was bringing home $150 a weekend working catered affairs. I knew the doormen at some of the hottest clubs on Long Island. Not bad for a thirteen-year-old. And now I was going to be forced to abandon it. For how long? A month? A year?

I didn't hear who asked the question, only McDonald's answer. "You're not coming back," he told us. "It's forever."

The words were like a body blow, hard enough to knock the wind out of me. *Forever.* The syllables kept echoing in my head. I couldn't believe forever really meant *forever.* How could it? How could we leave and never come back, ever? I didn't understand, and there was no time to figure it out. It had all happened so fast. Less than an hour ago, I was being dragged into Brooklyn to see my drug-dealing father, and now my entire world was being taken away.

There was no debate. In a way, the feds had made my father the classic offer he couldn't refuse. If he agreed to go into witness protection, he would be relocated somewhere in America with a new name and a monthly stipend and, best of all, a clean criminal record. In return, all he had to do was testify against people who wanted to kill him. He'd have been a fool, a dead fool, to turn it down, and he knew it. By the time Gina and I were brought to Brooklyn, the decision had already been made. And it was effective immediately. From that moment on, beginning the instant we walked out that door, we would be under the protection of federal agents.

Four of them drove us in two dark gray sedans with tinted windows to Rockville Centre. Another sedan followed with two more agents. My father remained in Brooklyn at FBI headquarters. I sat silently in the backseat next to my mother. My sister was on her other side. My mother was making small talk with the agent who was driving. Her measured words told me she was nervous. I wished I had the courage to say no, even if my mother didn't. *No,* I wanted to scream, *I won't go.* But I couldn't find the words. My head was spinning with anger and fear and confusion.

The sedans raced down the Southern State Parkway, past Valley Stream toward Rockville Centre. We were almost home. Then I thought how silly that was. Home? No, we were almost to the place we were leaving forever.

When we arrived at the house, the agents got out of the car first, then hurried us inside. One of them opened a box of black plastic garbage bags. "You've got an hour," he told us. Whatever we could stuff in a Hefty sack in an hour is what we could take with us.

I looked around my narrow room. It had had a strange feeling since the raid. Everything was neat, orderly, arranged exactly the way I'd left it, but slightly off-kilter, a reminder that someone had been through my things. My powerful Midland CB radio was on the desk, a gift to myself purchased with my restaurant earnings. Bumper stickers I'd collected from rock bands and nightclubs were on the shelves in front of my books, as were two cassette tapes I'd just bought, *Led Zeppelin II* and *The Worst of Jefferson Airplane*. My two compound bows were under the bed; my tennis rackets, baseball mitt, and hockey equipment were in my closet.

I couldn't fit it all into a bag. And how could I parse all my possessions? I was too numb to care.

I opened a dresser drawer, grabbed a handful of underwear and some socks, opened another and pulled out a pair of Lee jeans and some T-shirts, then dumped the clothes in a bag. I was done in three minutes. Then I lay down on my bed and tried to close my eyes, to shut everything out for a few minutes. My mom walked in, and I waved her out. I didn't want to talk to anyone. I stayed there for a little while longer, staring at the ceiling.

I walked into the living room and handed my

bag to an agent. My grandparents and aunts were there, all of them crying, Grandma still yelling through her tears. In one breath she'd try to comfort us—"Don't worry, we'll do something, we'll straighten this out"—and in the next she was screaming at the agents—"You heartless bastards! I don't even get a second to say goodbye? You care more about that piece of shit Henry than about my family."

All the hysteria was making a terrible situation worse. I knew if I stopped, even for an instant, I'd lose it too. I couldn't let myself cry. Crying would make me one of them, the same as my compliant mother or my powerless relatives who were weeping, wailing, but unable to just say no, to say, *Wait, let's think this thing through.* And that was the last thing I wanted to be at that moment. I ground my teeth together hard, and it made me squint like I was watching a gory scene in a movie. I followed an agent out to the car, and another one opened the door for me. I got in the backseat and waited. The crying and the screaming had spilled out onto the street. "Kaaaarrren!" my grandmother howled as the agents pried her away, literally tore her from my grandmother's arms. I stared straight at the seat in front of me, my vision blurred by the water in my eyes. I didn't say anything. I didn't even say goodbye.

GINA: When McDonald told us we had to leave, I felt so bad for my dad. "Oh my goodness," I thought, "my poor father—I can't believe he has to listen to these people." It was worse than the night the detectives ordered my mom around. Those federal men were talking down to him, telling him he had to go away forever because he'd get killed. They just didn't understand how smart my dad was. They didn't understand that none of this was his fault, that it was only a misunderstanding.

But he was going along with it, and he didn't seem frightened at all. So I decided not to be either. And if they were really going to make him leave, I was glad he insisted on taking my mom and Gregg and me with him. We would get through this, just like we'd gotten through everything.

Back at the house, I packed a few things, mostly clothes, and started to say goodbye. My aunts and my grandparents were so sad, all of them crying uncontrollably and my grandmother screaming. The rawness of their emotions washed over me, and I started to cry too. But I didn't feel their sadness. The idea of leaving forever hadn't really sunk in. I guess I was picking up on my mom's emotions. She was very upset, but she didn't believe we'd be going away and never coming back. Never is such a long, long time. She knew something would change, that somehow things would work out and she'd see her parents and her sisters again. My mom always had that kind of faith, and I suppose I inherited it.

I heard Alice knocking at the front door. She'd seen us come home, and she wanted to play backgammon. I was so relieved. Slipping out with my friend would be an escape from all that confusion and chaos. I wiped my tears away and asked my mom if I could go sit in the vestibule with Alice. She said yes. There was no reason for me to be in the middle of that scene anyway.

We could still hear my grandmother, but it was quieter once we got out of the living room. Alice, who couldn't help but notice strange men in suits crowded into our house, asked who they were.

"Some of my dad's friends," I said. "I don't really know."

It was all I could do to keep from telling her the truth. I wanted so badly to say goodbye, to tell her we were going away and never coming back and I would never see her again. But I knew I couldn't; the agents had told us we couldn't tell anyone. I wasn't sad, even though I knew I would miss her; it was more that I just wanted her to understand why I vanished. I held it inside, and we played backgammon without saying very much else.

And then it was time to go. We were out in the street now. I hugged my grandma, and she squeezed me tight, her tears wetting the shoulder of my shirt. Then I kissed my aunts and got into the backseat with my brother. When the car started to drive away, I watched out the rear window. My relatives were at the curb wiping their faces and waving, and as the car went faster, they got smaller and smaller. I remember looking at the sidewalk and the houses and the streetlights, and saying to myself at each little marker, "I'll never see that tree again. I'll never see that street sign again. I'll never see that lawn again."

Even that wasn't upsetting. I was shaken, if only because everything was happening so fast, and maybe a little melancholy. I wanted to ask my brother why he hadn't said goodbye, but he looked too upset to discuss it. Anyway, we were moving on, going somewhere else, maybe someplace better. And there was nothing I could do about it.

GREGG: The FBI agents took us to a hotel that night far out on Long Island, or maybe somewhere in southern Connecticut. It's hard to recall exactly. We bounced around so many hotels during the end of May and beginning of June that they've all blurred together into one anonymous Best Western. The feds were convinced one of Uncle Jimmy's henchmen would eventually track down my father if we stayed in one place for too long, so they moved us every couple of nights. We must have hit a half-dozen low-rent hotels in two weeks.

We fell into an agonizing routine. Every morning a pair of agents would drive us to Brooklyn so my father could be debriefed. It was a slow, methodical process. The FBI agents had my father walk them through his entire criminal life, from the time he was stealing bottles of olive oil from Brooklyn bodegas through the Air France heist up until the present. And then they would go over it all again because my father's memory was fuzzy. Partly that was because all the drugs had fried his brain and partly it was because my father had committed so many crimes it was hard to keep them all straight. "It was fascinating but also monotonous, just hours and hours of debriefing," one of the FBI agents, Ed Gueverra, would remember. "We'd have to go over it and over it and over it because Henry would remember one thing but not another thing, and then the next time he'd remember something else."

Of particular interest, of course, was the last half of 1978, the months between the time my father was released from prison and the Lufthansa robbery. The agents asked how he knew about it, and he told them what they'd long suspected: that Jimmy was behind it, but that he didn't want my father involved. My father's word wasn't enough to indict Jimmy for Lufthansa; his information was secondhand at best, and anyone who could have corroborated it was by then either dead or missing. But Gueverra and the other agents kept pressing him. And eventually he confessed to a crime they didn't know had even been committed.

"Where were you in December 1978?" Gueverra asked him.

"Boston," my father said.

"Boston? What were you doing in Boston?"

"Fixing games, Boston University basketball games. With some little black guy."

Ed McDonald had a perplexed look on his face. He'd graduated from Boston College in 1968, and he rode the bench for a couple of games during his freshman year. He didn't think he was good enough to ever be more than a fill-in, but he followed basketball and still played in some neighborhood games in Brooklyn. He knew which teams were any good in Boston, and he knew no one would bother fixing a BU game.

"You mean Boston College?" he asked. "And was the guy named Cobb?"

"Yeah, yeah, that's it," my father said. "Cobb. Little guy."

Ernie Cobb was a five-foot, eleven-inch guard and a cocaptain of the BC team during the 1978–79 season. He was a star, the third-highest scorer in BC history with 1,760 points, averaging 21.3 per game. He was also, according to my father, the last man to get in on the point-shaving scheme (although he would never be charged with any crime).

The idea started, he told the feds, when he went to Pittsburgh in July to see Paul Mazzei.

Mazzei knew a guy named Tony Perla, whose brother, Rocco, had gone to high school with a BC player named Rick Kuhn. The idea was to pay Kuhn and another player, Tim Sweeney, a starter who led the team in assists, to blow a few baskets, not enough to lose but enough to beat the point spread. (Sweeney would never be indicted either.) My father's role basically was to provide the "organizational strength," as he would put it later —the bookies who could handle big bets, the muscle to make sure everyone paid up, and the like. And that meant bringing in Jimmy and Peter Vario, Uncle Paulie's son.

As scams go, it wasn't very successful. My father once claimed that the wiseguys made millions from six fixed games that season, but the feds believe the operation was a wash. But that didn't matter. The important thing was that my father had implicated Jimmy in a criminal conspiracy.

And so it went, my father confessing to crime after crime. He ratted out Uncle Paulie, explaining how the nightclub job that allowed him to be paroled was a front, which meant the feds could get Paulie for making false statements to a federal agency, the parole board. The crimes and the names kept coming: drug dealers, bookies, hijackers. The word of one protected witness, especially a drug-addled wiseguy bargaining away a life sentence, usually isn't enough to go out and arrest someone, but my father was giving the FBI enough information to lay the groundwork for dozens of cases.

Those days might have been a bonanza for the FBI and federal prosecutors, but they were torture for me and Gina. They didn't think it was safe to leave us at the hotel, and they certainly didn't want us sitting in on my father's interviews, so we were shunted off to a spare and badly lit conference room down the hall. There was no television, no radio, no video games—just me and Gina, a telephone with no dial tone, and dozens of boxes of confiscated cassette tapes from Sam Goody's. It was like being a prisoner, locked away in an empty room for hours on end, having to ask to use the bathroom, waiting for someone to bring us lunch, not having anyone to talk to.

We passed some time playing "Name That Tune," but that got old fast, and the whistling made my head hurt. Nearly every day ended with a headache—not as bad as the migraines that used to make me sick, but painful nonetheless. Those first weeks were so tedious, so goddamned boring, that I didn't have anything to do except think about what was happening to us. I was so busy being angry at my father that I didn't have time to be afraid of getting killed on his behalf. Even worse, at night, back at the hotel, he treated the whole thing like a joke. "Quit fucking worrying about it," he'd say. "These guys are all right. They're my new friends. They're gonna protect us. Relax. I know what I'm doing."

It was like he was trying to convince us that he was the one running the show. We were ducking from hotel to hotel by night and stuffed in an office by day surrounded by armed federal agents, and he was practically mocking the fact that we needed to be protected. It was the same disregard he had for everything in his life. But even he should have understood how much worse it was this time. Our lives weren't just falling apart—they'd been vaporized, liquidated, erased. And it had happened in an instant. My father and mother had had advance warning, three weeks of federal officers massaging their insecurities and fears. Perhaps no one can ever fully prepare to give up his past, to run away and leave everything including his name, but my parents at least had those twenty-one days to think about it. Gina and I got nothing. Our lives as we'd known them were stolen from us in the half second it took Ed McDonald to say the word *forever*. No goodbyes, no last visits, no time to prepare. We were just gone.

My best friend, a kid named Mike, had no idea what had happened. We played tennis together all the time, but we went to different schools so he wouldn't have noticed that I'd stopped showing up at South Side Middle. I remember walking the halls shortly after the raid in late April, wondering what he thought, what his parents must have thought. They'd wanted him to continue in a private high school in the fall, but he'd talked them into letting him go to public school with me; I wondered if they'd still let him. I never got a chance to find out. At first I was too shell-shocked to call him, and when we were swept into protection, it was too late—we weren't allowed to make any phone calls. I felt guilty that I wouldn't be at school with him, and more guilty because I couldn't even tell him.

After a week or so in the conference room in Brooklyn, one of the agents told us we could call my grandparents from a secure phone. It was a relief to speak to them, to hear their voices and tell them we were okay. Aside from my mother, no one cried, which was also a relief—I didn't think I could handle more wailing. The agent let us stay on the line for ten minutes before he told us we'd have to finish up. We said goodbye, not knowing when we would ever talk to them again.

Before the agent left the room, I asked my mother if I could call Mike. She asked the agent, and he dialed Mike's house and handed me the phone. It was in the early evening, around dinnertime. Mike's mother answered. I said it was Gregg and asked if Mike was home.

Mike got on the phone. He sounded relieved to hear my voice. Then he asked me where I was.

"I can't tell you," I said.

"Well, when are you coming home?" he asked.

There was a long silence. I couldn't get any words out, and my eyes started to burn with tears. The sound of his voice hammered home the enormity of what was happening to us, of how much I was being forced to leave behind. I could hear him on the other end of the line. His breathing was short, like he was trying not to cry.

"We're not," I finally managed. "We're going away, and we're not coming back."

"What do you mean?" His voice began to break. "You're leaving? Can I call you?"

"No." I was holding back a flood of tears. I had to concentrate to speak, to squeeze the words past the lump in my throat.

"Can I write to you?" Mike was crying now.

"I don't know," I said. "I just wanted to say goodbye."

For almost a month, I'd held everything inside. I hadn't shed a single tear since we'd left. Then all that emotion came tumbling out at once. I started to sob.

I held onto the phone until I heard Mike say goodbye. Then I handed the receiver to the agent, who placed it in the cradle.

GINA: After about two weeks, the FBI agents grew tired of shuttling us to a new hotel every other night, so they found us a gray-shingled cottage in the Hamptons. I never realized it then, but protecting an entire family is incredibly complicated; the simplest tasks become very difficult when everything is shrouded in secrecy. How, for instance, do you go about renting a house? The FBI couldn't very well go to a real estate broker or a rental agent. The people who wanted to kill my dad had informants everywhere, and any piece of information that couldn't be bought could be extorted. If anyone outside of the small group of FBI agents and U.S. marshals who were watching us found out where we were staying, we would have been in terrible danger.

As it turned out, the place in the Hamptons was a summer house that was owned by a trusted friend or a relative of one of the agents. I never knew exactly who owned it, and I suppose that's just as well as far as the FBI is concerned. Not that it mattered anyway. I was just as miserable in the Hamptons as I had been in the hotels. In some ways it was a relief, being able to settle into one place for a little while, and the agents let Gregg and me stay there during the day so we were spared those awful afternoons in the conference room where I couldn't even go to the bathroom because the ladies' room was infested with roaches. But I was bored in the

Hamptons too. I remember sleeping a lot, even though I wasn't tired. I knew that place wasn't our final destination, and I was anxious to get moving.

The way my mom explained it, what was happening to us was actually wonderful. All the bad things that had come before would be erased and we'd get to start over. "Dad's going to work and he's going to do something good," she told me. "And Dad and I will be together, so we'll be a family, only someplace new." And the government was making this all happen, so it was totally official, very black and white and almost automatic. The bad life was over and a beautiful new life was beginning.

Of course my dad put his own spin on it, but even he was optimistic in his own way. He turned the whole thing into a grand adventure. "Don't you worry about a thing, Princess," he told me. "These guys are all chumps. I know better than any of those guys. Things are gonna be great. We're gonna get a big house and I'm going to get you a horse. Trust me, it'll be great."

I did trust him. And I wanted my horse. I'd learned to ride the summer before at Kutsher's Sports Academy, a camp in upstate New York, and sometimes my mother would take me to Hempstead Park to ride the old nags. The idea of having my own Arabian or Palomino was almost too exciting to bear. We were wasting time on Long Island. Every day in the Hamptons was one more day without my horse.

I asked the agents who were watching us to take me riding. Actually, they would say I whined about it constantly, and that I also whined about everything else. If they thought of me at all, they thought I was a spoiled brat. Well, of course I was. Partly that's because I was my dad's little princess and I acted the part. Yet I was also an eleven-year-old girl who'd been ripped out of her house and planted in an outdated, weather-beaten cottage where, I was repeatedly told, somebody might come by one day and shoot my dad. And these were FBI agents who worked organized crime cases—what did they know about baby-sitting?

There were about a half-dozen agents assigned to us, and they worked in rotating shifts. Someone was always at the house. When my dad left in the morning, one or two of them would stay behind to keep an eye on us, and when he came home at night, the next wave would stay for dinner and then spend the night. It never seemed like they were protecting us, though. I imagined they would guard the door with their guns drawn and patrol the yard, their eyes scanning the trees and everyone being tense and edgy. But it wasn't like that. Mostly they just sat around. Gregg used to joke that the only way they could stop someone from killing us would be if the assassin called ahead first.

On the other hand, if the agents had been peeking through the blinds all night, that probably would have made us more nervous. So maybe their laid-back manner was intentional. And they must have done a good job—we're still here, after all. For my part, I thought they were nice enough, but I still didn't like them because I could tell that they didn't think highly of my mom and dad, and whenever someone is in opposition to your parents, it's only natural to take your parents' side. I hated that they thought they were better than us. I remember one day when Ed Gueverra, who was young and handsome and actually very nice, played tennis with Gregg, who was very good. He drove us down to one of the public courts in town, and I sat behind the fence watching them bounce the ball back and forth. I wasn't really concentrating on the game, but I convinced myself that Gregg was killing him, just beating him senseless, my brother, whipping a grown-up federal agent. Gregg told me later that they didn't even keep score, that they were only volleying, but I wanted to believe that Gregg beat him. I was so proud of him for proving that one of us was better than one of them at something.

The only real fun I had in the Hamptons was helping my mom decide what our new names would be. When the government relocates you, they don't give you much coaching. They move you and give you a stipend every month to survive on and a U.S. marshal or two to keep an eye on you, but that's it. They don't give you a script to explain the rest of your life—where you came from, why you moved, why your parents have no credit or work history, or even a new name. That part we turned into a game.

My mom and I spent hours going through magazines and even the phone book looking for one that would be perfect, something that wasn't too ethnic or too plain but just right, something that sounded proper and sophisticated. She'd come up with one and say, "No, too Jewish," and then I'd suggest one and we'd decide it was too boring. Mom finally decided on Haymes, which was the name of a family we knew when my dad was in Lewisburg. Mr. Haymes was a convict, and Mrs. Haymes had a dog that my mom used to groom. I'd forgotten that, though, so the name didn't bring up any bad memories. In fact, I thought it was a brilliant choice. I could imagine Mr. Haymes strutting around a palatial mansion, like a character on *Dallas*. The other good thing about it was that my mom could take all of our things that had Hill written on them, like the guards for my ice skates, and with a couple of strokes of a marker, change the name to Haymes. She'd draw a loop off of the *i* to make it an *a,* use the two *l*s to form the *y,* and then add a flourish of *mes*. It was fancy in a way that seemed to befit a distinguished family such as ours.

I spent hours writing Gina Haymes on notebook paper. I liked the way it looked, the way it sounded, even the way my hand curled to form the swirl of the *y*. That was the only glimpse I had of our future, my made-up name, and I wanted to get it right, wanted to feel comfortable with it. We were working without a script—we never even sat down as a family to get our stories straight—but at least I would know who I was.

GREGG: My sister and her new name—what a pain in the ass. Gina and my mom spent hours giggling over Cohens and Johannsons and Ewings, like it was some kind of game. They tried to get me involved, ask my opinion, but I ignored them. "Who cares?" I told Gina. "Once you lose your name, what difference does it make what they call you? Call me whatever you want."

And then they settled on Haymes. My mother and my sister and I kept our first names, but my father switched his to Peter. "Ooooooh, Peter Haymes," my mother said, like she was introducing the Duke of Windsor. "Mister Peter Haymes. How does that sound?"

It sounded ridiculous. What the hell kind of WASP name was Haymes? As soon as my father opened his mouth, everyone would know he was Henry Hill from Brooklyn, *Noo Yawk*.

Like I said, though, I didn't really care what our last name was. I was just relieved to be out of the hotels. If I was going to live a miserable life on the run, I may as well be able to get outside in the fresh air. I'd never been to the Hamptons before, but I knew we'd be near the water, which meant I'd be able to fish. I was a pretty good fisherman. My Aunt Ellen's boyfriend, John, taught me when my father was in prison. He brought over a spinning reel and a rod and showed me how to cast in my grandmother's backyard, how to tie a basic fisherman's knot, how to clean and lubricate the reel. Later, he took me out on Sheepshead Bay in his boat, a twenty-four-footer with a center console and big outboard motor, to go after bluefish and fluke. We were planning on going shark fishing—John caught a 280-pound mako off Montauk Point once—but my father got arrested again before we had a chance.

The only problem, I realized on the way out to the Hamptons, was that I'd left my rods and reels on my father's friend Donald's boat. Then my father did something nice, something actually considerate. On the way to the Hamptons, he asked one of the agents to pull into a bait-and-tackle shop, where my father bought me new gear. I walked out with a graphite Shakespeare rod, what they called an "ugly stick," the kind where you could bend the tip all the way back to the handle, a Daiwa spinning reel, some tackle— all high-end stuff. It seemed like the first time I'd smiled in weeks. In all the gloom and darkness and misery, I had something nice. Those were my best possessions because they were, in fact, my only possessions. Things were starting to look a little brighter.

The first morning was bright and sunny, and I noticed the moistness of the sea air. I asked John Capp, one of the agents, if he'd take me down to Shinnecock Canal so I could catch some flounder. Capp was a nice guy, affable and easy-going, particularly considering the duty he pulled, watching over a wiseguy's kids. Gina and I called him Barney Rubble because he had the look: stocky without being heavy, a square face, and the same shaggy haircut as the cartoon character. He drove me down to the canal (which was close enough to walk to but he thought we'd be safer in the car) and helped me carry my gear—rod and reel, a small tackle box, a bucket, a carton of sandworms for bait—to the dock, a long boardwalk that ran parallel to the water. He waited while I put a worm on a hook and dropped the line into the canal, and he stayed until I caught a fish or two. After he was convinced I'd be safe, that there were no hit men or kidnappers hiding behind the trees, he left me alone on the dock and drove back to the house.

I was alone for the first time in weeks. The sun was warm on my back and the air smelled salty and the water lapped up against the pilings, and I was there for all of it, finally nothing more than a thirteen-year-old boy with a fishing rod and nothing else to do on a summer day. For weeks, everything had been moving at hyperspeed—the raid, the arrests, leaving, switching hotels. Even the interminable hours in that Brooklyn conference room were tense and edgy, boring but not in the way where you can relax. And now there was nothing but the water and the sun and a whole lazy day to waste.

A couple more flounders took the bait, and I reeled them in and deposited them in my bucket. My mind started to wander. I wondered where we'd end up. Someplace like this, near the water, would be all right. Maybe a big house on a cliff above the Pacific, or down south along the Gulf of Mexico where I could go after big game fish, tarpons and tunas. I'd buy one of those big, gold Penn International reels, charter a fishing boat, and strap myself into a fighting chair where I'd take hours to land a trophy marlin. Or a decent-sized city, like Pittsburgh, so I could go to Steelers games. I was a big Steelers fan. I could adjust somewhere like that. We'd moved so many times already that I'd gotten used to making new friends.

I chased the thoughts out of my head. I'd learned not to get my hopes up about anything, even in the best of times and especially when it involved my father. If I allowed myself to daydream about where we were going, if I started to get excited, even hopeful, about whatever our new life had waiting for us, odds were I'd be disappointed again. Every time my father promised things would get better, everything eventually went to hell. It was better to brace for the worst and be relieved if it didn't happen. The thing was, though, I wasn't sure anymore what the worst could be.

My line twitched in the water. I reeled in another flounder—six in all—and tried to forget about how miserable my life had become. I decided to just be a kid for a few hours. I brought the rod back over my shoulder, then flung it forward, throwing the line way out into the canal. Then I set the butt of my rod in a hole in the pier, positioned myself so I could watch the tip, and sat down with my feet over the edge to wait for another fish to take the bait.

A beautiful boat heading up the canal caught my eye. It was white and big, a forty-five-footer, I guessed, with a wide beam and a tall mast and a flying bridge, the kind I wanted to charter to go deep-sea fishing. I was fixated. I remembered my father's brief tenure as a captain, when he ran aground in Long Island Sound. I'd always hoped he'd get another boat and treat it better, actually learn how to operate it and keep it in working condition until I was old enough to take it out.

The boat was closer now, rumbling past the pier. I stared at it, admiring the lines as it headed toward the ocean. From the corner of my eye, I saw a black flash of movement. My rod flew off the pier and into the water. I'd been so preoccupied with the boat that I'd forgotten about the line I'd cast halfway across the canal. The boat had snagged it, and suddenly it was dragging my brand new gear out to sea.

I ran down the pier, chasing the boat and my gear, screaming as loud as I could. "Hey, hey, over here! My rod! Over here!" I yelled, waving my arms over my head, trying to catch the attention of anyone on the boat. No one heard me above the engine noise. I kept running and hollering along the pier, a couple hundred feet of board-walk, until the end. I flung myself at the fence, yelled one more time, then slapped the chain link while I watched the boat motor into the distance. *Fuck, fuck, fuck, fuck, fuck.* I threw my hands up, slammed them down, stamped my foot. *Fuckfuckfuck.* It was an omen, a sign. It had to be. I had one possession to my name, and I had only a few hours truly to myself, and now, no matter how hard I tried, the thing was gone and the hours were ruined. My father had so thoroughly and radically fucked up my life that I couldn't even have a peaceful afternoon of fishing without disaster striking.

My father. *Damn it,* I thought, I'm going to have to tell him I lost the rod and reel. No one would believe what had happened, that a big boat had snagged my line and snatched my rod away. I didn't want to face him with that tale. He'd think I tossed the rod to spite him. He wouldn't understand how much that rod meant to me, how the simple freedom of being able to pull a flounder out of the water was the only comfort I had left in the mess he'd created.

He'd probably laugh about it, or maybe call me a moron. And I knew how angry I'd get at him. I had an exceptionally long fuse, but on those rare occasions when it burned down, I could be a vicious kid. When I was seven, my father had bought me—bought, stole, whatever—a train set, an elaborate N gauge model railroad with expensive miniature locomotives. I thought he would want to help me set it up, but he got drunk instead and for some reason he was laughing at me with that maniacal staccato cackle of his. I don't remember why or how it started, but he just kept laughing and laughing and laughing. The fuse started burning, and then I was enraged. I took every piece of track and twisted it in half, just ruined the whole set. And he kept laughing the whole time, antagonizing me, until every piece was broken. If I got mad, I could destroy everything I loved. I might regret it later—I might even *know* I was going to regret it—but it wouldn't stop me. At that point, I was already so angry with my father that I didn't want another laughing episode to push me over the edge. When he got back to the Hamptons that night, I told him anyway. He did just what I'd expected. "What a fucking schmuck," he said. "A hundred and fifty fucking dollars and he throws it in the water." Then he laughed at me. I walked away from him, half surprised that I'd kept my temper in check.

GINA: We left the Hamptons in a hurry, and we didn't even know where we were going. One afternoon after we'd been in the cottage for a little more than two weeks, my father came home with the agents, and one of them told us to get ready. "Pack your bags," he said. "You're leaving tomorrow."

My mom asked where we were going, but all they said was we'd find out when we got there. At that point I don't think I cared where we went. That last night in the Hamptons was the only one when I wasn't depressed. I was keyed up, excited to begin our adventure. I could almost taste it. I felt as if I'd waited my whole life for that moment. Up until then, my life had been broken up by a series of temporary situations, some shorter than others, but all of them getting in the way of the happy future I had always dreamed of and that my dad had always promised was coming. I thought we'd had it, that normal life, for a few months when we lived in Rockville Centre. I'd even started to do well in school, which I think was because I was relaxed and content. But then he got arrested on the drug charges and we were in another situation that we had to get through. Finally it was coming to an end, and this would be the last temporary situation too. I really believed that. The government was helping us. Our new life was a matter of federal policy. You can't get more official than that.

We left early in the morning and drove straight to the airport, me and Gregg and our mom in one sedan with an agent, and my father in another with two other agents. They told us on the way where we were going: Omaha. I didn't know where that was exactly. Nebraska stuck in my mind, probably because it was an answer on a geography quiz I'd taken in elementary school, but I wasn't sure where that was either, only that it was one of those big states with straight borders somewhere between New York and California. It didn't matter, though. In the car I was as excited as if I were going to Disney World.

At the airport the agents flashed their badges and quickly led us past the security checkpoints. We didn't have to stand in line with everyone else—

because the feds were in charge, we got to go right to our gate. They gave us our tickets there, issued under fake names. Not our real fake names, the Haymes family, but completely made-up ones. It was funny to me, having *fake* fake names, but my mom had a dark thought: If the plane crashed, no one would know who we were. All of our original identification had been confiscated and shredded by the marshals, and we didn't have anything with our new names on it yet. She was right—we were in limbo, strangers to the world, people with old names that didn't exist anymore and new ones that had never been used.

I watched out the window through the flight. I wanted to see where we were going, to look out over Omaha and see what was waiting for us. The first thing I noticed when we got lower to the ground was how flat it was. And green. Not the dark green of trees, but lighter, like grass. Long Island is crowded, packed with houses on streets lined with trees; even from the air I could tell Omaha was different. It was wide open and uncluttered, fresh and clean. And once we were on the ground, the sky was amazingly big, a bright blue shell that spread all the way to the horizon. I liked the way it looked.

We didn't see much of the city when we got there, just the highway from the airport and then the few blocks of downtown before we got to the hotel. It was a Sheraton. I'd gotten to like Sheratons from all those trips to Lewisburg. And this was a fancy one, with a glass elevator that went up through an airy lobby, like an atrium. There was a game room and a pool and a gift shop in the lobby where there was a big stuffed monkey with long arms that I could wrap around me like it was giving me a hug. It cost thirty dollars, which to me sounded like a lot of money, but my dad bought it for me anyway. I took it as a sign, like an omen of how good our life as a family was going to be in Omaha.

My dad took us out for dinner that night, and even that was exciting because it was so different. We went to Godfather's Pizza, which was a chain, but I'd never heard of it because there weren't any in New York. And it was like no pizza I'd ever seen before, a thick, deep-dish crust and all kinds of crazy toppings. I ordered mine with Canadian bacon and pineapple. Who'd ever heard of such a thing? Less than twelve hours since we'd left our old lives behind and I was already making strange new discoveries. Omaha, I decided, was going to be great.

GREGG: My father never skipped a beat. Most men, you'd think they'd be humbled in that situation: running for his life, his past erased, his family uprooted, packed onto an airplane and flown into the bland Midwest so no one would pop a few bullets in the back of his head, stuff him in a trunk, and bury him upstate. Not my father. He was the same cocky bastard in Omaha that he'd always been in New York.

The marshals hadn't given us many instructions or much coaching, but what they did tell us was pretty simple to grasp. One, if people asked where we were from, we were supposed to say Stamford, Connecticut. A Connecticut accent isn't at all like our thick New York ones, but Stamford was close enough to Long Island that Midwesterners might not know the difference. Other than that, we were supposed to keep a low profile, try to blend in as best we could, the East Coast wiseguy and his family. It was the first time in weeks that we had no round-the-clock FBI protection. They told us that our best protection was our anonymity; we were safe as long as we didn't attract attention.

So what's my father do? The very first night, only hours into his supposedly low-key life, he takes us to Godfather's Pizza. He thought it was funny, eating at Godfather's, and maybe it was, but I wasn't in a laughing mood. Worse, he behaved like it really was some mobster's joint, like he was back at The Suite or Roberts Lounge. He started drinking as soon as we squeezed into a booth, going through two carafes of red wine, and got drunk almost immediately (as I've mentioned, my father has a low tolerance for booze, which I always thought was odd considering how much he drank). He started getting loud. It was nothing we weren't used to—a steady stream of *motherfuckers* and *cocksuckers* and *rat bastards*—but the families eating pizza in a Midwestern franchise clearly weren't used to it. No one said anything to him, but people stared, and then they glared. I couldn't help but stare back and wonder what they must be thinking: *New York hood on the run from the Mob.* I tried to envision some other thought: *Just some good ol' boy having a good time.* But that didn't seem right. The accent would have given him away. I couldn't shake the chilling thought that they could see right through us.

When he got the bill, he tipped the waiter twenty bucks, a ridiculous amount, probably a bigger tip than any Omaha teenager had ever seen. He slid it into the kid's palm and then grabbed him around the neck like he was embracing one of the regulars at the Copa. My father definitely didn't blend.

Maybe it was harmless. Hell, no one can tip too much, right? But I was in total despair over where we'd landed. When I'd first heard the word *Omaha* on the way to the airport, I was devastated. Those few moments fishing on the Shinnecock Canal, when I'd briefly fantasized about where we might end up, came racing back to me. I'd been right not to get my hopes up. There would be no big-game fishing in the Gulf of Mexico after all, no tailgating outside a big-league stadium, nothing at all, no perks to smooth the transition. I'd searched my mind for anything I knew about Omaha. Only two things popped up: *Mutual of Omaha's Wild Kingdom,* an animal show from the seventies that was hosted by a really old man, and corn. I was a born and bred New Yorker, headed into the bleakest, most boring heart of Middle America.

My first look at Omaha hadn't raised my spirits any. The first thing I noticed was how flat the landscape was, level and empty without even any trees to break up the horizon. The second thing I noticed was the heat. A marshal met us at the gate, and we had only a short walk to the car, but those few steps between the terminal and the curb had been like marching through an oven set on bake.

The next morning, after we'd had breakfast in the buffet at the hotel, I went out to explore the city, a few blocks of it anyway, since I didn't want to wander too far from the hotel. I wasn't worried about anyone finding us yet—Uncle Jimmy could scour the entire country for years and never think that Henry Hill would wind up in Omaha—but I didn't want to get lost in a strange place on my first day as Gregg Haymes either. I didn't know anyone. Not a single person to call or visit. No friends, no family. We were on our own.

The Sheraton was in a business district, and since it was a weekday, there were a fair number of people out on the streets. Far fewer than New York, though. And blonde people. I noticed that right away—compared to New York, Omaha had an astonishing number of people with fair skin and light hair. That didn't bode well for the rest of the Haymes family. I was the only blonde in a family of a dark-haired Irish-and-Italian father and a Jewish mother; my father used to joke that my mother must have had something going on with the mailman. As long as I kept my mouth shut, I could fade into the crowd. But my father and my mother and my sister would stand out like fish on bicycles. The accents, not to mention the constant cursing, would make my father the focus of all kinds of unwanted attention.

The sun was broiling hot, and the sky was clear blue, not a cloud above the city. I walked a couple of blocks in one direction, turned left, went a couple more blocks. I studied the storefronts, with their clean facades of gray stones and beige cement, and the sidewalks, which were wider and more even than any I'd seen before, like the concrete had been recently poured. There was no litter anywhere, not even in the gutters along the curbs. Omaha struck me as a very clean little city, but sterile and antiseptic. There's something about growing up in New York that can make a kid dislike a place for being too clean.

I made another left, walking a giant square loop around and back to the hotel. I was looking for something, though I wasn't sure exactly what. I'd know it when I saw it, *if* I saw it, something I could at least relate to or identify with, anything that would offer a hint of familiarity, some miniscule comfort.

I didn't find it. I walked maybe ten blocks that morning through what I took to be the heart of downtown, and the best I could say was that the city was unremarkable. It wasn't threatening or intimidating—it was just a plain, foreign landscape. And I was supposed to live in it forever. I knew I'd adapt because I'd always adapted. But I wasn't happy about it. I trudged back to the hotel, sweat beading on my arms and my forehead in the Nebraska heat, and went for a swim.

GINA: I was in the hotel pool one afternoon, which was surrounded by glass walls on three sides and covered by a glass ceiling, like a greenhouse. My mom was sitting in a chair near the edge of the water, keeping an eye on me and trying to relax. Then, from the corner of my eye, I saw her bolt out of her chair and start waving at me like she wanted me to swim toward her. When I got closer, I could see that her eyes were wide, and she kept shifting her stare from me to a spot behind me. She looked scared.

"Oh my God, oh my God," she said, frantically but softly, like she didn't want anyone else to hear her. "There's someone taking pictures."

I could feel my heart start to pound. My mom was understandably on edge, always looking, always watching for anyone or anything that seemed out of place. She tried not to show it, but she was like a mama bear protecting her cubs— the littlest thing would have her rearing up and rushing me and Gregg to safety. It's funny to think about now, considering the chaos in which we'd grown up, but my mom always had that protective instinct, even if it came out in weird ways.

That summer we went to Kutsher's Sports Academy, parents were only supposed to stay for the first couple of days, just long enough for the kids to get used to the place. But my mom and grandma didn't want to leave. They found a hotel nearby and every day they would sneak into the ice rink where I was taking lessons in a beautiful pair of Ridell figure skates my mom bought for me. They would peek out from under the bleachers and wave and giggle to themselves. "Oooh, there she is, there she is!" I liked it. I think I would have been terribly homesick if they'd left, and I think my mom would have worried too much about me too. It was like preventive medicine.

That was better than what Gregg got. The next summer he had wanted to go off to a survivalist camp where they drop you in the woods for a weekend and make you eat berries and build a lean-to out of brush and start a fire by rubbing sticks together. Mom wouldn't let him go. She said it was too dangerous. So he spent the summer around the house where Dad was selling drugs and shooting submachine guns in the basement and his friends were getting killed by the week. But she meant well.

Now her fear was infecting me. "Come on," she whispered at me as she bit her lip like she would do when she got angry. "Get out of the pool, right now, come on, get out."

My knee scraped the side of the pool as I pulled myself up, and my arms were shaking. I looked across the room, but quickly, stealing a glance so no one would get a good look at my face. I saw a man at the far end with a camera, and he seemed to be taking pictures of the atrium, the way any tourist who'd never been in a nice hotel might. In fact, that's what he looked like, a tourist. He was wearing trousers and a golf shirt, nothing out of the ordinary for Omaha and certainly not the kind of clothes my dad's friends would wear. But I remembered overhearing the agents back in New York saying that Uncle Jimmy wouldn't come after us himself—it would be someone we'd never seen before, someone we didn't recognize, someone who wouldn't seem threatening until it was too late.

Mom wrapped a towel around me and turned

me toward the door. She kept watching the man with the camera but with quick glances so he wouldn't catch her staring at him. I thought I saw him look back at us, but that might have been my imagination. My heart was thumping now.

We hurried into the hallway, my mom half pushing me and at the same time trying to look nonchalant, like we were just two more tourists going off to have lunch after a leisurely swim. As the door closed, I took one more look. The man was taking a picture of the garden beyond the glass wall. I had a panicky thought: Could that be him? Maybe he's blending in, trying not to draw attention to himself while he takes pictures of us to send back to New York to confirm that he'd found the runaway Hills. I felt myself shivering, but not from the chill of the air-conditioned hotel.

And then, as quickly as the fear had arrived, it vanished. By the time we got back to the room, Mom was already calmer, as if just having distance between me and the man with the camera was a measure of safety. It wasn't quite out-of-sight-out-of-mind, but it was something similar. My mom told me that she'd probably overreacted, that he was surely just a tourist or a businessman passing through Omaha. The government was protecting us, right? There was no way someone could have hunted us down so quickly. Right? The tone in her voice suggested she was trying to convince herself

as much as me. In my case, it worked. By the time I
dried off and changed into my clothes, I believed
that we'd been frightened by something completely
innocent.

It was easy to forget how much danger we were
in, especially in a quiet place like Omaha. As the
days unfolded, I became more encouraged that
everything would work out. The pieces seemed to
be falling comfortably into place. At the hotel—I
can't remember if it was before we saw the man
with the camera or after, but it was right around
there—I met my first friend in Omaha. She was
about my age, with blonde hair and blue eyes, and
when she introduced herself in the game room, she
said her name was Mary. Then she asked what my
name was.

"Gina Haymes," I said. It was the first time I'd
said my new name, and it just came right out, like
the most natural thing in the world, probably
because I'd practiced it so much. I thought, *That
doesn't sound so bad.* In fact, it sounded sophisticated.

Mary told me she'd moved to Omaha because
her father's company transferred him there. I told
her my dad had gotten transferred too, which
wasn't exactly a lie. Then she asked me who he
worked for. "The government," I said. I hadn't
thought that far ahead before, but it popped into my
head right when I needed it. And it was the truth:

My dad *did* work for the government. I knew I couldn't tell Mary precisely what he did—"He testifies against Mafia people who want to kill him"—so I told her his job was secret, which was also sort of true. It was a nice, compact story, short and to the point and very believable. Eleven-year-old girls don't really want more information about their friends' fathers' jobs anyway, unless they're a rock star or a professional athlete or someone famous.

We stayed in the hotel for a few weeks until we found a house to move into. It was a split-level in a subdivision away from downtown that was so new that none of the trees had grown up yet, and to me it was perfect. It reminded me of the houses I'd loved in Woodmere, when we'd drive by and I'd fantasize about who lived inside and if they dressed up for dinner when the father came home from work, except ours was brand new. I'd never seen new construction on Long Island. Every house I'd ever been in was at least forty years old, and now we were going to live in one that seemed to have been built especially for us. There were kids in the neighborhood, too, some old enough for Gregg and me to make friends with and, in the house next to ours, some younger ones that I knew I could probably baby-sit. Even my friend Mary from the hotel was nearby; her father bought a house a few blocks away, too far to walk but a pretty short drive for my mom.

GREGG: You can't tell just one little lie to explain your entire life. I know because I tried. Believe me, I tried. Even if people aren't probing, if they're just having a normal get-to-know-you conversation, one innocent question leads to another and another, and eventually you end up weaving a massive lie full of big, gaping holes.

When we moved into our house, kids in the neighborhood came over to see who we were. They were nice enough, and naturally they were curious about the new kids.

It began with the obvious: What's your name?

"Gregg Haymes," I said. When it came out of my mouth the first time, it sounded strange, almost unnatural. You know how you can tell when someone you're talking to is uncomfortable, the way they pause before they answer the simplest question? I tried not to be that guy.

Then: Where are you from?

"Connecticut," I said. We'd practiced that part, and keeping my answer to just the state saved the city for a follow-up. Which, of course, always came: Where in Connecticut?

"Stamford."

But the questions kept coming, questions I hadn't anticipated. Almost immediately, we were off script and winging it.

What's Stamford like?

I'd been to Stamford only once, in a snowstorm.

I had no idea what it was like. "It's okay," I said.

Where'd you go to school?

"I was supposed to go to Stamford High in the fall." I hoped there actually was a Stamford High School, or if there wasn't, that no one I met in Omaha knew any better.

More questions. Not all at once, but as we got to know people, they'd get curious and ask. What part of Stamford? What kind of neighborhood was it? Did you have a big house? Why did you move?

There were so many little details to keep track of that I was constantly scared shitless to say anything. It was hard enough remembering what I'd said, but I had to keep track of Gina too. What if I said we lived in a small house and Gina said we lived in a big one? Or if I said south side and she said north side? We had debriefing sessions, Gina and I, after we'd spent any time with other kids, going over our stories, comparing conversations, making sure everything we'd said had matched and, if it didn't, that we could explain why if it ever came up again. It was nerve-racking. I was serious about it, but I could tell Gina wasn't paying attention. It should have been a cinch because all we had to do was take our lives from Long Island and transfer them to Stamford—and then hope to hell we never met anyone from Stamford. The weird thing is, I could handle the questions about my father. Gina and I had that down. "He works for the government. It's confidential. We can't talk about it." That was easy.

In the end, it didn't matter. No one ever tripped us up, probably because no one was trying. We settled in soon enough, and my mother got us a membership at the local Jewish Community Center, where there was a tennis pro who ran a junior development program. That helped, having someplace to play tennis. That was something familiar, the thing I could relate to that I'd been looking for on the streets around the hotel. The kids in Omaha played different sports than New Yorkers, not so much on the organized-league level but in the neighborhood. On Long Island we spray-painted strike zones on the backs of apartment buildings and played stickball every day, or we'd get sticks and skates and play roller hockey in the streets. No one in Omaha played hockey, and they didn't even know what stickball was. Mostly they rode their bikes around or played basketball in their driveways, which wasn't really my sport. So finding tennis at the JCC was kind of a relief. And it turned out that I was pretty good by Omaha standards. In New York I'd been a mediocre tournament player who usually got bounced out in the qualifying rounds because the competition was so much stiffer—I was playing in tournaments with the likes of John

McEnroe's little brother. In Nebraska, though, I was one of the better kids, good enough to make the Nebraska State Open in the fourteen-year-old division of the U.S. Tennis Association.

The whole family drove up to Lincoln to watch me play, which was kind of cool, almost like we were a normal family. The tournament was held outside on a public court near downtown, and the registration desk was a long folding table set up courtside. I went over to sign in, not thinking as much about the form as I was about the game, getting myself geared up for competition. I had to enroll in the USTA all over again under my new name. The line for my name had three little headings above it, one each for first, middle, and last. I ignored them and just wrote *Gregg Haymes* in the space. Then I filled out the lines for my city and age and my home program at the JCC, put down the pen, and started to walk away.

"Excuse me." There was a woman behind the table. I stopped and looked at her.

"What's your middle name?" she asked.

I froze. My mind went blank. "What?"

"We need your middle name," she said. "What is it?"

My heart skipped a beat and my palms started to sweat. I hadn't thought of a middle name. I could have made up one, anything, but my brain was stalled. "Um, Matthew," I said, then immediately regretted it. I was suddenly very nervous, almost frightened. Matthew actually was my middle name, the one I'd been given at birth. I was now on an official USTA form as Gregg Matthew Haymes.

My father's friends—his old friends, the ones who wanted to kill him—all knew I played tournament tennis. What if one of them got the genius idea to comb through the USTA files for any fourteen-year-old playing under the name Gregg Matthew Something? Then they'd have the last name, they'd have the state, holy Christ, they'd have our address. They'd come after us. I may have just signed our death warrant.

I took a deep breath, tried to calm my nerves. None of my father's wiseguy associates would think to track down Henry Hill through junior tennis records. There were probably lots of Gregg Matthews playing tennis anyway. Right? I was trying to convince myself it was no big deal, but the pressure felt like my head was going to explode.

Haymes. Farrell. Court five.

I tried to bury those thoughts as they called my match. It was hard. I had trouble remembering the score, and I was playing in a fog. After some questionable calls by my opponent, I pulled out a narrow victory, 6–4, 7–6.

My father came down from the stands after my

first win. "What the fuck is the matter with you?" he said.

I could smell the liquor on his breath. He'd been drinking steadily. "What are you talking about?" I said. "I just won."

"Yeah, but you're playing like a fucking pussy. That cocksucker was robbing you on those calls, and you just fucking took it."

I was stunned.

"You've got no killer instinct," he said. "You play like a fucking pussy."

I walked away from him and seethed until my next match. My father deserved my wrath, but the kid I played next suffered it. He was better than me, and on any other day he would have beat me. But I wiped the court with him. Between points, I didn't walk to the ball—I sprinted. Months of pent-up anger exploded on the court. I played like I was possessed, and trounced him in straight sets, 6–0, 6–1.

When we shook hands after the match, my rage had been spent. But the kid on the other side of the net was wide-eyed. "Are you ranked?" he asked.

I shook my head and walked away. I won my next match, then the one after that, both convincingly. Word started to spread about the new kid from back East. My notoriety brought back that sick feeling that I'd had at the tournament desk.

It messed with my head. I lost my edge, and the second-seeded player beat me in the quarter finals.

GINA: In a lot of ways, our life in Omaha seemed better than it had been on Long Island. We had less money, but a nicer house and none of those awful parties. We went to the Jewish Community Center all the time, and I had friends to play with. We had most of our stuff too, our mismatched furniture and our dogs and my hamster and Gregg's cockatiel. Gram had taken care of the animals since we'd left Rockville Centre, and once the marshals told her we'd gotten settled—they didn't tell her where, though—she packed everything into a moving van. I counted the days until it arrived; I never liked the furniture we'd rented, and I thought the bedroom suite Aunt Ellen had given me would be pretty in my new room, which was painted yellow.

My dad still wasn't around very much, though. If he wasn't flying back to New York so FBI agents could interview him or federal prosecutors could prepare him to testify, he was hanging out in bars just like he'd always done. Not having Dad around seemed normal. The only difference was that when he was home he wasn't very happy. He could barely sit still, and he was always walking around like he was late for an appointment. My mom said the stress on him was terrible; he had become the thing he most despised, a rat. He was turning his back on everything he'd once held sacred, everyone he'd once depended on. "The government's heartless, making him do this," my mom said. "They're bleeding him dry." I accepted that. I believed it was only another temporary situation, that once he got through testifying we'd get on with our lives.

My grandma kept us up on everything that was going on back in New York. She wrote a lot, sending her letters through the U.S. marshals, who'd deliver them to us. But she called, too. Once we got the house, my mom slipped a few digits of our phone number into her letters home until my grandma had them all. Then every Sunday at noon, Gram would go to a pay phone on Long Island and call us. It was a horrible breach of security—the marshals had been adamant when they told us we couldn't have any contact with anyone from our past. But that's the way my parents led their lives:

Give them a rule, one simple rule, and they'd find a way to break it.

I didn't write as much as Gram wanted me to, but what eleven-year-old girl does? But every week, sometimes twice a week, she'd send a letter to my mom and one each to me and Gregg (or sometimes a single one to both of us if she'd already written a long one to Mom). They were typed single space at a small table in her basement, and so full of love and affection. They were always addressed to "My dearest darling Karen" or "My dearest darling delicious Gregg." For us children, she kept the topics pretty light, like how well she was doing in her temple bowling league—Gregg used to be her partner, and he was really good, so good that he won a trophy *and* a bag to keep his ball in—or how she'd hung our artwork behind the couch or asking us to take a picture of our new bedrooms so she could have a mental picture of where we were when we wrote our letters. In mine, she almost always included a few Yiddish words or phrases that she wanted me to learn. "Remember, Gina," she wrote in one letter, "when I see you I expect you to talk Jewish with me and you can if you memorize these phrases." That was the other thing about Grandma: She was convinced that somehow, some way, she would see us again, and sooner rather than later.

The letters to my mom weren't as cheery. She told my mom how disgusted she was at some of the things she'd learned, like about the parties where everyone was having sex and doing drugs. She kvetched that she hadn't been able to get back the bail money she put up to get my dad out of the Nassau County jail because the charges hadn't been formally dismissed yet, and she kept Mom up-to-date on how she was trying to sell Tri Gemini, my dad's silk-screening company, and a few other things, like some jewelry and a fur coat. Mostly, though, she wrote about how angry she was at my dad for getting us into this mess.

"I thought Henry was going to do all the talking so that none of this mess would continue," she wrote in one line. "So far it seems Henry is safely tucked away and everyone else is thrown to the dogs." Then her best line: "These things just don't happen to nice middle-class, hardworking Jewish people."

But I think even she had some hope for my dad—not the faith that I had, but at least some hope. At the end of one of her early letters to my mom, one she sent on June 20, 1980, she typed a half page to my father.

Dear "Heshy,"

I sat here, my son-in-law, and asked myself what do I want to write to you about. Some of the things were real pips, others were insincere, because, I really didn't feel them, and then it

came to me, the name "Heshy." That was an
endearing name my mother called my father and
since your Jewish name is "Avrum Hesh," I knew
what it was that I wanted to write to you. I
would love you to be "Heshy" and be a credit to
that name as "Gootman Melach" is a credit to
my mother's name. I resent the "thing," (I don't
consider it a person) that was responsible for
taking my daughter and her children away from
us, but, I want to love and respect "Heshy"!
Since we can no longer be close to those we love,
we want the security of knowing that "Heshy" is
there watching out for our interests. Taking care
at all times that no harm comes to them. Being a
husband and father second to none. Being
responsible for the love and respect in the home.
Don't ever use the name unless you intend to live
up to the standards that the name stands for.
I'm not asking that you call yourself "Heshy,"
I'm asking that you be a "Heshy," loving, giving,
unselfish, honorable, and proud. Your wife is
"Malach" (an angel), and you must prove
worthy of her love and belief in you. Alone
Karen's dream can never come true no matter
where she goes in the world, but, Karen, Heshy,
Gregg, and Gina can conquer anything they set
out to do. Daddy, I, Cheryl, and Ellen wish you
all the luck in the world. I want my children safe
and happy. We can live with the separation if we

can feel secure that you both are working at
building a new safe life.

Love, Mom

See, she even signed it "love." If Grandma could
believe in the man she liked to call "that dumb
bastard," then surely I could too.

GREGG: My father was drunk behind the
wheel. It was quarter to eleven on a July night, and
he'd pulled into the driveway with a bump that
snapped my head forward. Then he passed out.

I unbuckled my seatbelt and nudged him.
"Dad," I said. "Wake up." He didn't move. "Dad,
get up. We're home." He was dead to the world. I
shook him again, harder this time. No movement.
I stared at him and waited. Nothing. At least we
were both alive. I was grateful for that.

We'd been out all day. He'd gotten back from
another trip to New York the day before and wanted
to catch up with his son, I guess. It was early, before
noon, when we started. He was sober. I said okay.

The first place he took me was a bar. It was
nothing special, neither a good neighborhood
joint nor a fancy hotel bistro—more like a
Bennigan's or some other chain. They were set-
ting up for lunch. My father knew someone at the
bar because people like my father always know
someone at the bar. Drop him in the morning in

a new city, someplace he's never been, and he'll find a friend on a bar stool by nightfall. I watched TV while he made small talk for an hour or so, and then he announced it was time to go. Instead of going home, though, we went to another bar. And then another and another.

That's what we did all day and well into the night, drove to bars where my father talked and drank and I watched TV. After a half-dozen bars, he was hammered, and when he finally decided to go home, he could barely stand, much less walk straight. He wobbled to the car with my assistance and stood next to the driver's side door for a moment. Then he looked at me and held the keys out.

"Here," he said. "You drive."

I gave him a look like he was insane. "Dad! I can't drive," I said.

"You fucking drive. C'mon. Let's go."

"Dad," I said, "what are you doing? I don't know how to drive. You drive."

He was fucked up. But I was only fourteen. I'd never driven before, and I didn't think my wheeling around Omaha was any better an idea than helping my shitfaced father do it, especially since he'd had a lot of practice driving drunk. "No way," I said. "You're driving."

He shrugged and slid into the seat. It took him a couple of tries before he got the key in the ignition and got the engine started. He nudged the gas, but his foot was heavy with booze and the car lurched forward. "Hey!" I shouted at him. "Dad! Easy!"

"Don't worry," he said. "I got it."

He pulled into traffic and steered us toward home. He kept the car straight for about two blocks before he started drifting to the left, across the centerline. "Hey!" I shouted again as I grabbed the steering wheel. "Stay in the lane."

"Fuck you. I got it."

There were about six miles between the last bar and our house, which took my father almost twenty minutes to negotiate. He weaved, drove too fast for a few blocks, then too slowly. I sat next to him double-checking my seatbelt, then gripping the dashboard with one hand and the wheel with the other to help steer, every now and again screaming, "Red light! Red light! Red light!" until he would stop.

Somehow we got home, just in time for him to pass out.

I stared at him for another minute, then got out in disgust and started up the front walk. My mother was standing on the stoop holding the door open.

"Where's your father?"

I jerked my thumb over my shoulder. "He's in the car."

I knew it wounded her, my father's being an alcoholic. She'd been getting on him about it for the past year or so, ever since my grandfather, my father's father, died from cirrhosis. "Is that what you want for your son?" she'd yell at him. "It's just like that song, 'The Cat's in the Cradle.' Your boy is going to be just like you, *Dad*. Is that what you want? Remember how you felt watching your father drink himself to death? Is that what you want?"

He'd either laugh or tell her to fuck off or shut up. My father didn't have much capacity for guilt.

My mother went past me out to the driveway to rouse my father. I watched her open the door and lean in over him. I shook my head. *Mr. Peter Haymes,* I thought, *is home.*

• • •

My father always had an excuse for being drunk. During those weeks in Omaha, he would say later, he was trying to numb himself to the reality of what he'd become. "Yeah, it took its toll on me," my father recalled. "I couldn't forgive myself in the beginning for being a rat. I mean, I would have put a fucking gun to my head and blew my fucking brains out before I ever thought in a million years I would have become an informant, you know? I mean, that's how much I was into that shit, brainwashed or whatever you want to call it."

Brainwashed is exactly the word. Even at fourteen I began to understand the brutal truth about the wiseguy life. A few pieces—not all of them because I wouldn't learn all the details for years, but enough—had fallen into place for me. Stacks Edwards was dead, Marty Krugman had disappeared, and we were on the run. Even I could make the connection: The wiseguys, my father's friends, men I'd known my whole life, had turned on each other. There was no honor or loyalty; twenty years of friendship meant nothing once a man became a liability. Even *real* family members weren't safe. Remember Gerald Peters, my dad's drug partner whose son was the informant who got our house raided and started this whole thing? The son was dead within months, killed for being a snitch.

Now my father was next on the hit list. He had enough information in his foggy memory to destroy Jimmy, to destroy Paulie, to send dozens of men to prison for years or maybe forever. See, being a wiseguy isn't a series of distinct crimes— it's a way of life. There was no endgame, no ultimate goal. It wasn't like my father or Jimmy had a plan to steal enough so they could retire on the Jersey Shore; my father pissed through more money than most people make in a lifetime. They did what they did because that's who they were.

The thieving was so common and so continuous that individual crimes were forgotten (except, of course, for the really big scores or the ones they got busted for). I have a vivid memory, for example, of my father and Paul Mazzei stripping a room at the Sunrise Motel when we lived in Rockville Centre when I was twelve—unbolting the television, grabbing the linens and the furniture, all brand new, throwing it all in the back of a van. My father agrees that it probably happened, but he can't exactly remember because it was such a chickenshit rip-off. Asking my father to recount every illegal act he ever committed would be like asking the pope to name everyone who'd ever confessed to him.

But that's exactly what the feds were doing. The deal they'd made with my father required him to tell them everything. If they'd caught him in a lie, if they'd caught him holding back to protect anyone, they would have kicked him, and us, out of the program. So he was dredging his memory, pulling up details of hundreds of crimes he'd forgotten about. It wasn't just Lufthansa—it was a thousand rip-offs and drug deals and beatings and murders, any one of which might be good enough to make an indictment stick. Al Capone, as every wiseguy knows, went down for tax evasion.

That's why Jimmy and Paulie wanted my

father dead. And I knew they would stop at nothing. They'd already put a bounty on my father's head, half a million dollars payable to the man who put a bullet in his skull, and there were dozens of made men who would do it on a direct order from Paulie. That summer one of Jimmy's wiseguy friends offered my father's brother (who wasn't a wiseguy) a million dollars just to give up our address, which my uncle didn't know anyway. My grandmother told us that one of Jimmy's associates came to her house and promised her a quarter million if she'd testify that my father was a drug addict and a drunk and therefore a thoroughly unreliable witness. Other gangsters were harassing one of my father's girlfriends, a woman named Lucy, trying to get her to give up our location. And there were legitimate private investigators, hired by Jimmy or for Jimmy, tracking us down too.

There is nothing more terrifying than knowing people want to kill you, except knowing that they are *capable* of killing you. And being with my father made us all targets. I could only hope that we stayed one step ahead of them, and that the U.S. marshals were extremely good at their job.

GINA: So Omaha wasn't the dream come true I'd imagined it would be. I guess I expected a whole new life to magically appear, that once we'd gotten away from New York everything would instantly change. But it didn't. By midsummer I was still waiting for my dad to get a job, still waiting for my horse, still waiting for ours to be a normal family.

But we fell into a routine. I spent afternoons jumping off the diving boards at the JCC, I helped the Portuguese lady next door with her baby sometimes, and I played with my new friends. There were bouts of homesickness, and I especially missed Alice, but I knew there was nothing I could do about it, and eventually the feelings passed. Nothing had ever been stable in my life—no apartment, no house, no neighborhood. I was used to letting feelings pass.

I turned twelve in July and started getting ready for the new school year. My mom took me shopping and bought me Gloria Vanderbilt corduroy pants in rust and dark brown, though I'm sure the stores called them sienna and French mocha or something fancy, and matching shirts with small bows around the collar. I looked good, but I was beginning to feel a little anxious. When our family life was relatively calm, like it had been the previous year—my dad, despite his illegal dealings, was home and we had money—I did pretty well in school. But when there was chaos, like now, when Dad was gone so much, I got distracted and worried. I was trying to calm myself down, trying to be excited about starting in a new school, but it wasn't working.

And then, on August 1, 1980, Uncle Jimmy got arrested. For all the crimes he'd committed, federal agents got him on something incredibly minor: a parole violation. Like my father, he was still on parole for the Florida extortion case that had sent both of them to Lewisburg, which meant there were certain things—a lot of things, actually—that he couldn't do. He couldn't be around other criminals, for one, and he certainly couldn't carry a gun. The feds got Jimmy for both those things, and my dad helped prove it.

After the Lufthansa robbery, Jimmy had gone to Florida with an ex-con named Angelo Sepe apparently, the feds believed, to pay tribute to Paulie, who'd moved down there. My dad told the feds about that—they already knew, though, because they'd been watching Jimmy since the robbery—and he told them how he bought guns for Jimmy in the spring of 1979.

My dad had to fly to New York in early August to testify at Jimmy's parole revocation hearing. A marshal was bringing my father up to the hearing room in a back elevator, and when they stepped into the hallway, Jimmy was there. He glared at my father, then said something to his lawyer. The marshal overheard it: "I know that fucker's in the Midwest."

That was enough for the government to get spooked. I was snuggled on the couch with my mother that afternoon when the phone rang. She answered it, and I saw her face flush.

"Why?" I heard her say. "What happened?"

She listened some more, then hung up. Her hands were clenched.

"We have to leave," she said. Her words were clipped. But then she seemed to soften, and she hugged me. "Oh Gina, I'm so sorry. But we have to leave here."

She was squeezing me tight, but not hard enough to get rid of the pit in my stomach.

GREGG: I'd pushed the fear to the back of my mind that summer, not so far that I forgot it completely but enough that it didn't haunt me. I accepted my fate to be stranded in Omaha and decided, a deliberate act of will, to make the best of it.

By the beginning of August, things were looking up. The marshal assigned to us, a tall and ramrod straight guy with close-cropped hair named Llewellyn, drove me over to the high school where I was going to be a freshman. He wanted me to meet the principal.

"I've already spoken to him," Llewellyn said, "and he knows you have a . . . uh, you know, a special situation."

A special situation. Yeah, that was one way to put it.

"Anyway," Llewellyn said, "he knows that if you have any problems or issues, he should contact me. So that's all squared away. But we're going to go meet with him just to introduce you two. But there's nothing to worry about. This is all routine. I'm just going to make sure you get set up okay."

He led me into the office, and the principal got up from behind his desk to shake my hand. He was a big man, taller than Llewellyn and barrel-chested, maybe in his early forties. He was very cordial but serious too, not one of those goofy, overly friendly principals who wants to be every student's best friend. With his size and his demeanor, I imagined he was probably tough, which was reassuring, like he'd watch my back.

"If you have any questions," he told me, "any problems at all, you come and see me. If there's anything I can do for you, don't hesitate, all right?"

I nodded and thanked him. It was comforting, having those two men on my side, a federal agent, serious and professional, and a principal, big and intimidating. For the first time since we'd left, I felt like someone was really watching my back. I allowed myself to feel safe.

Then it all changed in a day. The next afternoon I came home from tennis and found my mother pacing the living room.

"There's been a problem," she said. "We have to go."

"Go where?" I asked. For a second, I figured she meant we had to run some kind of errand. But then I could see it on her face. Her eyes were red, like she'd been crying or was about to. She was trying to keep it together, and I realized she was talking in those short, clipped sentences again.

"They found us," she said. "We just have to go. The marshals're coming in the morning."

Terror stirred in my stomach. "Why? What happened?"

"I don't know." She was still pacing and muttering, more to herself than to me and Gina. "Why? God, I can't believe this. Why, why, *why*?" She was biting her lip and on the edge of hysteria. Gina started to cry.

"Mom, what happened?" I asked again. I was off balance, unsettled.

"I don't know," she said. "There's been a problem." Then, to herself: "Why, dammit, why?"

Following my mother around the house, I realized I was suddenly very afraid. The fear rushed forward from the back of my brain, flooding out everything else, blurring my vision. My stomach had that heavy, sinking feeling, like something tragic had just happened, and I was sweating and cold all at once. I could hear my heartbeat invading my thoughts, pounding a lightning beat through every panicked synapse. In an instant I was wrenched back to being Henry's Kid, the firstborn of a career criminal whose friends wanted him dead. I knew there was only one problem bad enough that the feds would want to move us again, and move us immediately: We were in immediate danger.

There was no point in asking any more questions because my mother clearly didn't have any answers, and she was too upset to give them if she did. I drew a deep breath. I knew I had to calm myself, slow down, think clearly. Panic was dangerous.

Where are they?

I was suddenly keenly aware of my surroundings, like a soldier walking point. I peeked out the window, scanning the rows of newly built houses and manicured lawns for any strange figures on the sidewalk or unfamiliar cars on the street. The trees were too new and young to provide any cover. But what would I do if I saw someone? I had no idea. Would I have time to duck? To run?

Wait. Deep breath. Think.

The marshals weren't coming until the morning. That gave us at least twelve hours. The feds believed we'd be safe for at least half a day. Whoever had found us couldn't be too close.

What if they're wrong? Oh shit, what if the feds got bad information?

I checked out the window again. Nothing suspicious. I did some quick calculations. A flight would take three hours, then another hour to drive to the house. But that would only be if they had our address. I dismissed that thought. The feds would have been at the house already if someone had our address.

But they could be in the city. They could be circling, waiting . . .

My father wasn't home. *Shit.* Maybe they'd already gotten him. No, no—I knew that couldn't be right. Someone would have told us. There would have been armed agents swarming over the house. My father must have been with the marshals. Or in a bar. I snorted at the thought, disgusted. He's the reason we're in this jam, and he's probably wobbling on a bar stool.

The fear was receding enough to clear my head. The danger, I figured out, wasn't immediate, only imminent. We were safe until morning if we just stayed put, and then the feds would take over. But how did it happen? We'd done everything right. It never occurred to me that my father had screwed up, that he'd given away the secret, that he'd talked to his old girlfriends in New York. I thought—I *knew*—his survival instinct would have prevented that.

Was it my fault? The tennis tournament, my real middle name . . .

That couldn't be it. No way Uncle Jimmy could have combed through all those obscure USTA tennis rosters in such a short time.

The phone calls from Grandma . . .

No, it couldn't be the calls. My grandmother was nothing if not stubborn. She could keep a secret, and she'd kill herself before doing anything that could harm us. No one tapped a pay phone anyway, and she always called from pay phones. She asked once in a letter which would be better, two five-dollar calls a week or a single ten-dollar talk on Sunday.

My mind was skipping through questions and scenarios. In rapid succession, I ruled out every possible connection between Henry Hill and Omaha, Nebraska. Which meant Jimmy or Paulie had thought of something I couldn't imagine, or had gotten to someone at the FBI or the Marshals Service who was supposed to be protecting us, had gotten some inside information. Terror welled up again, and I forced it down.

"We have to sell the car."

My mother was behind me. I spun around. "What?"

"We have to sell the car," she said again.

There was a crappy little hatchback in the driveway that she'd bought when we'd arrived in Omaha, an old beater worth a couple hundred bucks.

"Are you crazy?" I said. Selling the car would mean driving around Omaha, out in the open where anyone could grab us or take a shot at us. "Just leave the damn car."

"I can't just leave it," she said abruptly. "I paid eight hundred dollars for that car."

I was stunned. People wanted to kill us. Very dangerous men were at that very moment, as far as I knew, scouring Omaha for that rat bastard Henry Hill and his family. And my mother was worried about a shitty little eight-hundred-dollar car. It was a reckless gamble, risking our lives for less than a thousand dollars.

"I'll be back in a while," my mother said.

"Just leave it," I snapped.

"No. We need the money. Don't you understand? They give us nothing. Nothing! We have no money."

Shit. I didn't understand. She was taking a massive risk. I didn't want her to go, but I wanted her to go alone even less. I had no idea what I would do if we were spotted at some used car lot, but instinct told me I should be there anyway. At that point, which was safer—being home alone peering out the windows or being out in public? "I'll go with you," I said. "Let's go, Gina." Maybe there would be safety in numbers.

We drove to three dealers that afternoon. My mother couldn't just take the first offer. She had to shop around, get a deal, get a few extra bucks. At the first one, where she'd bought the car to begin with, I kept looking over one shoulder, then the next, searching the lots, the corners, the streets. My chest thumped while she dickered. When she walked away from the offer, offended that the dealer would only give her three hundred dollars, my whole body tensed, like a giant spasm. I couldn't believe she was dragging it out.

"Ma, what the hell are you doing?" I asked as we drove away.

"I paid eight hundred bucks, and that bastard won't give me half that," she said. "The car's worth more than that."

"We don't have time for this."

"Shut up! Just shut up!"

I suddenly regretted my decision to go, to bring Gina with us. I knew my mother was terrified. And I knew there was no point in telling her she was doing something completely fucking stupid. Instead, I watched out the windows and kept checking the mirror on my side to make sure no one was following us.

The last dealer gave her the best offer—I'll give my mother credit for driving a hard bargain even in absolutely horrible circumstances—and we were home well before dark with five hundred dollars in her purse. That was a small relief, still having sunshine left. Scared as I was in the daylight, shadows gave assassins a lot more places to hide. We drew the shades and spent the rest of the night packing. My father still wasn't around, so my mother got his things together.

My father showed up in the morning with the marshals, another bright, blue day, just like the one when we'd arrived. They herded us into two boxy Chryslers, my mother, Gina and I, and our three dogs and my bird in one, my father in the other. Marshal Llewelyn didn't have the cool swagger, that understated assuredness that feds often project. Instead, he was curt, almost like he was rattled.

"There's been a breach in security," was all he said as he pulled out of the driveway. He spoke in that monotone that feds use when they're being serious. "Your location's been compromised, so we had to make new arrangements."

I was right. They'd found us. I didn't know how, and it didn't matter. The only thing that was important is that they had.

In Omaha, Nebraska.

Omaha Fucking Nebraska.

And then the worst thought: If they can find us here, they can find us anywhere.

GREGG: Just like when we left New York, the marshals kept us in the dark until we were halfway to the airport. All we knew until then was that we were leaving, but we had no idea where we were going. I wasn't especially worried about it, though. For one thing, I had enough on my mind watching out for a hit man who might have already caught up with us. For another, I'd survived Omaha, and I never imagined they could send us anywhere worse. Finally, strange as it may sound, I was too dispirited to care. It hurt, having to leave. I'd gone against my will to a place I was determined not to like, and yet I'd sort of grudgingly opened up. I had tennis, I'd met a few good guys, a good coach, and eventually I had had a good day that turned into a good week that was beginning to turn into a good month.

Then—*boom!*—it's gone. No goodbyes. No explanations. No memories. This town would be erased from our childhood as if we'd never been there.

And we were running for our lives. Again.

"You're going to Kentucky," the marshal behind the wheel said.

Kentucky? I must have heard wrong. They couldn't send us to Kentucky. We didn't blend in Nebraska—how the hell were we supposed to fit in in the Deep South? Okay, maybe it's only the mid-South on the map, but as far as a kid from Long Island was concerned, Kentucky might as well have been Birmingham or Selma. I couldn't imagine anything worse for a kid from New York than Omaha . . . except Kentucky. And, unlike Omaha, I had a very clear mental picture of the Bluegrass State: It was rural, like dirt-road rural, and full of hillbillies who talked funny and chewed tobacco. I knew what we were in for. I'd seen *Deliverance*. Georgia, Kentucky— backwoods were backwoods as far as I was concerned. I didn't want anyone telling me I had a *real purty mouth*. They couldn't be sending us to Kentucky.

"Where in Kentucky?" my mother asked.

"I don't know," he said.

Shit. I'd heard right. I was too stunned to say anything.

We followed the same drill at the airport. The marshals got us tickets under fake names and flashed their badges and escorted us past security all the way to the gate. My father was muted that morning, more quiet than I was used to. He seemed tired and dejected. "This is terrible," I heard him tell Gina. "I'm sorry, Princess." But he wasn't really apologizing. If anything, he seemed to be blaming the feds, like they'd screwed up somehow, that it was their fault. At least he wasn't pretending things were good.

For years all I knew about the reasons we fled Omaha was that Jimmy had been overheard in the courthouse hallway muttering about the Midwest. Granted, the Midwest is a pretty big place—Jimmy didn't even have it narrowed down to a particular state—but he was guessing close enough to scare the shit out of me. I assumed that he was simply very good at hunting people he wanted to kill, that even from a jail cell he could orchestrate the search, command minions and associates. It wasn't until I was out of the program for more than a decade, long after I'd moved as far away from my father as possible, that I learned that my father had wanted to get out of Omaha, and that he was sloppy enough with his phone calls back home and yapping to old friends in New York that he made sure it happened. He boasted once, almost twenty years after the fact, that he did it on purpose. True? I don't know; I learned a long time ago not to trust anything my father says. But in his FBI file there's a notation about him making collect calls to "the danger area" from Omaha.

Anyway, that all came later. On that morning in the late summer of 1980, I didn't feel anything toward him—no particular anger, certainly no pity, and definitely not sympathy. I wasn't thrilled to be so physically close to him, though, because he was the prime target. You know how when someone you don't like or who smells weird puts his arm around you and you cringe? It was like that. When my father spoke, I tried my best to read my copy of *Tennis* magazine and ignore him. I just didn't want to be near him because, if the shooting started, I didn't want to be in the way. If he went down, I didn't see any reason why we had to go down too. And the airport is the last place you want to be if people are flying into town to kill you and your family—or if those same people know you'll be trying to leave town ahead of them. Despite the marshals' presence, I suddenly felt terribly vulnerable.

We headed down the jetway to the plane, my mother and sister and me. My father lagged behind with a marshal, who, after a few minutes, escorted him on board and sat in the seat next to him. They were about a dozen rows ahead of us, far enough away that no one would suspect we were together. That was the only bright spot in the entire morning.

As soon as we landed at the Lexington airport, I felt exposed again, like a target. We were never able to blend. The marshal from the plane handed us off to some other agents at the end of the jetway. The one in charge was a big fellow named Al with a redneck baritone. He didn't look happy to see us, like we were a shitty assignment dropped on him right before he was going to cut out and go fishing for the weekend. He barely acknowledged me and Gina. Maybe he'd take a bullet for us, but I got the sense that guarding Henry Hill was the penalty for drawing the short straw in the office.

My father didn't smooth things over either. Just the opposite. Marshal Al told him we were staying in Lexington.

"No fucking way," my father said. "You guys are crazy. There's a federal prison here."

He had a point. Wiseguys sometimes move their families close to the prisons where they're doing long stretches, or at least put them up in local hotels around visiting day. Any number of people—gangsters, their wives, their girlfriends—might recognize my father in Lexington. "No way," he said again.

"You're staying here," Marshal Al snapped.

"Fuck you. It's too dangerous."

"You're staying." Marshal Al was turning purple with anger, and a vein on his neck was bulging out.

My father grabbed a pay phone and dialed Ed McDonald's number in New York. I couldn't hear the conversation, but I knew he must be complaining about the new location. Then he hung up and slouched in one of the lounge chairs by the baggage carousel where we picked up the animals.

So much for keeping a low profile. We never seemed to get the inconspicuous part right. I wondered what could be more obvious in an airport than a family of four, three of them with jet-black hair and all of them with thick New York accents, surrounded by animal cages and federal agents, one of them big and surly and clearly pissed off. We looked like gypsy prisoners. People couldn't help but stare at us. I hoped none of them recognized us. I really hoped none of them wanted to kill Henry Hill.

We had to wait almost an hour until Marshal Al's beeper went off. The head office in Washington was paging him because McDonald had called there right after he spoke to my father. Marshal Al's bosses agreed with my father: Lexington was too dangerous. They would have to take us north, to a little town called Independence, four hours in a van.

GINA: I couldn't believe we'd landed in Kentucky. How lucky could we get? Kentucky—they may as well have told us we were going to live on the Ewing estate.

The summer of 1980 was the cliff-hanger break between *Dallas* seasons, when everyone waited all through July and August to find out who shot J.R. Maybe the whole dream sequence thing was a letdown, but I loved everything else about that show. It was my fantasy, the kind of life I knew we would always live once my father got a job and we settled down. We would have a big house with chandeliers and a stable out back, and we'd wear glamorous clothes to formal dinners. I knew *Dallas* was set in Texas, but as far as I knew, Kentucky wasn't all that different. There would be horses and people with funny accents and cowboy hats. Close enough.

My other favorite show was *The Dukes of Hazzard,* and that really was supposed to be Kentucky. Hazzard County was a great place, wild and chaotic and full of adventure and crazy hill-billies with cool cars. It was completely different from *Dallas*, but that was the beauty of it: We were going to where I'd have the best of both worlds.

We lived in a hotel for a couple of weeks. In

some ways it was like being on vacation. We'd run around all day or watch TV. I wandered around the hotel just listening to people—the guests, the clerks at the front desk, the maids pushing their housekeeping carts through the halls. They all had that accent, sort of soft and slow and romantic, the way the Duke brothers spoke. I really felt like we'd been teleported to a whole other world, someplace very far away from the bad guys and yet very close to where I'd always imagined we'd end up.

My mom took us to a couple of movies in those first weeks just to get us out of the hotel. When we saw *Urban Cowboy* I was transfixed. There it was on the big screen, people who lived in a city but wore cowboy boots and ten-gallon hats and went line dancing and rode mechanical bulls and fell in love with Debra Winger. That was my life. Or could be my life. I could line dance. I could be Debra Winger.

GREGG: There are all sorts of small things a kid has to give up when he's on the run that would never occur to anyone. The big stuff—abandoning your friends, most of your relatives, your school—are obvious. But there are other little moments, almost like the accessories of being young, that are abandoned or ignored out of necessity or fear.

Like Mean Joe Greene's autograph. See? No

Henry and Karen Hill were married on August 29, 1965. Karen's mother was always hard on him. "That gangster," she'd say, spitting out the words. She thought a nice Jewish girl like her daughter should have married a doctor or a lawyer, not some hoodlum Catholic from Brooklyn whom she'd met on a blind date. (*Hill family*)

As a little girl, Gina, shown here in 1974, was always the bubbly one in the Hill family. Though her father was in prison and her mother had to collect welfare to feed her children, Gina still believed her father was the best man in the world, which meant everyone else—the prison guards, the police, even her own grandmother—was wrong about him. (HILL FAMILY)

Their maternal grandparents were a stabilizing presence for Gregg and Gina before they were forced to join their father on the run. Here they're in their grandparents' driveway in Valley Stream on their way to see the 1973 New York Mets at Shea Stadium. (HILL FAMILY)

With Henry in prison, the rest of the family moved into a small apartment in Elmont, on Long Island. There were only two bedrooms, but instead of putting Gina (shown here in 1976 in front of their building) and Gregg in one and taking the other for herself, Karen slept on the couch in the living room. She never wanted her kids to go without anything.
(*Hill family*)

Gina was always excited to see her father when he was locked up in the federal prison in Lewisburg, Pennsylvania, in the early 1970s, but Gregg dreaded the trips. The drive from Long Island was exhausting, the days in the prison were boring, and the visits only reminded him how much he resented his father for being a criminal. And even if someone snapped a souvenir photo—like this one from 1975—to whom could he show it?
(*Hill family*)

Gregg was bar-mitzvahed in the spring of 1979. He was the only blond in a family that included a dark-haired Irish-and-Italian father and a Jewish mother; his father used to joke that his mother must have had something going on with the mailman. (HILL FAMILY)

In the spring of 1979, when eleven-year-old Gina practiced reading a prayer from the Torah for Gregg's bar mitzvah, life was good for the Hill family. Henry was out of prison and making money, enough to buy a house in Rockville Center with a swimming pool in the backyard. To the neighbors, they probably looked like any other suburban family. (HILL FAMILY)

Nassau County detectives arrested Henry Hill for dealing drugs on April 27, 1980. Two days later, Gregg and Gina were humiliated when the bust was reported in *Newsday*. The paper printed his whole name, his age, his address—everything except "Gregg's and Gina's father." But the embarrassment was short-lived: Facing a life sentence, Henry agreed to testify against his criminal associates, and the entire family disappeared into the federal witness protection program. *(FBI PHOTO)*

James Burke, a stone-cold killer who masterminded the Lufthansa robbery, was Henry Hill's main criminal partner. Gregg and Gina knew him only as Uncle Jimmy. Gina used to imitate him when she was younger. "Do your crazy Jimmy eyes," one of Henry's friends would say, and Gina would twist up her face until her eyes got weird and all the grownups laughed. In the spring of 1980, federal agents believed Jimmy would kill Gregg and Gina to get to Henry. *(FBI PHOTO)*

One of Henry's partners in crime was Tommy DeSimone, a flat-out lunatic with a boxer's build. DeSimone disappeared in early 1979; he is believed to have been killed in retaliation for killing a made man in the Mafia several years earlier.

Marty Krugman took bets in the back room of the salon he owned in Queens where Gregg would get his hair cut. He disappeared in January 1979, part of a string of killings connected to the Lufthansa heist. Eleven-year-old Gina overheard her parents talking about it. "They're never gonna find him," she heard her father say. "They cut him up in a million little pieces." *(FBI photo)*

Stacks Edwards was a big, friendly man whom Gregg liked a lot. He was also sup-posed to have gotten rid of the van that was used in the Lufthansa heist. When he didn't—and the police recovered the van—Tommy DeSimone shot him six times in the head. He was the first of the Hill family's friends to disappear. *(FBI photo)*

The one thing Gregg found familiar in Omaha, Nebraska, was tennis. In New York he'd been a mediocre tournament player who usually got bounced out in the qualifying rounds because the competition was so much stiffer. In Nebraska, though, he was good enough to make the Nebraska State Open in the fourteen-year-olds division of the U.S. Tennis Association. The Hill family lived there for only two months in the summer of 1980 before Henry blew their cover and they had to be relocated to Kentucky.

Gregg and Henry on the deck of the Ponderosa, the ranch house where they lived after the family was relocated—for the third time—to Redmond, Washington. Though Henry's boasting here about the sixteen-pound King salmon he'd caught fishing with his son, the two rarely did such things together. Their relationship was volatile at best: During those years in Redmond, Gregg attacked his father with a homemade mace, boxed his ears, and fantasized about blowing his head off with a shotgun. *(Hill family)*

Living in hiding just outside of Cincinnati, Henry decided to open the Queen City Trolley to show tourists the historic sights. Gregg helped refurbish the trolley, but he later decided the business was a misguided idea. He couldn't help thinking, "We're in witness protection—why are we running a tourist attraction?" *(Hill family)*

Gina went to her senior prom in 1986, but she didn't date much through high school in Redmond. After years on the run, moving from state to state, it would have been risky anyway. "What if boys from Redmond High School wanted to come home and meet my father?" she used to wonder. "What if a boy fell madly in love with me and wanted to know everything about me? How much would I reveal? How much *could* I reveal?" *(HILL FAMILY)*

one would ever see that coming.

The hotel we moved into in Kentucky was marginally fancy, a Mediterranean-themed place with wrought iron gates and faux stucco walls and a bunch of conference rooms big enough to host almost anything that would come through northern Kentucky. It wasn't the Ritz, but it wasn't a Motel 6 either. It was the kind of place where Mean Joe Greene would come to sign autographs on whatever promotional tour he might have been doing in the late summer of 1980.

I saw him one morning in the lobby, a huge man lumbering toward one of the conference rooms. I recognized him right away because I was a Steelers fan. Everyone recognized Mean Joe back then. Remember his Coke commercial? The man was more than an All Pro and a four-time Super Bowl champ—he was an icon.

And I was staying at the same hotel. I was six feet away from the man, close enough to touch him, close enough to feel that numb flush that usually happens in the presence of famous people. Plus I had the whole day to kill, nowhere else to be except cooped up in a rented suite where no one would think to come and shoot my father. I could wait in line with the rest of the fans who wanted him to sign a Topps card or a hat or a jersey or a poster and never have to worry about the time. I could even wait until the end, when he was all finished and walking to his room or the bar, and catch up to him in the hallway and shake his hand and get his autograph.

Except I couldn't.

We were no longer anonymous. Kentucky didn't feel safe to me at all, not then. I looked over my shoulder constantly, convinced that someone was watching us, stalking us. I spent my time mostly alone and secluded, playing pinball in the game room or watching TV or running sprints in my bare feet up and down the long hallways. That felt good, almost like running the 100 or 200 meters like I did on the South Side track team, except no one was keeping time or watching from the bleachers. Even at the breakfast buffet, if I felt a pair of eyes watching us—if I only *imagined* someone looking at us—I'd grab Gina's sleeve and say, "C'mon, let's get out of here." She always looked at me like I was paranoid, but I didn't care. Someone had to look out for us.

So how could I stand in line? I would be totally exposed. I realized no one was gunning for me specifically, but I still felt like a target. "Don't be crazy," my father said. "No one's going to recognize you."

"Why deprive yourself?" my mother said. "You deserve an autograph."

Why deprive myself? It drove me nuts. There I

was, being dragged into a life on the run, and as far as I could tell I was the only one in the family who understood that we should be afraid.

Yet even if they were right, if no one would recognize me and I was completely safe, just another kid waiting for an autograph, who would I tell Mean Joe I was? Who would I ask him to make it out to? Gregg Haymes? No. To begin with, that wasn't my real name, and now it wasn't even my fake name. Because we'd been discovered, so far as we knew, in Omaha, the marshals told us we'd have to call ourselves something different. I was a kid without a name.

Even that didn't matter. The point of getting an autograph, especially of someone like Mean Joe Greene, is to show it off. Who could I show it to? I had no friends. I didn't even have acquaintances. And once I made friends, how would I explain an autograph signed "To Gregg" if my new name was Carl or Steve or Bob?

I wouldn't be able to. And that was so frustrating. I was close enough to one of my idols to run a post pattern on him, and yet I couldn't approach him. I didn't feel safe enough to ask one of the biggest men in professional sports to scribble his name on a napkin.

GINA: We got to pick new names again, almost like we were reinventing ourselves one more time. My mom was stressed about it this time, though. She'd made it a game before, but now she wanted something simple, not quite as bland as Smith but not much more exotic either. Something along the lines of Hill, a generic name that wouldn't raise any suspicions at all.

She thought about Kaplan, which was Grandma's maiden name, but she decided that sounded too Jewish. So she considered a few more, all dull. Johnson, Andrews—things like that. She settled on Scott. I wasn't excited about it, but I can't say I was disappointed either. It was so generic that it held all kinds of possibilities. Mr. Scott could work as a garbage man or a farmer, or he could have a big estate with servants and gold fixtures in the bathroom. It would do.

My father got three new names. He was now Martin Todd Scott. I didn't want to change my first name; I'd been Gina my whole life. But Gregg didn't feel comfortable being Gregg anymore, not after that thing with the tennis tournament in Lincoln. He switched his middle name to his first, so now he was Matthew Gregg Scott. I hated that he did that. I felt almost abandoned, like I was the only one holding on to a piece of our past.

We had our new names memorized and practiced by the time we moved out of the hotel, which was about two weeks after we landed in Kentucky. My parents found a townhouse on a cul-de-sac in

Independence. It was rural, but not with dirt roads or anything like that—just a lot of hills and trees and two-lane highways, one of those places that's just starting to develop. Where we lived was actually like a development, a bunch of identical Tudor-style houses three stories tall and clumped around dead-end streets. There were kids in a lot of the houses, and, like in Omaha, we weren't the only transplants. I could still tell people my dad had gotten transferred and that he had a secret job with the government, and no one would question me. No one knew who we were, so we could be anyone we wanted to be. We could start to live a normal life.

GREGG: One night not long after we moved into the townhouse, I was riding with my mother in the used, cream-colored station wagon she'd bought so we could get around the back roads of Kentucky. It wasn't too late, but the sun had gone down and there were no streetlights on the narrow highway through the woods that led back to our house, so it was completely dark except for the headlights on the pavement.

"Is that car following us?"

My mother was glancing into the mirror, then back to the road, then at the mirror. She looked worried.

I turned in my seat to look out the back window. All I could see were two bright white spots, the lights from the car behind us. It was fairly close, maybe thirty yards behind, but I couldn't tell what kind of car it was.

"I don't know," I said, but I didn't really think it was.

The engine revved a little faster, my mother stepping on the gas, speeding up to sixty miles an hour. She checked the mirror again; the car behind us kept pace. She backed off the pedal and let the station wagon coast, slowing down to about forty-five. She was watching more closely now, her eyes looking at the mirror almost as much as at the road ahead. And still the car behind us kept pace, matching our speed, never losing ground or catching up, just hanging back there about the same distance.

"I think he's following us," she said. That clipped tone again. She was scared, gripping the wheel tighter.

I turned to look again. I was nervous now. He had been behind us for a while. How many miles? Two? Ten? I couldn't tell, but it seemed like a long time. And with the way my mother was driving, faster then slower, why hadn't he gone around us? I wouldn't stay behind someone so annoying.

"Why is he following us?" she said. "What's he want?"

"Maybe he's not." I was trying to sound calm, but I was scared. My palms were sweating. Fear is contagious. *They'd found us in Omaha,* I thought. *They found us here too.*

That went on for another mile or so. And then the inside of our car started to get brighter, his headlights flooding in from the rear window as he got closer to our tail.

"Oh my God oh my God oh my God," my mother said. She was shaking. "He's pulling up, he's pulling up."

I twisted to my left just in time to see a pair of headlights swing out from behind and start to move up the left side of our car.

"Oh my God," she said again. "Duck. Duck! Get down!"

She reached up with her right hand and pushed my head down between the dashboard and the front seat. She threw her own head back against the headrest.

It's amazing how much can go through your mind in a second. I got ready for a shotgun blast. I knew it would be a shotgun, something with some spread, something that can cover a large, moving target. I thought of that scene in *Walking Tall* where the rednecks destroyed Buford Pusser's car with shotguns. Then I wondered why I was ducking. What good is keeping my head down if they kill my mother and we crash at sixty miles an hour? Oh man, my head. *Please don't let me get hit in the head.*

The whir of tires on pavement, the growl of the engine growing louder then fading, the brief rush of wind. Then nothing.

I looked up to see taillights pull in front of us and then race away. It was only a stranger passing on a country road.

My mother let out her breath. Her shoulders slumped and her neck relaxed, but she was still breathing hard, almost hyperventilating. "Are you okay?" she asked.

"Yeah," I said. I didn't tell her I felt kind of stupid, or that I was exhausted. I'd only been ducking, but somehow I'd used all my strength. I was sweaty and tired and embarrassed, like a kid who gets scared by his own shadow.

"What's wrong with that person?" she said, but to herself as much as to me. "He was following so close, he got me so scared . . . what's *wrong* with people?"

GREGG: On a warm morning in September 1980, I got on a big yellow bus for the ride to my first day at Simon Kenton High School. The Pioneers—that was the mascot, and man, they weren't kidding. Independence, Kentucky, was the frontier as far as I was concerned. Daniel Boone country. The bus followed a two-lane road through tobacco fields and cropland where there were hardly any buildings and most of those were barns or grain silos. The school itself was nothing special, except I remember it being larger than I had expected. But the kids were definitely more rural than I was used to. Everyone wore blue jeans and flannel shirts, and a few of them had blue suede jackets with FFA stitched on the back—kind of a letterman jacket for the Future Farmers of America. I'd never met a kid who wanted to be a farmer. There are no farmers in Queens.

I was nervous. It was bad enough that I was a freshman, and worse that I was the new kid; those two things alone will put a target on a kid's back in any high school in America. But I had a whole other set of problems. I was walking into Simon Kenton with nobody, totally alone, with a huge secret and barely clinging to my new name.

Gina and I had already met some kids in our neighborhood, and even that hadn't gone all that smoothly. True, I did like the name Scott better than that pompous Haymes, but remembering a new first name is harder than you'd think. I'd have to concentrate when I introduced myself, try not to sound awkward when I said, "My name's Matthew." Then I'd have to worry about Gina. She kept calling me Gregg. And it never dawned on her either. She'd keep saying it until I shot her a look, and later, if I called her on it, she'd get angry and defensive. "I heard you already," she'd whine. "For the fifth time, I heard you." But then she'd do it again, and I'd give her another glare and tell her for the sixth time to stop calling me Gregg, goddammit.

The day I enrolled in the Simon Kenton High School class of 1984 was the first time since we'd left New York that I'd been alone in a crowd. I knew it would be easier to screw up. Anytime anyone asked me anything—What brought you to Kentucky? What's your father do? Where did you come from?—there could be a bunch of kids waiting to hear the answer. One on one, it's easier to fudge, easier to back up and cover your tracks if you slip. Or maybe one kid wouldn't pick up on something that didn't make sense. Now I would be trying to lie in front of an audience; any one of thirty kids might figure me out.

So I dealt with it by being incredibly aloof. I was short and curt, and I moved on as fast as I could from anything that had to do with me, my family, or my past. That made for some very disjointed conversations, which began my reputation as a space cadet. And it was cemented before the week was out.

I was in English class on the third or fourth day, after I'd already managed to gain some notoriety as the kid from New York despite my protests that I was from Connecticut. The English teacher was calling on a student.

"Matthew," he said.

I watched the teacher, waiting for Matthew to answer.

"Matthew?"

Why was he looking at me? Who was this Matthew character?

"Matthew!"

A switch went off in my brain. *Oh shit, I'm Matthew.*

"Yes," I said, sitting up a little straighter and sounding a little surprised. Just like Gina, I'd forgotten I wasn't Gregg anymore.

I heard laughter around me, the other kids giggling at the dope who couldn't remember his own name. It got around the school pretty quickly, and some of the kids started saying I must be on drugs.

GINA: After we'd been in Kentucky for about six weeks, I was watching TV one afternoon with my dad. We were sitting on the couch together. I can't remember what show was on but it doesn't matter because the important thing was this one commercial for Barbie's Dream Horse.

I couldn't believe it—Barbie had my horse! A little plastic version of exactly the horse I wanted, a golden brown color with a white mane and white tale. I'd been bugging Dad for weeks, every chance I got, to buy me the horse he'd promised, and now the perfect one was on TV. It was a sign.

"Dad, Dad! That's the color! That's the color horse I want!" I was so excited I was almost yelling. "Look! See the color? That's the horse I want."

He got this big smile on his face, and he edged forward on the couch like he was getting ready to stand up.

"Princess, let's go," he said. "I got the horse. I know where there's a horse just like that for sale."

I was stunned, but in a good way, probably the same way people are when they realize they've won the lottery. I'd hit the jackpot. Not only was I finally getting a horse—that by itself was exciting—but I was getting *exactly the horse I wanted*. Out of all the horses in all of Kentucky, my dad had found the perfect one for me.

He put me in the car next to him and told me we were going to the racetrack. My dad knew everybody at the track because that's the kind of man he was. Race tracks and bars, those were the places he was most comfortable. He liked to drink and he liked to gamble. It's kind of strange that men involved in organized crime gamble so much; they know better than anybody that the house always wins. My dad explained once that it was a release, a way to blow off steam and have some fun. And since they gambled with stolen money, I guess it didn't matter so much if they lost. But sometimes he won. I remember coming home one night and seeing him at the kitchen table with a big pile of cash in front of him. He was stinking drunk and my mom was screaming at him about fixing horse races and how he was going to get in trouble, but he was just grinning and laughing and counting his money.

We got to the track and he drove around back where the jockeys and the trainers work. And then the woman he knew came riding out on the most perfect horse I'd ever seen. She—the horse—was an Arabian-Saddle-bred mix the color of straw with the white mane and tail, like the Barbie horse had come to life. Her registered name was Sundance Tiara, but the trainer called her Banana Split or just Bananas for short. That's what I called her.

The trainer got down and held the reins so I could climb up. I was bursting with excitement, but part of me was scared to death. I recognized that feeling. Whenever something wonderful happened with my father, a little piece of me was waiting for something terrible to happen too. Like that day at FAO Schwartz when I was so overwhelmed by all the toys that I cried, or when he took me into Manhattan to see *Annie* and go ice skating at Rockefeller Center but drove like such a maniac that I was petrified the whole way. Even in the best of times, there was always the possibility of disaster. That's how it was the first time I mounted Bananas. I was afraid I wouldn't be able to handle her properly or that I would fall off or that my dad wouldn't have the money—that something would go wrong and jinx the whole thing.

But nothing happened. It went so smoothly. I rode Bananas like she'd had me on her back for years. I didn't go very far, just around a big barn behind the track. But the feeling of taking a horse outside of the little corrals where I had my lessons, of controlling such a magnificent animal on my own, was overwhelming. I stayed on her for almost an hour that afternoon while my dad patiently watched. Then I saw him pull a wad of money out of his pocket and peel off some bills, four hundred dollars that he paid right on the spot.

Bananas was mine. I finally had my horse.

GREGG: Despite my reputation as either a little spacey or a druggy—or maybe because of—I made friends fast. The first weekend after school started, I ended up going out with some guys on a Saturday afternoon. I was The Kid From New York, so maybe it was cool for them to hang out with me. Personally, I saw it as failure. I had so little to work with—*my father works for the government; we're from Stamford*—and I'd screwed up half of that. I couldn't do anything about it. Kids see New York on TV, they hear the accent, they figure it out. There's no point in arguing. And I guess it was cooler to be known as a New Yorker than as some Connecticut transplant.

There wasn't a lot to do in Kentucky except cruise or hang out and chew tobacco. One of the boys who was a year or two older had a convertible Triumph TR-7. Four of us squeezed into it and tore off down one of the back roads. It was a beautiful thing, teenaged boys in a speeding convertible, warm air blowing under a clear blue sky. *This isn't bad,* I thought. *Actually, it's pretty cool.*

Then I heard the twang.

It came from the speakers, that God-awful whelp of a guitar string that only guys with names like Waylon can make. It's the sound of rednecks and hillbillies. As far as I knew, those were the only kinds of people who made that music or listened to it.

It got louder.

"Country music?" I said. "You're kidding me, right?"

Three faces looked at me. "No," the kid in the passenger seat said. "C'mon, listen to this."

He twisted the volume knob. He was serious.

It wasn't southern rock, like Charlie Daniels or Lynyrd Skynyrd. Not that I liked any of that *Freebird* crap. I thought, hard rock's got to be hard rock. None of that Southern ballad garbage. But this was even worse. Those guys were listening to real country music. They might as well have been listening to opera. But they all loved it.

"Fuck that hard rock shit," one of them said to me. "You're in Kentucky now, city boy. Better get used to it."

I thought I heard a little emphasis on the word *boy*, like it was *bow-eye*. It made me smile, though. *City boy.* True, I was from New York, but I always thought I'd lived in the suburbs. And at least they were comfortable enough with me to indulge my loathing. I thought I could learn to get along in Kentucky. Maybe I could even get the hang of chewing tobacco without swallowing. But even if I stayed there for a hundred years, I knew I'd never like country music.

Of course, my father had to like it. I already hated Billy Joel and the smell of candles because of him; after a few months I had to add Willie Nelson to the list. He would crank up Willie on the boom box near the door to the backyard, all that raspy singing and twangy guitar. He'd even sing along. It was quite a sight. If he caught me giving him a look of disgust, he'd fire back with a fake redneck drawl, "What's the matter, boy?" I'm still not sure if that made me hate country music more, or if it only gave me another reason to hate him.

• • •

My father had an angle for everything. If there was a way to make a buck off a situation, he'd figure it out. And it was easy for him to pull it off because he never thought about or cared about the consequences. Plus, he had no shame.

In the fall of 1980, about the time my father was discovering Willie Nelson, the feds were moving ahead with the Boston College point-shaving case, tracking down leads, confirming information my father had given them, steadily building a case against Jimmy and the rest of the conspirators. Within a few months, by the end of January 1981, they would have enough to impanel a grand jury to hear testimony.

My father knew that a college sports scandal would be a huge story once the investigation became public. So he got ahead of the curve: He sold his version of the story to *Sports Illustrated*. It ended up on the cover of the February 16, 1981, issue, a photograph of a basketball net stuffed with cash, and the story started with a big spread across pages fourteen and fifteen. How I Put the Fix In was in block letters beneath a collage of pictures from BC games. Below that were two lines of italic type: *In this exclusive story, informer Henry Hill asserts that he and his associates rigged nine Boston College basketball games in 1978–79 by inducing BC players to shave points.* The byline said, "by Henry Hill with Douglas S. Looney." And then the first line of the story: "I'm the Boston College basketball fixer."

My father was a fixer?

That was my reaction. Not fear or anger, just flat-out, dumbfounded surprise. I'd never heard of the BC point-shaving scandal. And the feds, they were surprised too. They had no idea my father was blabbing to a national magazine. They went ballistic. Ed McDonald flew my father back to New York, sat him down in his office, and tore him a new one.

"I'm going to have you locked up!" he yelled. "Are you out of your mind? This is a breach of the agreement!"

My father shrugged it off. "Ah, what are you worried about?"

"It's a breach of the agreement," McDonald said again. "Anything like this, anything, again, I don't care what happens, you're going away. You're going to prison."

There were a couple of reasons why McDonald was so angry, both of them valid. First, my father was supposed to be hiding, which logically precluded talking to reporters or anyone else. Second, telling a story in print before you take the stand is a tactical nightmare. "That whole article was screwed up," one of the investigators would remember. "It was Henry's view of how things happened, when in reality things hadn't happened like that at all. But of course, we had to live with that at the trial." Any discrepancies between the *SI* story and my father's testimony could be used to shred his credibility, which was already paper-thin. Finally, my father was supplying a river of information to the feds. All those debriefing sessions in New York weren't just to prepare for trials. Tips he fed them were being used to get wiretaps, to authorize surveillance, to squeeze other suspects. The more his cooperation became known in the underworld, the less effective it might be (though, in fairness, I don't think it was much of a secret by then). And every time he popped his head up to thumb his nose at his old friends, they had more of an incentive to kill him, if just out of spite. Hell, they'd killed men for less.

I wasn't thinking about any of that, though. I was looking at my father's picture in a national magazine. Was that cool? I wasn't sure. Yeah, he was confessing to being a criminal, but kind of a clever one. And no one got hurt, not in that scam.

I heard him come through the back door. "Hey, Dad," I said. "What's this?" I had the magazine on my lap, opened to the page with his picture.

"Yeah, can you believe that?" he said. He had a big smile. "They paid me ten grand for that. Can you fuckin' believe it? Ten grand to tell 'em about fucking college basketball. How could I say no?"

He gave an exaggerated shrug and walked away. I felt a trace of a smile on my own face.

Yeah, how could he say no?

GINA: The bus from Twenhofel Middle School stopped at the corner of our cul-de-sac and the door squeaked open and I climbed down the steps to the sidewalk. It was a warm afternoon in September 1981. I was in the eighth grade and thirteen years old. We'd lived in Kentucky for a little more than twelve months, an entire year in the same place. I had my horse and I had friends and my dad was just one more scheme away from the big break that would get us into a plantation house where there would be chandeliers in the bathrooms and we would dress for dinner. When the bus pulled to the curb, I was about as happy as I'd ever been in my life.

I saw a man standing near our front door.

My pulse quickened. He was too far away for

me to recognize his face, but he was older, probably in his late fifties, with graying hair, and he was dressed conservatively—slacks and a dress shirt and a dark jacket—like he didn't want to stand out in a crowd. At the curb was a boring brown car, either a Chrysler or a Chevy sedan.

I felt nauseous, like my stomach was churning. I walked toward our house, first slowly, then faster so I could get past him as quickly as possible. I knew exactly who he was, even without ever having met him. He was with the government. He was a fed.

He saw me. I could tell he was watching me, staring at me as I hurried down the sidewalk. I was furious at him because I knew immediately why he was there. *Oh my God,* I thought. *We have to leave.*

I had my key in my hand before I reached the front steps.

"Is your mother or father home?" he asked.

"No." I didn't even look at him. I turned the knob and pushed the door open.

"Can I come in?"

"No!"

I was already inside, and I turned quickly, shoving the door so hard it slammed shut with a bang. I twisted again and leaned my back against the door. I could feel my heart pounding.

Then I started to cry. The tears just burst out of me, hard and fast, and I could barely catch my breath between the sobs. I saw my reflection, blurry through my tears, in the mirror by the door. My cheeks were red and wet and my mouth was contorted almost into a grimace.

Why? We didn't do anything wrong. Why?

I'd fallen in love with Kentucky. To me it was the perfect place. We were safe and secure there. My grandma and Aunt Cheryl had even come to visit us that summer, just to see how good and happy our life had become. They'd been careful about it, flying a convoluted route through four airports under fake names, Adele Black and Jean Decker, Black & Decker. Nothing bad had happened. No one found out. That's how safe we were.

And now we had to leave. I knew that's why the agent was there. He was going to take me away from Kentucky.

GREGG: My parents were so reckless in the summer of 1981. They just weren't capable of keeping a low profile, of following the rules. Sure, it was nice to see my grandmother and my aunt, but I was the only one who seemed to realize how damned dangerous it was. Uncle Jimmy, along with four other men, had been indicted on July 29 for the BC case, and he was looking at twenty years in prison, which only gave Jimmy more of an incentive to kill my father, and soon, before the trial started in the fall. The bounty was still out there, the private investigators were still looking for us—anyone could have tailed my grandmother to Kentucky. But no one in my family ever listened to me.

My father, in fact, was only raising his profile, exactly the opposite of what the feds wanted him to do. First there was the *Sports Illustrated* article, where he practically bragged about being a snitch and a master criminal. (The story said that the Lufthansa job "probably couldn't have been pulled off without Hill.") And then, while the feds were still sore about that, he opened the Queen City Trolley. My father, man on the run, wanted to show tourists the Cincinnati sights.

I wasn't opposed to it, not in the beginning. My only reservation at first was that it seemed so complicated. Why couldn't he just get a job? I'd heard all the excuses. He couldn't work forty hours a week because he had to fly back to New York and testify. The stress was killing him. He wasn't programmed for a working stiff's life. My father had a million excuses not to get a regular job. But at least he was getting into a legitimate business. I'd take what I could get.

He worked hard at it too. He found an old trolley car that had been used as a small diner, a complete wreck of a thing that had to be scraped and painted and refinished. Through a connection he'd met at the track, this guy named Joel, he found a pair of Belgian draft horses, and then he got some space in the basement of the old Cincinnati train station, which had been remodeled into a mall, where he could build some stalls. He convinced some people to put up capital, including—in hindsight, this was probably the dumbest part—an old friend in New York named Dennis and even my grandparents. And he hired a couple of rednecks to help us renovate the trolley and, once we were in business, lead the horses.

I hadn't spent a lot of time around bigots—I mean, serious, hard-core racists. My parents were never like that. Sure, sometimes my father talked like one, but not with any malice. For as long as I could remember, their friends, the people who came around our house and into The Suite, were an eclectic bunch: whites and Jews and Italians and blacks and Puerto Ricans and gays. In my father's world, the only thing that mattered was whether a man could make money. And my mother just liked everybody.

But these guys in Kentucky, man, they just hated black people. I was on a bus once with one of them, riding back from a store in Cincinnati where we'd bought some kind of acid or paint stripper. The two of us were near the back, sitting next to each other, the only two white people riding that bus through a not-so-great neighborhood. I heard the crinkle of the bag, and I looked over at the guy I was with. He'd taken the can out and loosened the cap.

He shot me a sideways glance. "Any of these fuckin' niggers makes a move," he muttered, "I'll be ready."

I realized I was more afraid of him than I was of anyone else on the bus.

We worked for a couple of weeks getting the trolley in shape and the horses stabled, and in July the Queen City Trolley opened for business. I was the conductor. I put on a crisp white shirt and a black bow tie and memorized a spiel about the historical sights along the route. "The oldest temple in Cincinnati was built in blah blah blah" and "German immigrants settled here blah blah blah" and "That's the fountain from the opening of *WKRP in Cincinnati*." Basic tourist stuff. I thought the idea had promise.

Except there was one horrible flaw: geography. To get to the historical sights, the trolley had to roll through one of the worst slums in the city. Dozens of kids would run to the curb and hurl rocks at the horses, and the people who'd paid good money for a quaint trolley ride would duck and cringe. My father—drunk, of course—would laugh and say, "Here come the Indians!" The redneck driving the horses would grumble about the fucking niggers and the goddamned jungle, mostly under his breath but sometimes loud enough for the passengers to hear, and the horses would buck and start so the trolley would kind of lurch along for a couple of blocks. I could never quite tell if I was angry or scared or frustrated or all three at once.

While the reality of the Queen City Trolley might not have been all that charming, the theory of it was good enough to catch the attention of a television show called *P.M. Magazine.* It was a national program that stations all over the country contributed to, filming short features that would be distributed into a pool that stations in San Francisco and Boston could use in their versions. The Cincinnati affiliate wanted to do a segment on my father's trolley that, if it was interesting enough, might be broadcast all over the country.

He said yes. He agreed to go on camera.

My mother gave him a home permanent and pasted a fake mustache on his lip and he used his new name, Martin T. Scott. But still, how bright was that? What were the odds that Jimmy Burke or Paul Vario or any of their friends and family would tune in to *P.M. Magazine* just in time to see a guy with a heavy New York accent and a bad perm boasting about his ghetto trolley? Even if they just heard the voice, the inflections, the way he talked, they could figure out it was Henry Hill. It was almost as if he was taunting all those guys who wanted to kill him, like he was playing some self-destructive version of a game show. *Will the real Henry Hill please stand up so we can shoot him in the head?*

That's about the time I understood what a misguided idea the trolley had been. It was getting way too much attention. I couldn't help thinking, *We're in witness protection—why are we running a tourist attraction?* And it wasn't even a *good* tourist attraction. "Ladies and gentlemen, boys and girls, children of all ages, welcome to Cincinnati's ghetto. Keep your arms and legs inside the trolley at all times, and your head down. And don't mind the bigot holding the reins."

In the end, it didn't matter. The Queen City Trolley lasted only a couple of weeks because it turned out that very few people wanted to duck stones on their way around the city. Even I quit after I got pelted in the head with a rock. And by the time the business closed, no one seemed to have figured out who Martin Scott, proprietor, really was. So far as we knew, anyway.

GINA: The next thing I remember was Alfie McNeil, the marshal who was in charge of protecting us from when we started in the program back in New York, sitting in our kitchen. My mom and dad were there too. It might have been that same day, only a couple of hours after I saw that other agent standing by the front door. Or it might have been the next day. It's all a blur.

I was screaming about Bananas. My parents were trying to calm me down, but I was inconsolable. I'd heard Alfie say, "You can't take the horse."

It was the government's fault. At that age, I didn't know enough to be angry with my dad. I didn't make the connections between all the stupid things he did and the danger that always seemed to follow us. I didn't see that hanging out at a racetrack with gamblers and other shady characters was probably the last thing a man running from the Mob should do. He certainly shouldn't be betting huge amounts of money or sneaking around the backstretch so often that one of the tracks finally banned him from coming in. The Queen City Trolley had seemed like such a good idea, something we could be proud of. I thought it was great when they put my dad on TV—that just proved that Marty Scott had done something great. I didn't think that it would put Henry Hill at risk, just like I didn't think that Gram coming to visit us or calling was dangerous.

And then there were things that I just didn't know, period. I didn't know my dad had been arrested. The first time was on April 16, 1981, when he got drunk and got into a fight with "a lady friend." That's what the U.S. marshals called her in a memo that was written years later. My mom would have called her "one of those whores your father's fucking." He got off with a fine for criminal mischief and endangering. Then he got arrested again in July for writing bad checks, four hundred dollars one time and thirty dollars another time. I found out later that when Alfie McNeil was sitting in our kitchen, the local police were investigating my dad for stealing some Belgian draft horses. It's not like he snuck them off of someone's farm or anything like that—he just never paid for them. Somehow the detective on the case had found out my dad was in witness protection. The detective wouldn't tell the marshals how he knew that, and I guess it didn't matter. My dad probably bragged about it when he was drunk or when he got arrested.

But like I said, I didn't know all that. So I was angry at the government for not protecting us better, and then for taking my horse away. After Alfie left, my mom and dad tried to calm me down. "Don't worry about what Alfie says, Princess," my dad said. "You don't have to give up Bananas. We'll make sure she's shipped wherever we end up living."

I believed him, and that made me feel a little better.

In the morning Alfie and some other agents were there with their boring sedans. I was on the sidewalk about to get in the car when I saw my friend Jibby lean out her bedroom window two doors down the street. She could see our luggage and the strange men escorting us.

"Gina!" she hollered. "Where are you going?"

I was startled. I didn't know what to say. I ad-libbed. "Back East," I yelled up to her.

The wind must have made the words sound different. She had a puzzled look on her face. "Seattle?" she yelled back.

Seattle? I didn't know where Seattle was exactly, except that Alice the housekeeper on *The Brady Bunch* was supposed to have been from there.

"No," I said. "Ba . . ."

Then I felt Alfie's hand on my arm. "Get in the car," he said.

I gave a little wave, slid into the seat, and Alfie shut the door with a firm thud.

GREGG: They didn't even tell us it was Seattle. "Washington State," the marshal said. That extra word at the end gave me a chill: The fact that they have to tell you it's a state only emphasized how far away it was, how distant, how fucking *remote*.

I was in the backseat of a government K car, scared but not panicky. I imagined it was how the mercenaries I read about in *Soldier of Fortune* magazine felt their second or third time under fire—no longer shit-the-pants petrified but edgy and hyperaware. Apparently the mercenaries got used to the fear, even inured to the fear, after ducking enough bullets. Maybe I would too. Just like when we fled Omaha, I was wondering how close they were, whether they had our exact location or only a general kill zone. By then I was certain that at least a dozen people wanted my father dead. His drug partners, the guys he fixed basketball games with, men who'd brokered stolen credit cards and hijacked trucks and boot-legged cigarettes. Even if they hadn't been arrested or charged, they were being harassed or bugged and watched by the feds. My father's information was like the quart of water that primes the pump: Every tidbit he gave up, every tangential wiseguy and half-forgotten score, led the feds to another target.

When I'd come home the night before, my mother was frantic, running around the house, stuffing things in suitcases. "They found us, they found us," she said. My stomach dropped. I knew who she meant, and I knew she was scared. It's weird how Gina and I have such different memories of how my mother reacted in those situations, of how she seemed to betray a different level of fear. It could be that I was more percep-tive, that I picked up on her clipped speech and shallow breaths, or it could be that she tried to be calmer around my sister. I was always the serious one; maybe she felt more comfortable letting me in on the reality of the danger, didn't try so hard to hide her own worry. I was also the cynical one; maybe I just interpreted everything more negatively.

"What are we going to do?" I asked.

"They'll be here soon," she said. I knew she meant the marshals. "We have to go." I knew that too.

"What happened?"

"Someone must've seen his picture," she said. She was still moving, racing around the townhouse. "Someone must've seen him on TV."

My stomach dropped another notch. We'd worked so damned hard on that trolley, honest work. Then I felt anger stirring, the pieces falling into place, raising questions, stoking a fury. He got some of the seed money from a guy in New York, a regular at The Suite named Dennis. Who else was he talking to in New York? Or at the track? Or when he was drunk? And what the hell was he doing on television anyway? The son of a bitch only had to lay low and keep his mouth shut—how stupid, how careless, how reckless could he be?

So we were fleeing again. After eighteen months on the run, things were getting worse. First Omaha, then Kentucky, now the edge of

Siberia, or so it seemed. I knew of only one major city in Washington—Seattle—and sitting in the back of the car on the way to the airport, I dredged up the only two obscure facts I knew about the place. Neither one was encouraging. One, which I got from *The Farmer's Almanac,* was that Seattle ranked second behind Juno, Alaska, in the number of overcast days. The other was that I remembered reading once that Seattle was closer to the Soviet Union than it was to Washington, D.C. I knew from basic geography that Seattle was as far away from New York City as anyone could get and still remain in the continental United States. Was my father so bad—and were the wiseguys that tenacious—that we had to be banished to the extreme edge of the country?

This was 1981, don't forget. This was before Starbucks, before Microsoft, before grunge. The only reason I instinctively thought of Seattle when the marshal told us where we were going was because there wasn't anything else out there. Washington State may as well have been Montana or Idaho—someplace huge and green and empty, only farther away. Wait—wasn't there a submarine base out there, a massive military base? Nothing for miles but a big, fat target for incoming Soviet missiles.

Perfect, I cracked to myself.

I watched the tobacco fields roll past. It was going to be hard to leave Kentucky. It wasn't my favorite place in the world, and I never would have chosen to move there. But it was all we had. I had no old memories I could share with anyone, no childhood friends. The only life I had was whatever I'd managed to create for myself in the previous year. It was like building something you were proud of, like a magnificent boat, and then watching it go down in flames. Only much worse. A boat is an inanimate object. You can walk away. You can't walk away from your life, even while it's burning.

I'd adjusted to our exile. I'd made friends. There was a guy I played tennis with that everyone called Preacher Jim for reasons I never understood. He drove a '69 Plymouth Road Runner with a Hearst shifter and a 383 cubic-inch hemi and a V-8 engine. I rode shotgun with him that summer when he drag raced up Empire Drive, a scene right out of an old movie, kids lining the road, some girl standing between the cars at the starting line, dropping the scarf. We hit 110 a quarter mile off the line.

I had a decent coach too, who might have been the only other native New Yorker in Independence. He drank those oil cans of Foster's beer and he drove a van everyone called the Jew Canoe, which I also never understood because I'm almost positive he wasn't Jewish. He didn't fall for that I'm-from-Stamford story, though. My accent was too familiar. But he didn't badger the point, so I didn't have to tell any more lies.

Everything during that past year was gone. Although it was impossible to get very close to anyone when you have to perpetually fib about who you are and where you came from and why you ended up in the backwoods of Kentucky, it still hurt to realize I now had no friends. None. Not a single person to share a laugh or a memory.

A memory. Tonight. *Shit.*

There was girl in my class, petite and blonde and very pretty. The other kids used to tease us that we should start dating because we were always hanging out at school together. We'd laugh about it, but I had a serious crush on her. I'd finally worked up the courage to ask her out, which for me was probably a bigger deal than it was for most fifteen-year-old boys, considering I couldn't tell her the truth about . . . well, *anything,* really. I was going to take her to dinner. It would have been my first real date.

It was supposed to be that night.

I should have been pacing my room, wiping sweat off my palms, trying to squash the butterflies in my stomach in anticipation of our date. It should have been a great night. A great memory.

Instead I was worried about getting shot on the way to the airport, where we'd get on a flight to the other side of the country all because my father couldn't get an honest fucking job and keep his mouth shut.

I didn't even get a chance to call her and cancel. I realized I was about to stand up a girl—to disappear on her—before I'd even had a first date.

I leaned my forehead against the car window.

Strangely, I didn't feel any sadness or even fear. There was no room. All I could feel was anger.

GREGG: We ended up in a little city of twenty-five thousand people or so called Redmond, about eighteen miles east of Seattle. To get there, we had to cross a long bridge across Lake Washington, which I initially mistook for Puget Sound because it was so huge. Redmond wasn't as rural as Kentucky—someone had anointed it "The Bicycle Capital of the Pacific Northwest"—but there was something about the place that made it seem like somewhere a New York wiseguy and his family could hide out for a while. There's a reason spooky shows like *Twin Peaks* and a lot of *The X-Files* episodes were filmed in the Pacific Northwest. All those giant conifers and gray skies and banks of fog give it a moody, almost gloomy feel, like it was designed for castaways and run-aways, anyone looking to escape from somewhere else.

Fear was not the predominant feeling. After a few days of running for your life, of believing the killers are close on your tail, you get used to it. It becomes almost normal, like a chronic illness you learn to cope with. We were never told of any *specific* threat. None of the federal agents ever said, "A hit man is on the way" or "Jimmy Burke found out your address" or "Someone is going to wire your car with dynamite." It was always oblique, never precise: *There's been a problem* or *Your location's been compromised.* It was a lot like the color-coded warnings for terrorist attacks these days: The government can announce that the level has gone up to orange or red, but what does that really mean? What are you supposed to do, or not do, when the color gets brighter? You don't know, so you do what you've always done—go to school, go to work, go shopping—except you feel uneasy all the time until you forget you're uneasy. So I got used to the twitch of tension when the ignition fired and started the green Pinto we'd bought from a used car lot. I often checked under the car too for any strange-looking devices; after a while my family would look at me like I was crazy, and maybe I was. But once you let your guard down completely, it becomes easier to forget about the danger completely. Better to get used to it.

If anything, I believed we were safer once we'd put a few thousand miles between ourselves and Kentucky. Washington State was so remote—the first thing I noticed in the airport were Japanese tourists and Native Americans and people who looked like Eskimos. I took that as a good sign; Eskimos were as far away from Queens as we were going to get.

Yet I could feel part of me starting to wither. We'd been moved twice before, and both times I'd allowed myself to settle in, to become comfortable, to start making friends. And both times I'd let my guard down and gotten burned. Those months in Omaha, that year in Kentucky, they were all erased. Whatever roots I'd begun to put down had been dug up, shredded, and discarded. Forever. They no longer existed, not on paper, not in any official record—only in memories I couldn't talk about. Each time we were relocated, our lives were reset to the same cover story: *We're from Connecticut, my father works for the government, we just got transferred here.*

I'd gotten good at that story. I'd told so many lies about my family so many times that they came out easily, smooth and polished, no glitches where I had to remember what details I'd made up, none of that awkward, reflexive blinking that happens when you're not telling the truth. By the autumn of 1981, eighteen months after we'd fled New York, I probably could have told the Connecticut story wired to a polygraph machine and passed.

But what was the point of telling it again? What was the point of opening up to people, of settling down, of investing anything of myself into another strange place? When would we have to leave again, just run away with no warning and no time to say goodbye? How long before they found us?

They would find us, too, unless we were extraordinarily careful. I really believed that. If they'd found us in Nebraska and Kentucky, they'd find us in Redmond. It would probably take them a while, maybe long enough that I would already be gone, grown-up and moved on, or so I hoped. But one day they'd find my father and put a bullet in his head. He'd slip up somehow. He'd say the wrong thing to the wrong person when he was drunk or feeling cocky or, most likely, both. Hell, he was already dead, a dead man walking as far as I was concerned. And we were shackled to him. I just hoped the rest of us, my mother and sister and I, wouldn't be in the car when it blew up.

Aside from the marshals, though, I was the only one who thought about those things. My father certainly didn't give a shit, my mother never put her foot down, and Gina still thought my father was going to turn into some kind of perfect human specimen, like a toad that becomes a prince. I knew better. Sometimes I could convince myself that I was the warrior of the family, but a lot of that also entailed being the worrier.

It would have been easier if anyone else had at least acknowledged my concerns, if my mother or my father had said, "You're right, Gregg. We're all in this together, so let's try to make it work." But I got just the opposite.

"What the fuck you worried about?" my father said to me not long after we'd fled Kentucky. "I don't want to talk about any of the bullshit. Quit being so fucking negative."

The fact that we were being hunted never registered with him. If anything, he seemed emboldened. He couldn't even behave on the flight to Seattle, for those few hours when we believed, or at least I believed, that our lives were in immediate danger. Alfie McNeil, the marshal who came from New York to get us out of Kentucky, flew with us to Denver, where we had to change planes. We were walking through the terminal to the next gate, under enormously high ceilings, when my father asked if he could stop in the lounge for a drink.

"Forget it," Alfie said.

"C'mon, we got a few minutes."

"No way. You're going to the gate, you're going to sit down, then you're going to get on a plane."

My father shrugged. Then he turned to me. I was carrying the cage with Rocky, my cockatiel. "Gimme that," he said. "I'll carry it."

I was too weary and distracted to notice what an unusual gesture that was, my father offering to do something nice for someone else. I said thanks and handed him the cage.

He took it in his right hand and immediately flashed his left to the door of the cage, pinched the latch, popped it open, and shook. Rocky tumbled out in a flutter of white feathers. My father dropped the cage and took a step to the side, toward the bar. He assumed instinct would overtake everyone else, that Alfie and I would chase after Rocky, that the bird would soar into the rafters. But Alfie was a pro. Before my father could take a second step, Alfie grabbed his arm hard and pulled him back. He didn't say a word either, just glared at my father. An airport security guard helped me catch Rocky, which wasn't very hard considering his wings had been clipped.

We got through the next leg of the flight without any drama, were shuttled to a hotel, and started looking for a house. We found one within a week, a big drafty thing with a wraparound porch that I called Tuxedo Junction because it looked like the house from *Green Acres*. My father fell back into his same routine, disappearing all day and all night to the local bars. He was still promising Gina that he'd get Bananas shipped up from Kentucky, even though the house had only a half-acre of land and it was in the middle of a residential neighborhood. No one would ever consider keeping a horse there. But what did he care? He had so many things to run from in Kentucky—the bad check charges, the investors he'd stiffed, the racetrack managers who'd banned him from placing bets because he won with suspicious frequency—that he was more than happy to be on the other side of the country. He'd gotten another free pass from the feds, had his troubled record wiped shiny clean again. At that point I think he believed he was above the law. I supposed in some sense he was, so long as the government needed his testimony.

GINA: We didn't stay in a hotel for very long after we landed in Washington. I think the government might have been getting tired of paying for a big suite by the night when it was cheaper for us to rent a house with the $1,500 we got every month for being in the witness protection program. That was fine with me. I always liked living in a house better, and my mom and dad found a nice one. It could have used some work, but it reminded me of a small-town train station, very cute and pretty comfortable. It had a big yard filled with apple trees, not like the open fields of Kentucky but bigger than anything on Long Island. It looked like it should have a horse grazing out back, but I knew it was too small, and besides, there was no barn.

My dad kept his promise, though. A couple of weeks after we moved in, a horse trailer pulled up in front of the house. I don't know how he did it, but somehow he managed to pay someone to ship Bananas. I couldn't believe it. I hated leaving Kentucky, but at least I had my horse. The only strange thing was that we kept her in the backyard. He said it was only temporary and that I could board her at a real stable as soon as he got settled. My dad and brother built a plank fence around the property so Bananas could roam without getting loose. We ordered bales of hay and I could ride her around the yard whenever I wanted. Sure, we caught the eye of our neighbors, but no one complained, at least not to us, anyway.

My mom, meanwhile, had a friend in Independence named Peggy who took one of our dogs when we left, a French Bouvier, the same kind of dog Ronald Reagan had, named Bar. Not long after Bananas showed up, Bar came. My mom had secretly kept in touch with Peggy and told her where we were. So within a few weeks, there were two people who had our new address.

But what did I know? I was thirteen and starting over in a new place where I didn't know anyone. I wanted my horse, and my dad got my horse. That was all that mattered.

And Redmond wasn't turning out so bad after all. Almost right away I found out something wonderful about myself: I was a good actress.

At the junior high school, where I was in the eighth grade, I signed up for a drama class because I thought it would be easier than math. Mrs. Tate was the teacher, but everyone called her Mom because she was so supportive and nurturing. I liked her right away. And drama *was* easier than math, but that might have been because I was good at it. I'd always been a performer, the little girl who wanted people to watch her, like when I did my Crazy Jimmy Eyes or, even before that, when I'd let Uncle Jimmy put a cigarette in my mouth so the grown-ups would laugh. Back in New York I used to put on short skits and act out commercials to make Gregg laugh.

My talents weren't always appreciated, though. One time when we were little and company was over, we were playing in my parents' bedroom and Gregg told me to interrupt the party and do the Charleston Chew commercial. You know, the one where some crazy cowboy says he can eat a Charleston Chew quickly. "I'll show you!" he yells, and then he starts chewing and he can't stop.

Gregg said that everyone would love it. So I went out to the living room and did it, and my father slapped me so hard on my behind that it was red for days. When I got back to the bedroom, crying, I chased Gregg and punched him and kicked him until we both started laughing.

I outgrew it, I suppose, not for any reason but just because kids find new things when they get older. But in the eighth grade, Mrs. Tate helped me find that natural talent again. We had class in the cafeteria because it was also the auditorium with a small stage at one end. We spent a lot of the year getting ready for the school play, but we also did a lot of exercises like writing and performing sketches and figuring out the staging and the direction. I was a good director; I could just see in my mind how things should go, where the actors should be and how they should say their lines. But I was good on stage too, especially when it came to accents.

Early in the year, only a few weeks after we moved to Redmond, Mrs. Tate had us put on a short play during class. I can't remember exactly what the plot was, but it was funny and I played a disheveled housekeeper who had a thick New York accent. That was easy for me, of course, but no one else knew that. My natural accent had smoothed out after spending the last eighteen months in the Midwest and Kentucky, and besides, I'd told everyone I was from Connecticut. Speaking with perfect

New York pronunciation must have seemed like quite a feat, especially in Washington where no one has any kind of accent.

When the play was over, a girl walked up to the front of the stage. She had brown hair and she had the same expensive taste in clothes as me. I'd seen her in class, but I didn't really know her before then.

"I just wanted to tell you," she said, "that you have the greatest New York accent."

I'm sure I beamed. That's when I knew I had a fan. My first fan. "Thanks," I said. I tried to brush it off like it was nothing, but I was flattered.

"Really," she said. "That was really great."

She told me her name was Kathy and that her family had just moved to Redmond. I told her mine was Gina. She was my first friend in Redmond.

GREGG: Redmond had a junior high, which was seventh, eighth, and ninth grades, instead of a middle school, so high school started in tenth grade. That meant I was in the youngest class, a freshman again, no matter that they called us sophomores. The new kid again too, the one who *tawked* funny, the one without a good explanation for what his father did for a living or why the hell he'd moved to Redmond, Washington.

My first class on my first day was English. Mrs. Harkins—I can't believe I still remember her name—introduced me to the class. She kept the story short and simple. "Class, I'd like you to welcome Matthew. His family just moved here."

I got the usual nods and stares and a couple of grunts from the rest of the kids. Then I took a seat next to a tall, husky kid with thick black glasses and dark curly hair.

"Howdy," he said, only he didn't pronounce the *w* so it sounded like *ha*-dee. "My name's Chris."

I shook his hand. I can't explain it, but I liked him right away. Just a feeling.

"Where you from?"

"Connecticut," I said, nice and smooth.

"Cool. Glad to meet you."

Just by watching him, I could tell Chris was kind of a loner, a free spirit who did things in a confident way, like he was his own man, like he didn't have any need or desire to be part of a clique. He had a streak of rebellion in him a mile wide, and he loved to buck authority—all of it, from the principal on down—just because it was there. Everyone knew him, but no one seemed to really *know* him, if you know what I mean.

That made us a good pair. His reasons might have been different, but we were both independent, secure in our own selves, unafraid to think maybe the adults were wrong. And the fact that he wasn't part of a clique made it easier for me to be friends with him. I could deal with Chris one on one without having to contend with a half-dozen other kids. I knew we'd be friends from the day I met him.

In some ways he was a good distraction for me, kind of a release from the pressure of carrying the secret that I was Henry's Kid. Chris was crazy, not in a malicious way, but rambunctious, daring. Like if we'd be driving around in his Plymouth Champ, a small economy car that was known more for its gas mileage than its muscle, and someone cut him off, he'd jam the gas pedal into the floor, rip through the gears, and bury the needle at the far end of the speedometer, past the eighty-five-mile-an-hour mark on the gauge, and fly down the road until he caught up and inched ahead so he could swerve back in front of the guy who'd cut him off to begin with. Chris would race anyone. He wasn't picky. Didn't matter whether he was driving the Champ or his parents' Oldsmobile—if someone wanted to go, or if someone was dumb enough to cut him off, Chris hit the gas. It sounds kind of silly now, but back then it was a good way to blow off some steam.

Not that I was completely honest with him, though. I was always cautious and reserved, partly out of concern for our family's safety, mostly because I knew in the back of my mind that any friendships I made in Redmond could evaporate literally overnight with a single, indeterminate breach of security. A marshal would knock on our door, tell us we had to move, and I'd be gone forever. But after a few months, Chris was the best friend I'd had since leaving New York.

One thing that drove our friendship was Chris's family. I loved hanging out at his house. Chris's family was solid as a rock. His parents had been high school sweethearts in Rockford, Illinois, where his dad used to manage a chain restaurant. He plugged away at it, put in his hours while he raised his family, and eventually rose to vice president of the largest franchiser of Chi-Chi's Mexican restaurants in the United States and Canada, which is why they moved to Redmond. Maybe it wasn't a glamorous job, but it was honest and it was stable. It was *normal.* The whole family was normal, Norman Rockwell normal. I mean, they sat down to dinner together every night. His mother volunteered for community groups. His father went to work every day and came home every night and he paid his bills and he hadn't spent half of his kids' lives in prison and nobody wanted to kill him. He went fishing and hunting with his son, and even reloaded his own ammunition.

God, I wanted a father like that. I longed for a family like that.

GINA: We stayed in Tuxedo Junction until the early part of 1982 when my mom and dad found us a bigger house. We needed one. A bigger piece of land, anyway, because I think the neighbors were getting annoyed watching Bananas tear up our yard. And we needed a different house because my mom was getting tired of the drafts blowing in through the loose windows.

The next house was beautiful. It was on five acres on a ridge with a view to the north of the Sammamish Valley in Woodinville, and on a clear day I could see all the way to the vineyards in the distance. There was a long driveway that curved up from the street, and the barn was off to the right, even though it looked more like a big suburban garage than anything I'd seen in Kentucky. Then the main house was next to that, sort of a fifties-style ranch but huge, four thousand square feet, with a half-finished basement and picture windows all around. It was more room than we'd ever had. There was a stall for Bananas and five more to board other horses if we wanted, and all that land to ride across. I called it the Ponderosa. So did Dad. It fit.

I guess I was happy, or as happy as anyone could expect me to be. But I could tell even then that things were changing. Every girl goes through it to some degree—you know, those awkward years when your parents are the most embarrassing people on the planet. It usually happens right around puberty, so I was right on schedule. But I think it was different for me because my father was so different from other girls' fathers.

Looking back, it was when we moved into the Ponderosa that a small crack in my faith started to open up. For years I'd always known my dad was right and everyone else was wrong. When he went to prison, it was because the government didn't understand how smart he was, how generous he was, how he saved a little black boy from drowning at the beach. When we had to run away from New York, it was because Uncle Jimmy got mad because he didn't understand either. My dad made all those promises to me and he kept the ones that he could. Our life *did* get better, I *did* get a horse, we *did* get a nice house. Even when the government made him travel all the time, my dad always told me we were one step away from a nice life, a normal life, and I always believed him.

So where was he now? He wasn't flying to New York much at all. He'd been there in October and November to testify against Uncle Jimmy and those other men in the basketball case, but that was all over. Five men—the Perla brothers, Paul Mazzei, Rick Kuhn, and Jimmy—were convicted, and the judge sentenced Jimmy to twenty years. But my dad still wasn't home. I didn't understand why he didn't want to be with the people who believed in him, the people who loved him. And when he was home, he was usually drunk. I don't think I blamed myself the way you hear kids do when their parents have problems. I knew I was a good kid and that I hadn't done anything to make him stay away. But that only made it harder to understand.

I didn't dwell on it, though. There were too many things going on—I was still adjusting to a new city and a new school, still making friends, still settling in. I suppose I cut my dad a lot of slack back then because of the testifying and the stress and everything else.

At about the same time, I was learning more about my dad and the life he'd led. You have to remember, for all that we saw, that Gregg and I were sheltered from the worst of it. It's not like my father took us out on hijackings or came home and bragged about different jobs he'd pulled or told us bedtime stories about the Lucchese crime family. We knew he didn't work a real job, but I never thought of him as an actual criminal. He was a wangler. That's what I'd always thought.

Then I started to do the research.

About halfway through the eighth grade, my social studies teacher assigned us a research report on the Mafia. I was smart enough to realize my dad would know something, so I asked him if he could help me. Remember, I was thirteen. I'd never seen *The Godfather*. I didn't really know what the Mafia was, not in any detail.

"Oh sure, Princess," my dad said. "I've got a whole box of stuff for you."

He went to a closet and moved some things around until he found a cardboard crate stuffed with papers. A lot of them were reports written on FBI stationery with whole sentences blacked out. There were other things too, like magazine articles and books or sometimes just a few pages copied from a book. I remember the pictures the most, though. There were dozens of them. Some were of famous things, like the St. Valentine's Day Massacre, a bunch of bodies lying in puddles of blood. But there were other dead people too. They'd been shot or strangled or stabbed, and I'd never heard of any of them. They seemed like regular people, men just like my dad. I felt a shiver. I'd never known how violent that life was.

"Where'd you get this?" I asked him.

"Ah, it's just some research," he said.

I didn't ask anymore questions about that. I don't think he wanted to talk about it, and I don't think I wanted to hear the answers. But I asked my mom about it later.

"Oh, Daddy knew bad people," she said. She was washing dishes and she didn't even stop. She said it like it was nothing.

I felt very small, like I was treading on delicate ground.

"What about Uncle Jimmy?" I asked.

"What about him?"

"Did he really want to kill us? Did he really kill

Marty?" Those had always been abstract concepts to me, death and dying. Now I was confronting them.

Mom put down the dish she was holding and looked at me like I had a fever and needed to take more Children's Tylenol.

"Well," she said, "Uncle Jimmy had different sides."

I stared at her. She could tell I wasn't satisfied with that answer.

"Yes," she said. "I mean, I don't know. But, yes, he's capable of that."

That didn't make sense. Uncle Jimmy? He'd always been so nice to us.

Mom went back to wiping a dish. "You know Mickey?" she said.

Of course I knew Mickey. That was Uncle Jimmy's wife. I nodded.

"Well, before they got married, she had a boyfriend. And I don't know what happened, if he was bothering Mickey or what, but the day Jimmy married her, they found her old boyfriend cut up in pieces. They found him, parts of him, in his car."

She was so calm about it, like she was telling me about an old car we used to own. Was it that common? Was there so much bloody violence that everyone just got used to it?

"Uncle Jimmy chopped someone up?"

Mom turned to look at me, and I saw her

expression change, as if she suddenly realized what a horrible story she'd told me. She leaned down so her face was closer to mine.

"Oh, Gina, I don't know if he really did that."

I could tell she was lying. She believed it.

"It's just that your father really did know some bad people. He was never like that, but some of those people could be. They have different sides to them. I don't know what some of them are capable of."

Yes, she did. Uncle Jimmy was capable of cutting a man into pieces. Uncle Jimmy who had every new toy in his basement, who thought it was funny when I made Crazy Eyes, who was always so sweet to me—*he chopped up a man*.

I didn't know what to say. I didn't know if I could speak. I knew my father wasn't like that, wasn't capable of those things. But I also knew, better than I ever had, why we had to leave New York.

GREGG: By early 1982 things were looking pretty good for the Hill-Haymes-Scott family. We had a big, new house and, in theory, we were completely unburdened by the past. My father had gotten full immunity for all the crimes he'd committed before May 20, 1980, the day we went into witness protection. The Kentucky charges—which were all minor compared to the rest of his criminal résumé anyway—were meaningless because the suspect, one Martin T. Scott, had vanished behind a veil of federal secrecy. Jimmy Burke would be locked away for two decades, and the feds weren't dragging my father back to New York nearly as much now that the BC trial was over.

My mother, meanwhile, was going back to cosmetology school to get her license again. She'd had one in New York, but Karen Hill didn't exist anymore; she too would be starting over, fresh and clean, as Mrs. Martin Scott. She'd be able to get a legitimate job cutting hair and applying makeup.

Even Gina and I could make do without having an official history. We were young enough that no one really cared about the details of our lives from three or four or five years earlier. Who thinks a clean-cut sixteen-year-old boy is hiding a dark secret? No one does, and no one pressed us for details beyond our sketchy cover story.

We'd been given a fresh start far away from anyone who wanted to hurt us or who knew rotten things about us or who didn't trust us. All was forgiven and forgotten. How many people ever get that kind of break? Not many. Especially not people like my father, who did everything wrong. For the first time since we'd left Rockville Centre, we didn't stand out. We didn't sound as funny, partly because our accents had started to fade and partly because no one in Washington spoke with the pronounced drawl of the South that only made us stand out in contrast. Unlike Omaha, there were people with black hair in Redmond. Gina had her horse. And now she, we, had the big house where we could all sit down for dinner together.

My father was cooking on a winter night in early 1982. He spent the day hovering over a stew pot on the stove filled with his Sunday Gravy, which is what everyone who isn't from New York or didn't have a Sicilian mother would call pasta sauce. He'd start by sautéing onions and very finely sliced garlic in olive oil, and then he'd add the tomatoes, pouring in the juice from the can before the actual fruits that he'd crushed in his hands and pushed through a sieve to get the seeds out. When that mixture boiled, he'd add a little Chianti and give it a quick stir, then skim off the acid that foamed at the top. While that was simmering, he'd get started on the meatballs his mother taught him how to make with ground veal and pork and beef, and then he'd brown the sausages, two hot and two sweet. The smell wafted from the kitchen and filled the entire house, a gorgeous aroma.

We sat down at the dining room table, a long oak rectangle that had matching chairs like Gina had always wanted, shortly before the sun went down. If you stood, there was a great view out the window of the valley beyond the deck. Oh, wait— we didn't have a deck. We had a *lanai*. That's a fancy Hawaiian word for "porch," and my mother and father insisted on using it even though we were nowhere near the tropics.

It bugged me that they called our deck a lanai.

The whole house, as a matter of fact, bugged me. The fact that we were living there wasn't sitting right in my gut. I wanted to be an optimist like my sister. I really did. Except for my father's being a barfly, our life appeared to be as good as it had ever been or as I had ever expected it to be.

But something was off. How could we afford this place? That's what I didn't get. I knew my father had some weird arrangement, not really renting but not exactly owning. He'd met some old Italian guy who wanted to unload the property and agreed to take balloon payments for it—so much up front, so much more later, and on and on until my father had the deed. But where was he getting the money? My father still didn't have a job, and the stipend from the marshals was a poverty wage, fifteen hundred a month, eighteen thousand a year. The arithmetic didn't add up to a house with four thousand square feet and five acres of land with a barn and a view.

I hadn't said anything, though. There was no point. My family lived in a fantasy. Any dose of reality I tried to throw in would be met with a sharp, "So we'll deal with it!" I would be told I was *negative* and *ungrateful.* After all, as I was often reminded, *I never went without anything.* I worried alone.

My father sat at the head of the table with his back to the window and the view. He'd been drinking wine all afternoon, but, for him, he was basically sober. And he was smiling. A big mischievous grin, like he was busting to spill a secret.

He lifted his glass and touched it to my mother's so it made a fragile tinkling sound. He winked at her.

"All right, listen up. I got a book deal, baby."

My mother was smiling. She already knew the secret.

"I did it," he said again. "I got a fucking book deal."

He lifted his glass in a toast to himself and took a big swallow.

"They want me to tell my fucking story," he said. "No shit. They want the life and fucking times of Henry Hill. It's gonna be huge. Bestseller, you'll see."

My mother lit up like a Christmas tree. Gina sat up straighter in her chair, beaming.

"No shit," my father said. "This is what we've been waiting for. We're gonna be set for life."

My father still had that big grin wrapped around his face. He was very proud of himself. It turns out that he'd been trying to peddle his life story almost from the time he found out his life was in danger. He'd been working on it for at least six months by then. When we were in Kentucky, his lawyer arranged for him to meet with a magazine writer who knew a lot about organized

crime. My father's role in the Mob—not actually
in it but enmeshed, observing for decades—was
compelling enough for a publisher to pay for the
details. He'd signed the contract in September
1981, right about the same time Alfie McNeil was
telling us our security had been "compromised."
But that's how my father thinks: *There's a half-
million-dollar contract on my life. How can I make a
buck off it?*

I stared at him. Now it made sense. Now I
understood how we could afford the big house.

"You're kidding me," I said.

He turned toward me. The smile slacked, but
it didn't disappear.

"No, I'm not fucking kidding." He took
another drink. "What the fuck's the matter with
you?"

I glanced around the table. Gina opened her
eyes wide and glared at me as if I'd said the wrong
thing at a formal dinner. My mother looked
disappointed that I wasn't as thrilled as everyone
else.

Was I the only one who understood? Hadn't
we fled for our lives three times in less than two
years? Weren't people looking to kill my father,
and us if we got in the way? Weren't we hiding?
Telling *Sports Illustrated* how he fixed basketball
games was one thing. That was on and off the
newsstands in a flash. With Jimmy and the other

four guys in jail, who was going to come after us for that? The BC Alumni Association? Some gangly point guard? Even I could understand the appeal of grabbing a quick ten grand for that article. But now he was going to talk about his life in the Mob, reveal all the gory details, confess all those crimes that had never been solved, name all the very dangerous names. If there was anything more reckless than thumbing his nose at all the guys who wanted him dead, all the guys he was going to help put in prison, I couldn't think what it would be.

"What the fuck is wrong with *me*?" I said.

I'd never been that blunt with my father before. Maybe I'd never been big enough. Or maybe I was just tired of running. For eighteen months I'd lived with a constant dread. At sixteen, the things I wondered about were whether someone would point a high-tech, laser-scoped rifle from two hundred yards or wire a half-pound of C4 to the ignition or do something low-tech like run us off the road. I wondered whether I'd get in the way, if my mother and sister would be dead too. I wondered how long we could hide, whether I would slip up or already had, whether I'd given away a clue, some snip of the secret that had gotten back to my father's *friends*.

My father just wanted to make a big score and maybe get famous too. I just wanted to stay alive.

What he was doing was putting all of us at risk.

There was a long silence, my whole family staring at me.

"Look," my father said. "This is what we've been waiting for. This is the big score. I tell my story, I get paid, we're set."

Another score. Another goddamned score. My entire life had been lived score to score, and none of them ever mattered. My mother and father spent money they didn't have, blew thousands and thousands because there was always another score down the line, another pile of cash waiting to be spent. That's how wiseguys live. But he wasn't supposed to be a wiseguy anymore. That was the whole point, the reason we were on the other side of the country. If he wanted to be a wiseguy, let him go get a .22 in the head and be done with it.

I sat there and seethed. My appetite was long gone. Finally, I said the only thing I could think of. "Why don't you just drop dead and write your fucking book without us?"

My father's eyes turned wide and watered, as if I'd enraged him and hurt him at the same time. "Fuuuuuck yooooooouu," he said as he got up and rushed out the door, almost as if he'd planned for a quick exit.

My mother gave me a pitiful look, like it was my fault my father walked out. "Do you always have to be so negative?" she said.

Did she expect an answer? That was like asking a drowning man why he had to be so wet.

I pushed my chair back, stood up, and walked away.

GINA: My dad was redeemed. He was a writer now. He'd left that old life behind, and now he was a professional. He would be in bookstores. People would respect him. I could tell people what he did and be proud of him. The story I'd been telling about his secret job with the government had always seemed like such an obvious lie. I mean, if you had to make up something about your father, isn't that what you'd say? Even if it had been true—I mean really true, not the sort-of-true way that it was—it wouldn't have been something I could brag about because it was so nondescript. But a writer—that was cool.

Okay, maybe technically my dad wasn't going to be a writer. A professional named Nicholas Pileggi was actually writing a book *about* my dad, which I knew was different. My dad was going to be the subject of someone else's book. But it was still going to be the story of his life, which meant he'd get to tell his story to Pileggi so Pileggi could write it down. My mom said dad was a ghostwriter. That's the wrong word too—a ghostwriter would write the book for him under his name—but it sounded good. Either way, Dad was going to be famous and he'd make some money and the rest of the world would finally know his side of the story. I was still clinging to that dream that one day we'd be a normal family. The book could be the thing that finally made that happen.

Still, I knew I wouldn't tell too many people, at least not right away. By that age, I'd learned not to talk about my family more than I had to. But if someone like Kathy did ask what he did, I could say, "Oh, he's a ghostwriter." I'd say it nonchalantly, like the way rich people talk about money, like it was no big deal but I knew it was intriguing. Ghostwriter sounded like a pretty important job, especially if you'd never met one before.

Kathy and I spent a lot of time together after we met that day in drama class. There were rehearsals for the school plays, *David & Lisa* in the late fall—I played a den mother—and *The Wizard of Oz* in May of 1982, when I was the Wicked Witch of the West. We were friends outside of school too. I think Kathy looked up to me a little bit, as if I was more worldly or wiser because I came from the East and I smoked cigarettes. And our house, our family, was so different from hers.

Kathy's mom and dad were very nice people, upstanding citizens and all that, who lived in a nice, clean house a couple miles from the Ponderosa. But they were also strict. Like when Kathy was old enough to drive, they would clock her mileage to make sure she was going where she said she was. And they would ground her for every little thing.

My house, then, was like an escape. It was like a clubhouse for teenaged girls. There was no real discipline. We could sneak out to the barn and smoke and talk for hours and no one would come looking for us. There were cats and dogs all over the place, and the place was always a bit of a mess. That part bothered Kathy. I remember she would never take her shoes off in the house because we had this dark beige carpet that, when we eventually cleaned it, was more of an off-white.

Kathy liked my mom a lot too. Everyone did. She was so sweet, exactly the kind of mom that everyone wishes they had. Mom was one of those people who always thought it was better to have her kids and their friends around the house instead of out in a parked car or in an alley doing something wrong. So she was pretty lenient. But not in a lazy way, like she ignored us. Mom was very involved in the things I did, very supportive, especially of my acting. If we needed furniture for a set, my mom would always let us borrow a chair or a sofa or a table. She even did all the makeup for *The Wizard of Oz*. My mom was cool.

My dad, on the other hand, was more of a mystery to Kathy. I think she sensed at first that I was embarrassed by him. Part of it, I'm sure, was just being thirteen, but a lot of it was how unpredictable he'd become. I never knew if he'd be home or what kind of mood he'd be in if he was or even if he'd be dressed in something other than that ratty white bathrobe that was a little too short. If he was sober, he was very charming. But that didn't happen very often. In the morning he was usually sick from the previous night. By midafternoon he was often well on his way to getting drunk. That left few chances to catch him in the right mood.

But Kathy asked questions. A lot of questions. God, she was nosy. She would ask about everything. I let it slip once that we'd lived in Omaha for a while, and it turned out that she'd lived there too until she was in second grade. She asked where we lived exactly and where I went to school and had I ever been to this place or that place. I didn't have any answers. "We weren't there very long," is all I told her. "But it was hot." And then there were questions about Kentucky after I told her that's where I got Bananas. I had a few answers for that, but nothing specific. At some point I'd even confessed that I was from New York, but I didn't give her any details. I was used to keeping secrets. I think she figured that out.

Of course, all the questions eventually led back to Dad because he was the reason we'd had to move.

"He got transferred," I'd say.

That answer always begged the next question

—"What's he do?"—and I always had the short, easy story of his job with the government.

I can't remember if I'd ever fed that line to Kathy. I must have because I can't imagine someone that nosy wouldn't have asked the question. But she asked again one day after school in early 1982, right before we started rehearsals for *The Wizard of Oz*. We were at my house, in the barn, with a pack of Marlboro Lights. I don't remember why it came up. There probably wasn't any particular reason other than Kathy's being curious.

"So what's your father do again?" she asked.

I was ready this time. "He's a ghostwriter," I said. I flicked an ash and tried to look bored.

"What's that?"

I took another drag. I was talking about something very sophisticated. "It's like a regular writer, only a little more, like, secret. Like he uses a different name."

"Oh."

That seemed to satisfy her. She didn't say anything for a few minutes. She looked around the barn, then at her shoes, then at me, then back around the barn. I could tell she was pondering the idea of a ghostwriter, maybe thinking it was mysterious or glamorous or something.

"Gina?"

"What."

"Where's his typewriter?"

"What do you mean?" I hadn't thought of that. I was buying time.

"I've been all around your house," Kathy said, "but I've never seen a typewriter."

"Oh, that's because . . ." I was thinking fast. ". . . that's because he's a consultant. He, like, consults and comes up with the story. He gets other people to type it."

Kathy nodded slowly. I couldn't tell if she'd bought it.

GREGG: Chris was on to us early. He never believed the lie about my father's working for the government, not after meeting him. Chris was a bright guy, but most fourth-graders could spend an hour with my father and realize the government wasn't trusting him with any responsibilities. Not someone who smoked pot and got drunk every day.

As much as I liked hanging out at his house, Chris liked being at mine. That was the funny thing about our friendship, two guys who shared similar interests but liked each other's families because they were complete opposites. When a kid grows up in a stable household, he probably gets bored with it. So a place like the Ponderosa must have been like a real-life Wild West theme park; in fact, Chris used to call my house the O.K. Corral.

Eight months after landing in Redmond, my father was in his same routine, if you could call it that. The odds of his being home on any given day were less than fifty-fifty. He would be out drinking at the Fraternal Order of Eagles lodge, which sounds weird because my father wasn't much of a lodge man, but the Eagles didn't have much of a lodge, just a battered gray shed with cheap drinks on a two-lane highway on the outskirts of town. Or he'd be at the Workshop Tavern, a roadhouse with a hammer and a saw on the light-up sign out front and a couple of moldering salmon hanging from the ceiling beams. The décor was sparse so as not to distract from the serious drinking going on. The regulars, drunk women and seedy men, gravitated to him. Or was it the other way around?

If he was home, there was no telling what kind of spectacle he'd put on. He might be screaming at my mother in a drunken rage or he might be sitting on the couch in a bathrobe rolling a joint. Or on a good day he'd be dressed and sober and gregarious, rattling around the kitchen cooking a huge Italian feast. I'll give him that: When he wanted to, my father could cook. On those days, the good days, Chris ate well, and no one said anything if he wanted a couple of beers or if he mixed himself a Scotch and soda. It's hard for any kid not to like that kind of atmosphere. And even on the bad days, I think Chris found the chaos endlessly fascinating.

At four o'clock on a Sunday afternoon in the spring of 1982, Chris and I were in the dining room, just hanging out. From where we sat, Chris had a view into the living room. He could see my father sitting on the couch in that ratty white robe. He was rolling a joint and screaming into the phone.

. . . fuck you, you cocksucker. . . . Tell him I'll cut his fucking balls off. . . .

"So," Chris said, a little too casually, "Gina told me your dad's a ghostwriter."

Fucking Gina. She just couldn't resist. For almost two years I'd managed to keep my father's life story separate from my own. I gave no details, engaged in no long discussions—just mastered the ability to change the subject as quickly as possible. But once Gina started bragging about her dad the writer, it was only a matter of time before it got around school.

"Sort of," I said. I felt that old hitch of being caught in a lie.

"What kind of stuff does he write?"

I hesitated, trying to figure out what to say. I heard my father's voice from the couch.

. . . you cocksucker, gimme my fucking money. . .

The *Sports Illustrated* story was the only thing that came to mind. It *was* the only thing. "It's not like he's a big writer, you know," I said. "Magazine stuff, mostly. All kinds of topics. Sports. Gambling."

Shit. The story was getting messy already, even if everything I'd said was technically true. I tried to cover myself, divert the story into a gray area. "I mean, he tried to do some writing, but it's not like he made a living out of it. But, you know, he was in the restaurant business for a while too."

"Really?" Chris raised one eyebrow. He was very well read, a literary type who devoured serious books by famous authors. He knew my father wasn't a reader, let alone a writer. Anyone who spent five minutes with my father could figure out he wasn't especially literate. He didn't read at all, except for *Penthouse* and *Hustler*. The only time I'd ever heard him mention an author was a few months earlier when he was drunk and rambling about how "that fucking Machiavelli was right on the money." I'd never read Machiavelli, so I didn't know what he was talking about.

I shrugged and tried to let it drop.

Chris's stare shifted back to the living room.

. . . *no, fuck you, you fuck.* . .

"So, what's he working on now?"

"He's got some kind of proposal in the works, but nothing steady."

We were both quiet for a moment or two, listening to my father holler into the phone. Then

Chris looked at me again. I could tell he had another question.

"Why would a writer move to Washington?"

"Well . . ." Oh hell, why would anyone move to Washington? This was uncharted territory. I couldn't simply say he'd been transferred, like I did when I pretended he worked for the government. "My parents thought about California"— where did *that* come from?—"but they just like it up here. And it was cheaper."

Chris nodded, but one of those slow nods, like a detective's listening to a guy explain how he happened to find a stereo just lying on the sidewalk. My father's voice was in the background.

. . . don't fuck with me, you cocksucker. . .

"Yeah, sure," Chris said. "I got it."

GINA: I slept over at Kathy's house one weekend in the fall of 1982. Actually, I slept over at her house a lot, and she slept over at mine. We were in ninth grade and she was my best friend, probably the best friend I'd ever had, definitely the best one since we'd left Rockville Centre. There was still a part of me, a big part, that she didn't know, but it hadn't gotten in the way. Teenaged girls share all kinds of secrets, but I had one that I'd been too afraid to confess.

We wanted to watch a movie that night, so I made Kathy rent *American Gigolo* because Richard

Gere was hot and it looked really sexy. I was fourteen and thought I was ready for a movie about a gigolo. I was wrong. We didn't like it. Kathy called it "truly awful."

When the pizza came, I started doing an impersonation of my grandma's friend Mildred. She always said she was allergic to MSG, so I took a bite, swallowed it, and clutched my throat. "Saul!" I said in a perfect Long Island Jewish voice. "Saul, I'm dying here! I said no MSG, Saul! No MSG! Oy, what are you doing to me, Saul? I'm dying!"

Kathy laughed so hard I thought she might choke. When she caught her breath, she started asking more questions. *So* nosy. She wanted to know about my grandfather, and I told her how he sold hats and how he sent me the English riding helmets, and then she wanted to know about Gram and Valley Stream and why we left.

Why we left. It always came back to that. For more than a year, Kathy kept coming back to it. There were so many holes in any story I'd told about my dad. Where did he get his money? How did we afford the house? Why wasn't he around very much?

I wanted to tell her. I knew I shouldn't; I knew it was dangerous. But I wanted to so badly. I'd been forced to abandon my past, to change my name, to move to strange places, to pretend to be someone else, someone I wasn't. Now I'd found a friend that

I cared about and liked hanging out with. I wanted Kathy to know me, the real me. And I wanted an ally. I wanted to share the burden, to have at least one other person know what I was going through.

I had to tell her. I couldn't be alone in this anymore. I couldn't keep lying, not to my best friend.

I wrestled with my thoughts. We were sitting at her kitchen table, in a nook with a big bay window that looked out over a manicured lawn. It was dark outside, so I could only see my reflection in the black glass. I stared at my own face. Then I took a deep breath.

"If I tell you something," I said, "you have to promise you'll never tell anyone."

Kathy's eyes got wide. "What? What is it?"

"I'm serious," I said. "There's something I have to tell you, but you can't tell anyone, not a soul. Ever."

She shook her head. "No, never. I wouldn't tell anyone."

I could tell she was dying to know. She was almost drooling.

"You promise?"

"Yes, yes, I promise. What is it?"

"Swear on your life," I said. I meant it too.

"I swear, I swear on my life."

I looked at her and took another breath. "I'm only telling you because you're my best friend and I want you to know because maybe you'll understand more."

Kathy nodded her head, eager like a puppy.

I changed my mind. "I can't tell you," I said flatly.

"Yes you can! I swear I won't tell."

I changed my mind again. But I was enjoying it, toying with her. "It's too dangerous," I said. "People could get killed."

Her eyes got wider and she leaned across the table so her face was closer to mine. "What is?" she whispered. "What's too dangerous?"

"Maybe it's not such a good idea. For your own safety."

"Gina! I can handle it. Tell me. Please, tell me."

I stared at her like I was sizing her up to see if I could trust her, but really I was figuring out the most dramatic way to tell her.

"My last name's not really Scott," I said. "It's Hill."

I waited for a flash of recognition. Nothing. I was mildly surprised until I remembered how far we'd traveled. Where I came from, being Henry Hill's daughter meant something. In Redmond, Washington, Henry Hill was a nobody.

Kathy was rapt, though, waiting for the good part of the secret.

"Well, the reason we had to leave New York . . ."

What was the best way to say it?

"We *had* to leave. Because of my dad. He's, was, um . . . involved with people in the Mafia."

Kathy sat bolt upright as soon as I said "Mafia." She looked to her right, at the reflection in the window, then got up and pulled down the shade closest to her. She pulled the second blind and the third, then sat down again and leaned in close again.

"Oh my God. Oh. My. God. Your father's in the Mafia?" She didn't seem horrified, but I think it definitely caught her off guard.

"No, no. He's not *in* the Mafia. He's just involved with people who are. Was. He was."

"Oh my God. What do you mean, *involved*?"

"Involved. He knew people. And that's why we had to leave New York."

"What's why?"

"Some people got mad at him and wanted to kill him, so we had to leave."

"Somebody wants to kill your dad? Oh my God."

There was a break while Kathy digested that information.

"Wait," she said. "Did your dad, you know, did he ever kill anyone?"

"Oh God, no!" I said. "He's not like that. He just knew people."

A million questions followed, one after another. It was as if Kathy had hit the mother lode of nosiness. So many interesting details to be dug out. I didn't give her many, though, mainly because I didn't have a lot. So I'd say, "Oh, you don't want to know," or "Don't get me started," or I'd just wave my hand dismissively and shake my head.

But it felt good, like a weight being lifted from my chest or a slime being washed off my hands. I'd told someone. My best friend knew who I really was and how weird my life had been. Just the fact that I let myself get that close to someone, close enough to share the secret I was never supposed to tell, felt good.

We stayed up for hours, Kathy asking questions, me not giving very good answers. I made her swear a couple more times not to tell anyone.

Of course, first thing Monday morning she told two boys at school, who immediately came and asked me if it was true. I told them that was the dumbest thing I'd ever heard and I couldn't believe they'd fall for such a stupid story. It worked, I guess, because I never heard anything else about it.

But I was so mad that I didn't talk to Kathy for a month.

13

GREGG: The FBI and the U.S. Marshals Service saved my father's life. There's no doubt about that. My father knows it too. Ed McDonald, the prosecutor who sat us down in his office in Brooklyn and told us we would have to leave forever, didn't need to do a whole lot of convincing. Sure, my father put on a show, acting all tough and full of bravado. But he knew he was a dead man if he stayed in New York or even if he ran away under his own name. As a marked man, he could never run far enough or fast enough to get away from Uncle Jimmy and the Lucchese family. Without the feds, my father would have been nothing more than a brief story buried inside *The Daily News*. MOB ASSOCIATE FOUND DEAD IN DUMPSTER.

The government most likely saved my mother's life too. When my father was in the Nassau County jail after the raid in Rockville Centre, Uncle Jimmy tried to sell her some blank T-shirts for the silk-screening business. The shirts were supposedly in an empty storefront in a warehouse district in Queens, and Jimmy was standing on the sidewalk telling her where to go, telling her he had great stuff for her. She got spooked—something in Jimmy's tone, the way he was smiling at her—and ran to her car. She knew too much. She could say too much. To Uncle Jimmy, a friend for twenty years, she'd become almost as much of a liability as my father. He would have killed her that day. She believes that, and I do too. It was business, like getting fired, only more permanent. And how many bodies had there been already? Six? Seven? I'd lost count. In my father's world, after a while even murder seemed routine.

By saving my parents, the feds probably saved me and Gina too. The feds had warned us that if we'd stayed in New York, we could be kidnapped or killed to prevent my father from testifying. Yet joining our father on the run didn't make me feel any safer. In some ways it felt *more* dangerous, as if we'd crossed a line and had become stool pigeons too. We were still targets; I doubt any hired killer would have thought twice if I or Gina happened to be in the way when he pulled the trigger on our rat father.

So I don't want to sound ungrateful. But the fact is, I can't help but feel that we survived *despite* witness protection, not because of it. See, the feds weren't protecting us out of the goodness of their bureaucratic hearts. My father was an asset, a body worth more alive on the witness stand than dead in a shallow grave. The point was never to rehabilitate him or care for us so much as it was to remove him from the people who wanted to kill him. For guys like my father, protection isn't about redemption; it's about surviving long enough to testify. Period.

And that was a problem. My father was a career criminal. It's the only life he'd ever known, the only skills he'd ever developed. Worse, he was an alcoholic and, depending on the month and his supply, a drug addict too. He was utterly incapable of functioning in the straight world. Yet in witness protection, there was no alcohol rehab, no job training, no reprogramming—just a few hundred bucks every month that wouldn't cover his bar tab. So the marshals never felt like our saviors. They were simply our last resort. It was a little different in the beginning, when FBI agents were guarding us around the clock. I felt protected then, like one of those guys might actually risk his life for me or my sister or my mother or even my father. But to the marshals, my father always seemed to be just another assignment, and a dreaded one at that, who came with extra baggage—a wife and two kids. They were indifferent, remote; except for some early contact in Seattle, the marshals seemed totally uninvolved.

All of that was hard to figure out at sixteen. I never blamed the feds—and I still don't—for my father's predicament, but I resented their exploiting it for his testimony and leaving us with the mess. How many close calls would it take, how many second chances would they give him before they finally straightened him out?

Redmond was his fourth chance, another bite of the apple, almost down to the core now. The feds had to put up with his behavior because they still needed him to testify at trials that wouldn't begin until 1984 and 1985. But he was getting worse, spiraling down fast. He was still trying to tell me that the only way he could get through what he was doing—ratting out his closest associates and friends, turning his back on the life he loved—was to drink and get stoned. Bullshit. Every drunk and junkie has an excuse. My father's was just more interesting than most. But it was still an excuse, and I wasn't buying it, even if my mother and sister did.

If he'd only been screwing up his own life somewhere else, I probably could have ignored it.

If he'd kept his antics out of the house, they would have been *his* problem, not mine. If only he'd risked his own life, not ours.

But he didn't.

I was in my bedroom one night near the beginning of 1983, halfway through my junior year in high school. Everything was in its place, neat, tidy, the same way I'd always kept my room, my sanctuary from the chaos around me. I was in bed, the lights out, drifting off to sleep, when I heard my father slam the front door behind him when he came in. There was a soft, shuffling sound, his footsteps on the carpet, moving past my door and down the hall to my parents' room, then another door banging shut.

I closed my eyes again. A minute passed, maybe two. A muffled rumble jolted me fully awake. My father's voice was loud, angry, but I couldn't make out the words through two closed doors. Then I heard my mother's voice, also loud but not so angry, almost conciliatory, like she was trying to calm him down.

. . . *fucking cunt* . . .

The sound was clearer. Experience told me what was happening, what was going to happen next. How many times had he come home hammered and screamed at my mother, slapped her, taken a swing at her? I couldn't count that high. Was it getting worse, happening more often? Or was I just getting bigger, older, sick of it all?

. . . don't you fucking start with me . . .

I reached under my bed in the dark, found the ax handle, and slid it out. I sat up, swung my legs over the side, and held the mace in both hands. It was a vicious tool. I'd been nosing around the library a few weeks earlier and found a book on World War I trench warfare that detailed the weapons doughboys used in hand-to-hand combat, the clubs and truncheons they'd make from scrap and spare parts. I'd checked it out, took it home, and rustled around the barn for materials.

. . . fuuuuuck yooooou . . .

I'd wrapped a length of chain around one end of the ax handle and secured it with ten-penny nails so it was like a hard, knobby ball. Then I covered it with black electrical tape to hold everything in place. It had a good heft to it and nice balance. I imagined it could have taken a good-sized piece out of an unlucky German on the Western Front.

. . . Henry, be quiet. You'll wake up Gregg . . .

My mother knew I'd step in. Since the night he announced his book deal, I'd been standing up to him. Not every time, but more and more with each passing month. "Why don't you go back to wherever the fuck you've been for the past three days?" I'd yelled at him just the week before when he was screaming at my mother. "Just get the fuck out of here." He didn't take it well. He told me to go fuck myself. "You don't fucking tell me what to do, you little fuck."

. . . fuck Gregg . . .

I gripped the handle. It felt good in my hand.

My fuse was burning.

We'd had to move three times because people wanted to kill my father.

I'd had to say goodbye to my best friend in a two-minute phone call.

I'd had to change my name, abandon my past, dissolve my roots.

My father was going to get us all killed.

. . . shut up, you fucking cunt . . .

The fuse burned down.

My legs uncoiled like springs, and my left hand tore open the door, my limbs moving like they had minds of their own, individual motors controlling each muscle. My legs took two giant strides down the hall and then the right one was up, karate-style, my foot flying toward their bedroom door, crashing through it, smashing it open.

My right arm was raised high, my homemade mace above my head. It had to come down. There was a desk, an antique rolltop, against the wall, within reach. I swung. The chain and the nails and the tape collided with the wood, splintered it, shattered it.

I lifted my club again. My heart was racing, pounding, and adrenaline flooded my veins, my muscles, my brain. I looked at my father, my eyes wild.

"Get the fuck out of here," I said.

My father smirked at me. He started to get off the bed, and as he rose, he said, "Fuck you."

I kicked him in the stomach, hard, as hard as my leg would let me. He dropped back on the bed with a wheeze and gasp, all the air rushing out of him. He grabbed his side, near the rib I'd just broken with my foot, and grimaced.

"You little fuck . . ." He gasped. "Ow, sonofabitch. You fuck . . ."

"Get out."

"Who the fuck are you telling me to get out? This is my fucking house!"

Give me a reason, you piece of shit.

I squeezed the handle tighter. I could see how his head would split, the black tape cracking into his skull, the small bones around the temple crumbling. One swat would take him down, maybe even kill him.

Just give me a reason.

A shadow crossed behind his eyes, doubt or surprise or maybe even fear, like he knew what I was thinking. It passed almost immediately, and he started yelling again, trying to intimidate me. But he was doubled over, hobbled, screaming in pain. I was standing my ground.

He limped out of the room, then out of the house, cursing over his shoulder, promising he'd kill me. After a moment I heard the car start and pull away down our driveway.

My heart began to slow. I was trembling and sweating. My rage had been blind, uncontrolled, and it frightened me. One more reflex, one more provoked spasm, and I would have killed my own father. In that moment, in fact, standing there in a rage, I wished I had. He knew it, too. A line had been crossed, a boundary breached. My father had never been able to buy me off like Gina. But he'd never had to fear me either. And the feds couldn't protect him, not from me nor me from him.

I looked at my mother sitting on the bed. The room was silent. I could still feel my heart beating in my chest. She had a sad expression on her face, more relief than gratitude.

"I hope you didn't hurt him," she said. "Gregg, you've got to control yourself."

"He got what he deserved," I said.

We stared at each other. Then she looked around the room. "Oh no," she said. "My desk. Look at my desk. It's broken."

She started to cry.

I stood there for a moment. Suddenly I felt ashamed that I'd destroyed her desk. I walked away, slowly and still shaking, feeling lightheaded the way you do when adrenaline starts to dissipate and the rush subsides.

I realized then that I was in this alone.

GINA: My dad and Gregg were at each other's throats. I didn't see anything physical like my dad's shoving him or Gregg's taking a swing, but the verbal abuse was terrible. The only way it could have been worse was if Dad had been around more so they could scream at each other more often.

I was spared my dad's rampages. I was getting more frustrated with him, but he still called me Princess and I still hoped, beyond all common sense, that he would straighten out, that things would get better. He was working really hard on the book, and he seemed excited about it. "Just wait," he kept saying all through 1982 and into 1983. "This is gonna be big. We're gonna be set for life."

I wanted to believe him. Really, I wanted to be an optimist. But my dad made it so hard. His behavior was so erratic then, just outright bizarre and cruel. Even his princess couldn't be insulated from the worst of it.

One day in school, when I was standing in the hallway by my locker, a boy walked up to me.

"Are you Gina?" he asked.

It was the middle of the ninth grade, more than a year since I'd been in Redmond, so I'd seen him around the school before. We weren't friends, though. He was a little geeky, but not the dorkiest kid in school. I wondered why he was talking to me.

"Yes," I said.

"I'm your new brother."

Huh? What kind of nerd joke was that?

"Excuse me?" I'm sure I said it sarcastically.

"Well, stepbrother. Your father married my mother."

I didn't say anything. He must have had me confused with someone else because that couldn't possibly be right. My parents hadn't gotten divorced. I knew no one could be married to two people at the same time.

"That can't be right," I said.

"Yeah, it is. They went to Reno and got married over the weekend. So I guess that makes us brother and sister."

He wasn't saying it in a mocking way, like he was messing with my head. I realized he was serious—he really believed my dad had married his mom.

Someone had lied to him. That had to be it.

"No," I said. "That's wrong."

I turned and started to walk away. "I just wanted to introduce myself," I heard him say behind me, but I kept walking.

I stewed about that all day. My dad had done some crazy things, and my parents had had some terrible fights, but they hadn't gotten divorced. I would have known about that. And if my mom hadn't left him by now, it probably wasn't going to happen.

After school I went straight home. My mom was in the kitchen. She didn't seem to be in a good mood.

There was no easy way to ask, so I just spit it out. "Mom," I said, "did Dad marry someone else?"

Her face flushed, and she leaned on the counter with both hands. "That sonofabitch," she said.

Then she turned toward me. "Yes, Gina, your father got drunk and married some whore he was fucking."

I guess there was no easy way to answer, either.

It took the wind out of me. I could feel my own face flush. We were so close to being a normal family, and now he was starting another one on the side?

"Why?" I asked. "I mean, who?" That seemed like the more important question.

"Staci." My mom's voice was dripping with disgust and contempt. Staci was a friend. She had been, anyway. My dad met her through this guy he knew who was dating her. Staci was an amateur beautician; she came to the house once and cut my hair and gave my mom a perm. She seemed nice.

But one afternoon, probably in the fall of 1982, I found my mom in a complete rage. She had a length of pipe in her hand, a big, heavy one from a hammock stand in the yard, and she was cursing when she yanked open the door to her car and tossed the pipe on the seat.

"Mom, what are you doing?" I'd never seen her so mad. It was scary.

"Your father's fucking that woman Staci," she said. She was fumbling with her keys, trying to jam the right one into the ignition.

"Wait, wait, slow down," I said. I was trying to be calm so she would be calm. There was no telling what she might do in that state. "Tell me where you're going."

"I'm going to go bash Staci's face in," she said as the engine roared to life. "And then I'm going to beat your father." She put the car in reverse, backed up with a squeal, then floored it down the driveway.

She was gone for a long time. But Staci got lucky because she wasn't home. Instead, my dad answered the door wearing Staci's bathrobe. I don't know why my mom didn't club him right then, but she didn't. In fact, she had calmed down by the time she got home—but she was still pretty upset—and within a few days she'd forgiven him. My mom always forgave him. She blamed the alcohol instead. Psychiatrists call that codependency, I think.

But this? Marriage? Forget moral—it wasn't even legal.

"*Staci?*" I repeated. "How could he marry Staci? How could he marry *anyone*?"

Mom threw up her hands. "I don't know. Because your father's an asshole. Ask him."

I couldn't, not then. He wasn't home and wouldn't be for days. I was dizzy, anyway, confused and furious at the same time. What would I say to him?

The story eventually came out, weeks later, after I'd calmed down a little. I confronted him in the living room. He was sitting on the couch rolling a joint—he was smoking a lot of pot then—and only half listening to me, not seeming to understand the hurt he'd caused.

"How could you do that?" I demanded.

"Ah, Princess, I was drunk," he said. He waved his hand at me like he was shooing away a fly.

"You were drunk? That's your reason?"

"It was nothing. It was no big fucking deal."

"You *married* her!"

He grunted dismissively. "I thought she had some money. She thought I had some money. I was just trying to get some land her father had."

I was speechless. After all the reckless things he'd done, this was just creepy: committing bigamy, betraying my mother, to swindle a piece of property.

"But you're already married," I said. "Remember? Wife, two kids?"

"Ah, that's the beauty of it. Your mom's married to Henry Hill. Staci's married to Marty Scott. They're two different people."

I was stunned, and then I was livid. I could tell by his tone that he actually believed that. He thought his secret identity, the one the government gave him to keep him alive, was a ticket to bigamy and a land scam. And why shouldn't he believe that?

But, like everything, it passed. The marriage to Staci was annulled not long after. My mom seethed for a few weeks, but eventually she forgave him. And I guess I did too.

GREGG: There were two bedrooms in the basement of the Ponderosa, and I moved into one of them not long after I went after my father with my homemade mace. I needed the distance, even if it was just one floor down, a buffer between me and my father.

Attacking him with my mace had unleashed something in me. It was almost as if that first violent outburst had stoked a fire. My temper was short and vicious, and we'd gone back and forth with nearly psychotic outbursts. A few weeks after, early one afternoon, I saw my mother in the kitchen. She had a bruise under her eye. I asked her what had happened. "Nothing," she said. "It's nothing."

I was emboldened, and I was crazy with rage. I knew he'd hit her. Without saying a word, I grabbed a filet knife from the counter, then stalked down the hall to my parents' bedroom. I went to the closet and tore open the door. I reached in, swept my arm across, and grabbed everything on a hanger—my father's suits, his shirts, his trousers. I didn't stop moving, just turned with all those clothes on my arm and stormed out to the porch. I dropped them in a heap, then picked up the first suit from the pile. I held the knife in my right hand with the blade down like Anthony Perkins in that famous shower scene from *Psycho*. I stabbed into the back of the suit coat, right between the shoulder blades, and ripped downward, slicing all the way through. Then I threw the shredded fabric over the railing and grabbed the next piece from the pile. My mother was screaming at me to stop, but I ignored her, focused on my work. I kept stabbing and ripping, suit after shirt after trousers, until I'd demolished his entire wardrobe. Then I dropped the knife and left to go find Chris.

Chris spent a few hours calming me down, waiting for my fury to dissipate. Later, when the sun had gone down, he went back to the Ponderosa with me. My father had already come and gone. I knew because of the wreckage he'd left in the driveway: my motorcycle, a 1972 BMW R60/5 that I'd bought with the money I'd earned waiting tables. He'd wailed on it with a baseball bat, then yanked out all the cables and wires until it was a twisted wreck, my vintage bike totaled. I stared at it in silence. My father had taken so much from me—my friends, my past, my whole childhood. The only things I had were what I'd worked for. And now he'd taken one of those, one of my prized possessions.

I snapped. I lashed out at the first thing I could grab, which was the patio furniture, a red-wood table and four bench seats. I lifted the first chair and slammed it into the pavement. A piece flew off. I picked it up again, heaved it down again, then again and again until it was in splinters. Chris stood off to the side, begging me to calm down. I ignored him and grabbed the second seat, the third, the fourth. Then I turned the table on its side and kicked off the legs before lifting the top and smashing it on the ground. I kept lifting and slamming until the furniture was in splinters and I was exhausted.

Three weeks had passed since then, and we'd avoided each other, my father and me. It wasn't hard because he wasn't home much, and if he was I retreated to the basement. I wished he was like Chris's dad, an honest guy, a hardworking guy who didn't get drunk and abuse his kids. I lived vicariously through my friend. I could spend hours at Chris's house, listening to his father tell stories about drag racing when he was a kid in Illinois. He called me *easy money* when we played pool on his antique table. And I'd tag along with them when they went goose hunting in the sagebrush of eastern Washington or fishing for steelhead trout in the Snoqualmie River. We were wading up there one day, the three of us, when a big, flat rock I was standing on tipped over and dumped me backward into the water. It was deep and freezing, and I lost my rod as the current grabbed me and swept me down the river. I was struggling to keep my head above water; I'd heard stories of people drowning because their hip waders flooded and pulled them under. But Chris's father saw me coming. He was fishing downstream, and as the river carried me close to him, he reached out and grabbed me with one hand and my rod with the other.

I could count on Chris's father. I craved that feeling.

My father hadn't destroyed all my possessions. I'd also bought a shotgun, a 12-gauge Browning Pump-Action. It had a full choke, which meant the pellets fired in a tight cluster that could hit a goose in high flight. That was a great gun. I used to sit in my room and polish the bluing, oil the slide, feel that satisfying click when it passed over the loader, then again when it released.

Sometimes I'd close my eyes and listen real hard until I couldn't hear anything except silence. Then I'd pump the slide and listen to that steely click. *Chunk-chuck.* Such a beautiful sound, crisp and simple. I wondered what that would sound like in the darkened hallway outside his bedroom, if the dingy carpet would muffle the shell loading into the chamber, if he'd hear it through the closed door, if he'd recognize the double clunk in his drunkenness. I wondered if it would scare him.

I'd look down the barrel, a deep, black hole, perfectly round and smooth and clean. The barrel looked bigger straight on, close to the eyes, like an abyss, an endless, empty tube. Except there would be a hunting load at the other end; a high-brass cartridge would explode like a bomb and throw buckshot out of the hole, a thousand pellets moving so close together they'd act almost like a single slug. At close range, bedroom range, a single shell could take his head clean off.

I closed my eyes again and wrapped my hand around the slide.

Chunk-chuck.

GINA: My mom was holding everything together as best she could. Whatever money my dad got from the book was spent as soon as he got it, and the stipend from the government wasn't enough for a family of four to live on, especially not with my horse and all those cats and dogs to feed too. So Mom figured out a way to make ends meet. She was resourceful like that. With all the horrible things that kept happening, she was determined to make sure her children had everything they needed and most of what they wanted.

She got her cosmetology license the first year we were in Redmond so she could work in a salon. Then she started studying for a nurse's license. Our house was so big and had so many bedrooms that she thought she could take in an old person who needed some basic care. Not someone who was really sick or was bedridden and had to be monitored around the clock, but someone who just couldn't live alone anymore because she was too frail or forgetful or just lonely. It would be kind of like baby-sitting for an old person.

Betsy moved in with us in the late summer of 1983, just before I started the tenth grade at Redmond High School. She was a tiny old woman, very prim and proper, and suffering the early stages of Alzheimer's. She was functional—she could feed herself and dress herself and do all those basic things—but sometimes she'd get confused. Her children and grandchildren all lived far away, and they didn't think she needed to be in a nursing home, not yet. So they paid my mom eighteen hundred dollars a month to let her live with us. It was a good deal for everyone. Our house with the deck and the view was nicer than an institution, and Betsy didn't really need much. Mostly she just sat around and watched TV and ate meals my mom fixed for her. She wandered off one time and went to a neighbor's house, all scared and nearly crying because she thought she'd been kidnapped and was being held in our house. My mom went and got her and explained everything, so it was fine, but sort of embarrassing because the neighbor happened to be Gregg's math teacher, which was just our luck. Other than that, though, Betsy was all right.

After a few months, my mom wanted to go back to the salon, so she had another idea. Betsy was deteriorating just a little, enough that she needed someone around all the time just in case she fell or wandered away again or needed help turning on the shower. So my mom put an ad in the paper offering free room and board in exchange for keeping the house clean and looking after Betsy.

That's how we met Flo. Oh, she was a character. She had big glasses and her hair was so black it looked like it had been wiped with shoe polish. She had a dramatic voice that always sounded like she was straining to make her words important, like whoever she was speaking to was the most special person in the world and whatever she was saying was the most interesting. She'd been widowed three or four times—Gregg called her the Black Widow—and divorced a couple more and was looking through the personal ads for husband number seven. My mom liked her right away and invited her to move in late in the fall of 1983. She brought a few pieces of furniture with her—some chairs, a table—that filled the gaps in our own stuff and her dog, a gold terrier that looked like the head of a mop. "Come here, Goldie Doggers," she'd say. "Sit by mommy."

I'll admit I wasn't crazy about the idea of another old woman living with us, especially after Flo put a lock on her bedroom door so I couldn't steal any more of her cigarettes. But, looking back, she really kept things together. Flo was orderly and tidy, two things the Hills (or the Scotts) weren't known for. She loved to clean and she loved to cook. Nothing fancy like my dad, just basic all-American food, but she did it every night so that dinner would be waiting for us. Then, at three o'clock every day, she'd shower and get dressed up nice and put on her makeup and mix herself a martini. A *martooni,* as she preferred to call it. She'd sit at the kitchen table with Goldie at her feet, sipping martinis and smoking Marlboro 100s, the long ones, until it was time to eat.

That was our household for almost a year, and it

worked out pretty well. We got used to Flo, and then we got to like her, and the extra money helped pay a lot of the bills. It was a good situation, but Betsy continued to get worse. She wasn't completely senile at the end, but physically she was having more and more difficulty. Going to the toilet was getting to be too hard for her, and she probably needed a full-time nurse. But Flo was doing her best to keep up with the cooking and the cleaning and Betsy.

She was making breakfast one morning—Flo loved to bake—and Betsy was in the bathroom that was just off the kitchen struggling to get her panties up. She couldn't do it by herself, so Flo went to help her, but since she was cooking, Flo didn't want to get her hands dirty. So she held them up like a surgeon who'd just scrubbed up and balanced on one foot while she used the other one to nudge Betsy's underwear up. It was kind of comical.

My father walked into the kitchen right about then. Maybe he was hung over or still drunk, or maybe he was just being territorial. Even though he didn't cook as often as Flo, he considered the kitchen his private domain. He looked around and saw eggs frying on the stove and pancakes waiting to be flipped on the griddle. Then he looked through the open bathroom door and saw Flo in her Chinese robe and hair net standing on one foot with her hands held up in front of her.

He snapped.

"Who the fuck asked you to cook?" he yelled.

Flo was so startled she almost lost her balance.

"You're supposed to be taking care of that old lady, you stupid bitch," he said. "No one told you to fucking cook."

"I am taking care of Betsy," Flo shot back. "And someone had to cook. People have to eat."

My dad reached for a skillet on the counter, not a hot one but that hardly matters. He threw it at Flo. My father could throw, too. I'd seen him throw knives dead-center into a target in the basement in Rockville Centre. He used the same motion with the pan.

Flo got her hands in front of her face just in time to knock the pan away, but the impact broke a finger. All hell broke loose for the next few minutes. Flo was screaming and my father was screaming and Betsy was crying and food was burning and Goldie Doggers was barking. It was awful.

Flo moved out that day. My father was gone for the next two, though I don't know where.

GREGG: By the fall of 1983, two years after we'd moved to Redmond, my father and I had reached an uneasy détente. The violence between us, as terrible as it could be, was never a normal part of our relationship, like an inevitable spark of friction. After each episode, I would be filled with self-loathing, knowing that my temper had spun out of control, that I'd been powerless against my emotions. Destruction simply wasn't in my nature; I had to be driven to it. After every brawl my father would slink off for a couple of days, finish his bender, and then dry out. "I'm sorry," he'd mumble when he came home. "I was out of my mind. I was crazy." I'd tell him I wished he wouldn't get like that, that I hated being pushed that far, that no son likes to fight with his father. And then there'd be a long lull until the next bender and the next blowup.

There was always a next one, too. More than three years removed from his wiseguy life, my father was spiraling downhill. He still didn't have a job, other than telling his story to Nicholas Pileggi, which wasn't the same as being employed. He'd blown through the advance he'd gotten from the publisher, spending it on the house and gambling away thousands in barroom card games. He was picking up some cash from two friends in California who were importing huge quantities of hashish and cutting him in on the profits, but he went through that just as quickly. The only thing even close to labor that he was doing was tending a field of marijuana plants in the cellar. He'd met this guy named David who rented houses—that way, David wouldn't lose his own property if he got busted—and turned them into grow labs for weed, incredibly potent stuff, too, some kind of Hawaiian hybrid. He got my father into the business—gave him some starter plants, showed him how to arrange the grow lights and space the beds and fertilize the roots. About a third of our basement, the unfinished part that used to look like a dungeon, had been transformed into a botany experiment almost overnight.

While his own crop was growing, my father

was smoking enormous amounts he'd buy or barter from one connection or another. He even smoked in public. He would take a toothpick or paper clip and hollow out a Winston cigarette and stuff a joint inside. He got back into cocaine too, snorting lines almost every day and dealing some to fund his own supply. Between the drinking and the drugs, he was in worse shape than I'd ever seen him, worse even than those last frenetic days before the raid in Rockville Centre.

With all those chemicals coursing through his body, his behavior, just day to day, was getting increasingly unpredictable. We had three horses in the barn then, Bananas, a colt named Logan, and a quarter horse named Bondora. I don't know where they came from, if they were stolen or borrowed or if we were boarding them for someone else or if he'd actually bought them (though with what money I have no idea). My father claimed the quarter horse as his own. "The Big Bondora," he called him. He'd go out in the afternoons and saddle him up and ride down to the Workshop Tavern, hitch him up out front, sit at the bar all day, and ride home drunk. If we'd still been in Kentucky or in some small town in Texas, or if the Workshop hadn't been three miles away via busy blacktop roads, maybe it would have been quaint. In Redmond it was stupid, something a crazy man would do.

One afternoon around that time, I was in the living room when I heard the roar of an engine out back. I figured they must be doing some construction on the polo field in the valley below our property, which wouldn't have been that unusual, but the sound kept getting closer. It revved faster, and there was a crunching sound, followed by a high whine, like the transmission had slipped and the tachometer was redlined. The engine slowed, then sped up again, more crunching, another whine. Over and over. I went out on the deck and looked toward the sound, but I couldn't see anything because our property sloped sharply down a hill that was covered in thick brush eight feet high.

The noise started again, and I saw a sapling start to bend. A thicket tumbled over, and the front end of a Toyota Land Cruiser appeared through the undergrowth. My father was in the passenger seat, navigating. His friend, an Indian he called Chief, was behind the wheel. Both of them had beers in their hands, my father with a cigarette dangling from the corner of his mouth.

They kept coming, forcing the Toyota through the brush until it got hung up on a tangle of vines. Then they'd roll back a few feet, gun the engine, and plow forward again. It went on for a half hour, maybe forty-five minutes, two drunks crawling up a hill. They stopped when they crashed through the plank fence at the top and killed the engine. My father stumbled out of the cab. He was laughing when he saw me.

"I'm clearing the land, boy!"

That's what I mean—*weird.*

Those were the harmless antics. But he was becoming unpredictably violent too, and not just with me. He didn't go after my mother, at least not when I was around—I think the mace episode had left an impression—but there was no telling who might be a target. Like Porky, this big waiter at a Mexican restaurant called El Toreador. That was one of my father's regular haunts, and his friendship with the owner, a guy named Wayne, helped land me a part-time job. I'd been working there for about six months when my mother came in one night with my father. He got drunk pretty quickly, but he didn't seem to be behaving any differently than usual.

But then poor Porky said something friendly to my mother, maybe mildly flirty but surely nothing offensive. My father, in his drunken haze, took it as an insult, convinced that Porky was putting the moves on his wife. He lurched to his feet, slurring curses. And then he pulled a gun out of his pocket. He was staggering around, waving his pistol and menacing Porky, my father, the ex-con on the run. Wayne managed to calm him down enough to get the gun away from him and chase him out the door. So no one got hurt or arrested. But the next day I got fired. Wayne was afraid my father might come back if I kept working there.

That's how far my father had fallen. Back in New York no one would have even thought about firing Henry's Kid. In Redmond, Marty Scott's kid wasn't worth having around.

• • •

In the spring of 1984, when his crop in the basement was just about mature, the deal my father had brokered to sell the weed fell through. I don't know the details, and they aren't really important, but my father was suddenly stuck with something like a quarter of a million dollars of marijuana that he couldn't sell, unless he wanted to retail it a dime bag at a time. David, the guy who got him started in the business, came over and told him the bad news. My father freaked. He started screaming, calling David a cocksucker and threatening to cut his balls off—a full-on blowup. David, a much larger man who always struck me as a pretty quiet guy, yelled back at first, but then realized he was dealing with a crazy man and walked out the door.

I followed him toward his truck. I noticed he had a lever-action rifle in a gun rack behind the seat.

"Hey, David," I said. "Wait up."

He stopped, stood there with his arms folded.

"Look," I said, "I'm sorry about my father. When he gets like that, he's just . . . you know, you can't reason with him. He's just fucking crazy."

It struck me as odd that I was apologizing to a drug dealer for my father's lunatic ratings. I had fantasies—detailed, graphic fantasies—of killing him myself. There'd been times when I was frightened by my own rage, by how virulent my own hatred could be. But I didn't want him dead; I didn't want to hurt him or see him get hurt. I hated my father reluctantly. I hated him, *when* I hated him, for making me hate him. I hated him for not being the father I wanted him to be. But he was still my father. It's complicated.

David nodded as he got into his truck, like he already knew everything I'd just told him. Then his eyes shifted up, so he was looking at something behind me.

I turned just as my father came through the door. He was screaming at David, and he had a kitchen knife in his right hand, a big carbon-steel blade that could debone a turkey. He was waving the knife above his head and running toward David.

I thought of the rifle in the truck. My father was too wasted to notice.

I moved toward my father, met him halfway, grabbed onto his wrist, squeezed, and swung his arm down onto my thigh. "Drop the knife!" I said. "Drop the fucking knife!"

I lifted his arm, banged it off my thigh, again and again, yelling at him to drop it. My muscles were aching, and my thigh stung something awful. And then he just let go. The knife clattered on the blacktop. I got a foot on it so he couldn't grab it, but he didn't even try. He just straightened up and stormed back into the house, angry that I'd interfered in his business. It never occurred to me that I'd probably saved his life.

GINA: No one who knew me knew how strange my life was at home. To the outside world I was a normal high school sophomore. I had the big eighties hair and the shoulder pads tucked into my blouses. I acted in school plays. People in the houses behind ours, the ones lining the polo field at the edge of the valley, hired me to baby-sit their kids. I was always on time, always responsible.

Part of me held on to the hope that everything would turn out all right in the end. My dad was excited about the book. He kept saying how big it was going to be and that maybe they'd even make a movie out of it. If that happened, if he finally had money, he wouldn't be as stressed and he wouldn't drink as much and he wouldn't fight with my mom and he'd stop sleeping with every woman he met.

All he needed was that one big break. Everything else, all the craziness, it was like my mom said—a temporary situation.

But temporary seemed to be lasting forever. And it seemed to be so hard on my dad. Or maybe he was the one making everything harder. I couldn't decide, and if I did I would change my mind. But he was getting worse in every way, to the point where I was embarrassed by him.

I started playing tennis that year. I wasn't anywhere near as good as Gregg, but I made the junior varsity team. I didn't expect my dad to come and watch any of my matches because during those years I didn't expect much of anything out of him. But I saw him in the bleachers one afternoon. He waved at me and for a moment I was happy. I thought it meant he was trying to be a better dad, taking an interest in his daughter.

I walked toward the stands, and he started coming down. When I got closer, I could see that he looked like hell. He hadn't shaved in days, his clothes were filthy, and he was so drunk I could smell him from five feet away. I was mortified. I motioned for him to follow me and led him around the corner, out of sight, and begged him to go home. He resisted, but not for long. He was too drunk to argue.

His friends had a lot to do with it. He was spending a lot of time with people I'd never seen before, and from the moment I met them I could tell there was something off, something not quite right. I didn't know why, but they made me uncomfortable. Considering the people I'd grown up around, that's saying something.

A bunch of them came to the Ponderosa early that summer on a beautiful warm day. My father was barbecuing. That was when I first noticed the purple marks on their arms and the backs of their knees, like small bruises. At fifteen, I didn't know what track marks looked like. My father's friends were junkies. He'd moved up from marijuana and cocaine to heroin.

I wasn't enjoying the barbecue. All I wanted to do was get on Bananas and ride away for a few hours and get away from all those people. I was riding Western style then, so I needed help cinching up the saddle. I called for my dad, but he didn't answer. I called again and he said to wait a minute. I called for half an hour before he finally came to help me tighten the straps.

Then he stuck a foot in a stirrup, swung his other leg over Bananas's back, gave her a nudge, and took off at a gallop. I could hear his staccato laugh as he rode down the hill.

"Hey Dad," I screamed at his back. "Fuck you!"

His laugh echoed over the valley as he rode farther away.

I was furious and, in a way, humiliated. He'd

never pulled something like that before. He was screwing with me like I was some mark he could take advantage of in front of all his creepy friends. I stomped around the barn, then sat down and waited for him to bring my horse back.

About ten minutes later I heard the thump of hooves coming back up the hill. I stood up and scowled at my dad. I couldn't read the expression on his face. He passed me at a trot on his way into the barn. I started to follow, but before I could get there he came charging out. He was running toward me. He had a two-by-four in his hand.

I stood frozen, not believing what I was seeing. He was halfway into his backswing when I turned and ran. He swung forward, still in a full sprint, and the board clipped me on the hip, hard enough to sting but not to slow me down.

"Don't you ever fucking talk to me like that," he yelled at me. "I'll fucking kill you, you ever talk to me like that."

I didn't dare stop. I pounded into the house, down the hall, and into my room. I slammed the door behind me, locked it, then sat on the bed panting and crying. I stayed there all night, and in the morning neither one of us said a word about it.

GREGG: It was getting harder to keep the secret about my father. Or rather, it was becoming impossible to pretend he led anything close to a normal life, that he had any kind of legitimate job. His slide continued through the summer of 1984 and into the fall.

Technically, he was still working for the feds. Uncle Jimmy would die in prison partly because of my father. The twenty years he got for the BC point-shaving was only the beginning. In February 1984 he was indicted for murdering Richard Eaton, the guy whose frozen corpse the feds showed my mother a picture of when they were trying to scare her into the witness protection program. That trial was coming up in a couple of months, and Jimmy was looking at a life sentence. Uncle Paulie was locked up too because of my father. Earlier that year he told a jury about the no-show job Paulie got him at the nightclub when my father was released from Allenwood. After a life of crime, that's how he got tripped up, making false statements. Paulie was almost seventy years old, and the judge gave him four years, which would be a death sentence.

With the two top targets, and a few smaller ones, already in prison, the government's patience with my father was growing thin. The marshals had moved us twice because of, as one agent would put it in a memo, "security problems that are self-created." Now he was doing it again. He just didn't learn. He truly believed he had a free pass.

The marshals were still steamed about my father's arrangement to have Bananas shipped to Seattle. That was a huge security breach, giving out our address to whatever track rat ran the horse shipping business out of Kentucky. The feds probably didn't know about all the drugs, or maybe they didn't care. I was naive enough then to believe the government would at least try to rehabilitate my father, but I realize now that the agents' job was merely to protect him until he took an oath and said his piece on the stand. And they didn't know about the book, not yet. In August 1984 my father got in trouble again and tried to play his marshals trump card.

Compared to all the other illegal things he was doing, it was minor: a drunk driving arrest on August 5. A smart man, a guy who understood that people wanted to kill him, would have taken his probation and paid the fine and gone to alcohol counseling as Martin Scott. My father, a habitual wiseguy, tried to tell the cop who arrested him that he was part of a special presidential commission against organized crime. The cop didn't buy it. So when he sobered up, my father told the prosecutor who he really was, Henry Hill, and that he was in the witness protection program.

The marshals weren't happy. He's not supposed to be breaking the law to begin with, and he's certainly not supposed to be revealing his identity. The feds had invested a lot into the making of Marty Scott, too much to have it pissed away on a DUI.

The feds were even less happy when they got their phone bill. My father ran up eleven hundred dollars in long-distance charges, six pages of calls, that he billed to the Organized Crime Strike Force in Brooklyn. Most of them were to New York, "the danger area," as the feds called it. Even worse, some of those calls were made *from* New York to our house in Redmond. He was scamming the feds so he could take phone calls from people who weren't supposed to know where he was.

It was as if he had a death wish. That, or an invincibility complex. Either way, the stress was eating away at me. We'd been on the run for more than four years, and I'd faithfully kept the secret the entire time. That's an awful way to live, especially for a kid, being afraid to let anyone know who you are, having no confessor for your fears. And how far did that get me? It seemed like every time my father got drunk or arrested, he told someone else. My mother and my sister weren't concerned about the consequences of telling others who we really were. How many people knew? How many people had they told? What was the point of preserving our secret from my closest friend?

"Chris, there's something I've got to tell you."

We were at my house, just hanging out, not doing anything in particular. We'd graduated in the spring, and I'd be leaving for college in a couple of weeks. Not far, just sixteen miles away at the University of Washington, but I'd finally be out of the house. I'm not sure why I waited until then to tell him. Maybe I knew it was going to come out sooner or later, probably sooner, and that he should hear it from me instead of reading it in the newspaper.

"What?"

"My father," I said. "He's not a writer."

Chris laughed. "Yeah, I know. I figured that out a long time ago."

He noticed I wasn't smiling. He stopped laughing.

"His name's not really Marty Scott," I said. "It's Henry Hill."

No recognition. I hadn't expected any.

"And my name's not really Matthew. It's Gregg Hill."

He looked at me sort of quizzically, as if I was laying the groundwork for an elaborate conspiracy.

How do you explain all those years, condense them down to a manageable nugget? I figured the saga would be best stripped down to the essentials.

I took a breath so I would have enough air to get the whole long sentence out. "My father used to be in the Mafia and we had to go into the witness protection program."

Chris seemed to freeze, stunned like a squirrel that had taken a good rap on the skull.

"And that's why we moved to Washington."

The silence was deafening. And it went on. Chris just stared at me, completely blank, until his face slowly began to shift, to stiffen. I don't think I'd ever seen him with a serious expression. Chris was a joker, the guy who liked to have fun, who'd look for a laugh and almost always found one. Now he looked like one of those prison guards from Lewisburg.

I didn't say anything else. I let the silence hang between us. It was as if a giant vacuum had sucked all the air from the room so there was nothing for the sound waves to travel through.

"Whoa . . ."

That's all he got out. He swallowed hard, took a deep breath, gave his head a little shake, like he was clearing out some cobwebs.

"Wow," he said. "The *Mafia*. I can't believe that."

"Yeah, well . . . it's true."

"Whoa."

More silence.

"When did you guys move?"

Okay, this was good; questions were good. The shock was wearing off.

"A couple of years ago."

I waited for the next question. Nothing.

Chris abruptly stood up. "I gotta go."

"Why? Wait . . . is everything okay?"

"I don't know," Chris said. "I just don't know." Then he left.

I sat alone in the living room wondering if I'd made a mistake. I shouldn't have told him. He couldn't handle it. Why would I think he could? I told him my father was in the Mafia, for God's sake. The Kiss of Death, horse heads in beds, bullets through the eye, all that scary Hollywood shit. Damn it, I should've kept my mouth shut.

I tried to see it from his perspective. Maybe he thought I was crazy, that I was making up a bizarre story to explain my bizarre father. Or maybe he felt betrayed, like I'd been lying to him all this time, which in truth I had been. Hell, my whole life was a lie, or based on one.

Son of a bitch. I may have just lost my best friend.

And the damnedest thing was, we weren't even in the witness protection program anymore. No one told me then, but it's true. I've seen the memo in my father's FBI file. "During August 1984," it says, "Mr. Hill and family were formally removed from any further program services based upon his continued arrests and breaches of security."

We were on our own, and we didn't even know it.

GINA: It was like old times in the late summer and early fall of 1984. Not old times in a good way, but familiar. My mom would get a phone call and then she'd pick up her purse and her car keys and I'd ask where she was going.

"Your father got arrested," she'd say. "I'm going to get him out of jail."

It happened three times, right in a row. There was that first drunk driving arrest and then, in September, another one, which was strange because he had a goat in the backseat. Apparently he'd gotten it from a friend; he thought the goat could wander around the yard and graze so he wouldn't have to cut the lawn. Six weeks later, in the middle of October, the police arrested him outside a deli standing in a pile of shattered glass. They charged him with burglary, but he really only wanted a pack of cigarettes. He was drunk, the store was closed, so he smashed the window. That's all he took, though. But that's how he looked at the world: If he needed smokes, what's the big deal about a broken window?

Actually, he figured out a way to get cigarettes delivered so he wouldn't even have to get off the couch. He'd call Domino's pizza, which I know because I got a job there and my friends would say, "Hey Gina, I'm talking to your dad." All the delivery guys liked taking pizzas to him because he gave them five-dollar tips, which was big for a high school kid in Redmond in 1984. Anyway, he'd always order an anchovy pizza. That was his angle, because he knew Domino's didn't have anchovies. So while the pizza was baking, someone would have to run to the grocery store to get anchovies and since they were going anyway my dad would have them pick up a couple packs of Winston Lights. Then he'd pay for the pizza and the cigarettes and give a five-dollar tip.

That always seemed very complicated to me, as well as expensive because half the time he didn't even want the pizza. But that's how his mind worked. To him, he was getting one over on someone. He'd found a way to use someone to do something for him. And since he was willing to pay for it, what was the harm? Everyone won.

I'd decided that the time he tried to beat me with the two-by-four was just a terrible mistake, one of those freak episodes that everyone has once in a while. I mean, he was still a mess—a lot of drugs, a lot of fights with my mom—but he didn't hit me again, or try to. And he would get into these terrible funks and go on long benders, especially when there was a lot of stress in his life, like at the beginning of 1985 when he had to testify against Uncle Jimmy again.

It was for the murder case this time. That was really hard on him because he knew Uncle Jimmy would go to prison for life. My dad always struggled with being a rat. I understood that too, even though I was old enough then to understand that Jimmy would have killed him in a heartbeat. But they'd been through so much together. My dad lived by that code, and he was betraying it. I think even the interviews for the book were hard for him in that way, telling all those secrets.

He was a good witness, though. I read about it later. When he flew to New York, the FBI assigned agents to protect him, and they made sure he didn't drink or get high so he'd be sober on the stand. He told the jury that Richard Eaton, the dead frozen man, was killed for stealing a quarter-million dollars' worth of cocaine from Uncle Jimmy. He said that Jimmy bragged about it. "Don't worry about him," he said Jimmy told him. "I whacked the fucking swindler." The jury believed him. Uncle Jimmy was sentenced to life, which would last about eleven years before cancer killed him in 1996.

With all that going on, it made sense that my dad would have problems. That was a lot for any man to deal with. That's how I thought then, anyway. Yet there were still times when he'd be his old self, the good self, the sweet and charming and generous dad that I'd always hoped would be permanent. He would be sober for days at a time, and he'd cook for us and go riding with me. Usually I tried to keep my friends away from him because I never knew what shape he'd be in. But if he was straight, my friends adored him. And they should have. I remember he made a wonderful dinner for Kathy's birthday that year, a pasta dish with a garlic sauce, and he even gave her a present, a gold bracelet. I didn't realize he'd lifted it from my mother's jewelry box. Except for that, it was very sweet.

GREGG: I escaped in the fall of 1984, disappeared across Lake Washington to college, away from my father and the disaster unfolding around him. It was a strange sensation, a feeling of relief and regret and frustration all at once: relief that I'd gotten out, regret for leaving my mother and sister behind, and frustration at knowing there wasn't a damned thing I could do about it.

It's funny, but my whole life I'd been the straitlaced member of the Hill-Haymes-Scott family. I got good grades and I worked for my own money and I didn't really drink or do drugs and I never got in trouble. There's a scene in *The Wild Bunch* where someone asks Brando what he's rebelling against and he says, "Whaddya got?" I was the opposite of that. My father was a cheating, wife-beating, drug-dealing, thieving, gambling, alcoholic ex-con drug addict. I had *nothing* to rebel against. My only rebellion was to behave.

But once I got out of the chaos, I created a little of my own. I lived in a dormitory and gravitated to a floor known as The Zoo. I became, for the first time in my life, a terrible student; I had trouble just showing up for class, even though my first one didn't start until 12:30. My grades hovered around the D-plus level, earning me the distinction of academic probation, and I partied constantly. I could drink with the best of them— rum, tequila, vodka, beer—and easily put away half a fifth in a single night. I was a different kind of drinker than my father, though. I was a happy drunk, more carefree, never at all violent. I made dozens of new friends and lost my virginity to a beautiful coed named Rachel, who became my girlfriend. It was an adventurous semester that helped numb years of open wounds I didn't want to feel. It felt like my first burst of freedom, and it was exhilarating.

I fear what would have happened if I'd stayed in the house in Redmond. I was deliberately oblivious to what was going on, but the stories my mother told me later were chilling. I'd come to blows once with my father (twice if you want to count taking the knife away from him) and had been one provocation away from killing him. It scares me to say it, but I believe one of us might have killed the other, that my father in a psychotic rage would have caught me in an unguarded moment or that I, my fuse burned clean away, would have shot him or clubbed him to death.

He was heavy into heroin then. My mother later told me he'd started shooting it because the membranes in his nose were burnt out from all the coke. And of course he was drinking heavily. The combination made him meaner and meaner. My mother would pick him up at the airport when he flew back from testifying in New York and watch him weave down the jetway. She'd think to herself, "Oh no," and then try not to betray any emotion, not let him know that she knew he was shitfaced because that might set him off. My mother was the one person he could always vent his frustration on, because he knew she'd take it.

She waited for him one afternoon at SeaTac

Airport when he was flying in from the Eaton trial, right after helping put his old friend away for life. My father got drunk on the plane and passed out, so he didn't get off before the flight went on to Portland. My mother stood in the airport waiting for hours, and when he finally flew back, he was in a vicious mood.

She didn't say anything, not wanting to stir anything up. They got in the car, and she drove north toward Redmond, when, out of the blue, he leaned over and punched her in the face. He shattered her glasses, drove shards into her face. Her eyeball was okay, but she still has a scar above her cheekbone.

It didn't make sense to me why someone would put up with that, why she would take it once, let alone for twenty years. But she could always rationalize it. She'd say it was the alcohol or the booze or the stress. She'd say that she brought out the worst in him, that she would get him revved up, that she would raise her hands first and that would start the brawl. Whatever the reasons, there were astonishing episodes of violence that winter.

During one of the brief times when they were basically getting along and he was supposedly sober, my mother and father had a couple of friends over. Nothing fancy, just a little dinner. At one point she realized my father had disappeared. She went looking for him, figuring he was probably in the kitchen. He wasn't. Then she noticed the bathroom door was closed. She knocked.

"I'll be right out," my father said.

"Open the door," my mother barked, like an order.

"I'm going to the fucking bathroom."

"Open the door!"

"Wait a minute."

She reached over to the kitchen drawer, opened it, and pulled out a ball-peen hammer. Then she kicked the door in. (Our house got busted up a lot.) My father was sitting on the toilet, the lid closed, with his sleeve rolled up, one of my mother's belts tied around his arm, and a needle in his hand.

She cracked him with the hammer. She just kept swinging, calling him a bastard, hitting him in the shoulder and his tied-off arm.

"I'm sorry," my father said. Over and over, that's all he said—"I'm sorry, I'm sorry"—until my mother's arm got tired.

The thing is, my mother didn't tell me that story until years later. Gina didn't call me at school and say that something terrible had happened. At the time, in that context, neither my mother nor my sister thought to call me. That's how low things had gotten—beating a junkie with a hammer just wasn't that big of a deal. It was one of the bad things they overlooked because they were waiting for the good things.

GINA: I didn't date much in high school. I guess a lot of it was growing up the way Gregg and I did, but I always felt a few years removed from kids my age, like I was a little older, a little wiser, a little more world-weary. I wasn't a snob or antisocial—I had lots of friends—but having a boyfriend just didn't interest me. And I liked spending time with Chris more, anyway. He still came around the house after Gregg went away to college, and soon he became as close a friend to me as he was to my brother.

And what if I had wanted to date? What if boys from Redmond High School wanted to come home and meet my father? What if a boy fell madly in love with me and wanted to know everything about me? What would I say? How much would I reveal, how much *could* I reveal? See, it would have been very complicated.

My whole life I just wanted to be normal. When I was a little girl, it meant having my dad home and having a house. For a couple of years there was the fantasy of the plantation house and the horses, the dream that we'd seemed so close to in Kentucky. At sixteen, though, it was simpler. I wanted a boy to be able to come to my house and pick me up for a date and not have to worry about my father getting drunk.

And I couldn't have that. Not for sure. The risk was there, and it was too high.

In the spring of my junior year, my psychology teacher paired up students for a research project about how people relate to one another. Part of the assignment involved taking pictures of people in public, like couples in the park and mothers with their children, that kind of thing. My partner was this senior boy named Jeff who was incredibly cute and funny as hell. I had a massive crush on him.

We went out one afternoon and took all of our pictures and had a really great time together, laughing and kidding around and talking about all sorts of things. Then we went to a diner and got something to eat and talked some more. I knew it wasn't a date, but it kind of felt like one because we got along so well. And when we were done eating, he offered to drive me home.

He pulled off the main road onto the side street and made a right into our driveway, which immediately turned to the left. It was a long driveway, and partway up, about even with the barn, my father had installed one of those log arches like a ranch would have. He pulls through the arch and the headlights hit the house and he sucks in his breath, like he's surprised or impressed.

"Oh, wow," he said. "You live *here?*"

The house always looked better from the outside, and even better at night. But I felt a little jolt of pride.

"Yeah," I said. "For a couple years now."

"Wow," he said again. "Very nice."

He turned into the parking area in the front of the house and put the gear shift into park. "I really need to use the bathroom," he said. "Do you mind?"

My heart skipped a beat, then started pounding. My palms were sweaty. I had no idea what was lurking on the other side of the door. My father could be passed out on the couch. Or he could be rolling a joint in his robe, wearing nothing underneath, his balls flopping on the couch. My parents could be throwing plates at each other. There could be a half-dozen junkies nodding off in the basement. Maybe someone had smashed all the furniture that afternoon or bashed out the windows above the deck. I was terrified of being embarrassed.

"No, I don't mind, not at all," I said. *What the hell am I thinking?* "That's fine."

We got out of the car and started up the front walk. My feet felt like lead, and my hand was shaking when I turned the knob. I tried not to flinch when I opened the door.

The first thing to hit me was the smell. It was vaguely sweet, like onions sautéing. The second thing I noticed was the noise, because there wasn't any. I stood in the doorway for probably a second too long, looking around. The house was tidy, even clean. There were logs burning in the fireplace. No one was smoking dope or snorting coke, because no one was there.

I tried not to look relieved.

"The bathroom's this way," I said, heading toward the kitchen.

Jeff followed me. My dad heard us coming and met us in the doorway. He was wearing a sweater and corduroy pants, like he'd stepped out of a Norman Rockwell painting.

"Dad!" I said, probably too excitedly. "This is Jeff."

"Hello, Jeff," he said. There was no alcohol on his breath. He held out his hand. "Nice to meet you."

"Nice to meet you, sir."

Jeff excused himself to the bathroom, then came out and made small talk with my dad, who said absolutely nothing stupid. Jeff asked if we had horses, and when I said yes he asked if he could see them, so we walked down to the barn and petted Bananas and Logan and Bondora. Then I walked him back to his car.

"So," he said, "is your dad a doctor or something?"

I laughed, then caught myself. "No," I said. "He's a writer."

Nothing came of me and Jeff. I didn't think

anything would. But God had spared me for one night. Or He'd given me a sign. When I needed him most to be the dad he could be, my dad came through. It was still possible.

GREGG: In the summer of 1985, my father's brother arranged a family reunion back in New York. It sounds stupid, but we decided to go, all four of us. We'd be traveling without any protection, but it had been almost four years since we'd last had to flee. Jimmy and Paulie were in prison and we had our new identities that weren't so new anymore. My father had been back and forth to New York so many times that he didn't think twice about it. Gina had snuck back the summer before for a quick visit with my grandparents, and she told me she was far more afraid of the marshals finding out than any wiseguys grabbing her. If anyone was going to worry about the danger, it would have been me. But even I missed New York, and the thought of seeing my family again was enough to make the trip worth the risk.

For some reason—I can't remember why, but it isn't important—my mother and Gina took one flight, and my father and I took another. I hadn't seen him much in the past year, hardly at all from the start of classes in the fall until the end of the spring semester. Strange as it sounds, I missed him in my own way. He missed me too.

That didn't last long. Our seats were in the back of the plane, near the rest room. As soon as we were off the ground, my father slipped into the bathroom to snort a few lines of coke. He came out, animated and loud, and started calling the stewardess, except he kept saying "waitress." He got some miniature bottles of vodka, swallowed one, then opened the next.

"This is great," he said. He scratched his nose. "Me and my son."

He reached into his carry-on bag and pulled out a *Penthouse.*

"Let's talk," he said. "C'mon, it's been years since we've had a heart-to-heart talk. We don't talk enough. I miss these talks."

His voice was loud enough that the heads in front of us turned around.

"That's great, Dad. Keep it down, though, huh?"

"Oh, c'mon, don't fucking shut me out."

He opened to the first pictorial.

"Yeah, I miss these talks. Me and my son." Another nose rub, another belt of vodka. "Waitress!"

"Shut up, Dad."

"Don't fuckin' shut me out, c'mon, please. Waitress!"

He didn't wait for her. He got up and disappeared into the bathroom again.

I spent the rest of the four-and-a-half-hour flight pretending to be asleep and trying to ignore him. My father hadn't changed at all. The only difference was that the marshals weren't watching his back anymore.

GREGG: The reunion in New York was bittersweet. Or maybe that's too dramatic a word because it implies more melancholy than I actually felt. It was good to see some of the old faces and places, though there weren't many of those since we were cautious enough not to go gallivanting through my father's old haunts or neighborhoods where someone might recognize the Hills. Gina snuck over to my grandparents' house in Valley Stream one afternoon, and *snuck* was the operative word. My grandmother pulled the car as close to the house as she could and had Gina practically sprint the four steps to the door. Uncle Jimmy had been in prison for years, but one of his friends might have been tenacious enough to sit on the house. Why take the chance?

Thomas Wolfe was right, though: You can't go home again. New York wasn't home anymore. There would always be, for me, something sinister about the city. The fond memories I had—stickball, street hockey, my friends, typical kid stuff—had been overwhelmed by the bad. *People want to kill your father. You have to leave. Now. Forever.* Five years had passed, I'd grown from a gangly kid into a (very) young adult. But the memory of that fear, that feeling of helplessness and desperation and vulnerability, lingered. Away from the city, it was easier to forget who we really were. But being in New York dredged it to the surface. We were the Hills again.

And where was home? Omaha and Kentucky had been fleeting, and I'd never expected to settle in either of those places. Was it Seattle? In my own way, that's where I'd come of age, crossed that boundary between childhood and adulthood. It was familiar, comfortable. Chris was still my best friend—he'd gotten over the shock of my revelation pretty quickly. I had a girlfriend in college whom I was madly in love with.

But I'd been a lousy student; my freshman grades were so bad that I was considering taking the next year off. Then what would I do? I couldn't live at home. My father was a cancer. Even now that he was safe—and he seemed to be, relatively speaking—he was a junkie and a violent drunk. I knew I'd have to cut him out of my life, if only to save myself.

For a while, after the academic disaster of my first semester, I thought the army might be the answer. When I was thirteen, I'd wanted to be a Green Beret. At nineteen, when I had a murky past, an untenable present, and an uncertain future, it seemed like the way out. So I went to see a recruiter near campus. He was salivating after he interviewed me, a college boy who'd gotten stellar grades through high school. I could graduate an officer and then begin active duty. The army would even pay for part of college. It was perfect.

But then I started filling out the application. It was detailed, far more so than I would have suspected. The military wanted to know every place I'd lived for the previous decade, the name of every school I'd attended. I didn't have the answers. My official past only went back to Stamford Junior High School, and I wasn't even sure there really was such a place. I had no address before Omaha, and I couldn't remember that one, anyway. I struggled for more than an hour, sweating, trying to conjure information out of thin air. After what seemed like an eternity, my mood changed from exhilaration to defeat. The recruiter thought I was having second thoughts, so he put on the hard sell. I told him I needed to get some information together, then lied that I'd be back the next day. My life had been so strange that even the army wouldn't have me.

But at least the immediate danger had passed. We'd made it through a weekend in New York with no one menacing us, no one threatening us. A friend of Uncle Joey's took us to LaGuardia, walked us to the gate, and waited until we walked down the ramp to a jet scheduled to fly nonstop to SeaTac. We had that going for us. We were safe.

Until we weren't.

We took separate flights again, my father on one plane, me, my mother, Gina, and my Aunt Ellen on another. We all adored Ellen, and she wanted to spend some time with us in Seattle, visit the Ponderosa and catch up after so many years. Our seats were near the back, my mother and I in one row, Gina and Ellen in front of us. We fastened our seatbelts, settled back, and waited for the jet to push back from the ramp.

One of the flight attendants clicked on the PA. There'd been a schedule change. Instead of flying straight to the West Coast, we'd be stopping in Las Vegas.

Okay, not a big deal. That would add an extra hour or so to the trip, but we'd get to stretch our legs on the stopover.

The plane was full except for three seats in the rows behind us. The attendants were going through the cabin, reminding people to put their seats upright. We'd be off the ground in less than five minutes, out over the ocean in ten.

There was a mild commotion up front. The last three passengers were coming through the door, panting because they'd apparently had to hurry to catch a last-minute flight to Vegas. They were all men, and the lead one, the guy waddling up the aisle first, was a human mountain—six-foot-six and almost as big around. He looked familiar, but I couldn't place him.

I looked at my mother. She was pale, and her jaw was clenched. I looked back at the fat man in the aisle, now only three rows ahead of us and still coming.

Big Vinnie.

That's the only name I had for him. He'd been an everyday regular at The Suite, a guy who'd seen my mother's face every night for years, a gambler who ran up a ten-thousand-dollar tab he never got around to paying. None of the wiseguys paid at The Suite. That's why it got closed down and my mother went back and busted it out, stripped everything—the glasses and stools and registers and liquor bottles, anything that could be sold as swag.

I didn't recognize the other two guys, but if they were with Big Vinnie, they had to be wiseguys too.

We were dead.

I flashed back to a Christmas long ago when my father was locked away in Lewisburg. He had his friends on the outside throw a party for us kids at the Kew Motor Inn in Queens. Big Vinnie was there. He brought Henry's Kid a nice present. Just like Santa Claus. But like most of my father's friends, Big Vinnie had a violent side; I remembered how he once got so angry at this one guy that he kicked the man's car so hard and so many times that he totaled it.

I knew the rules. Big Vinnie was a wiseguy and my father was a rat. He had a duty, a perverse obligation, to finger us. That's the way the wiseguy world works: If Vinnie saw us and didn't tell Paulie or Jimmy, he'd be a rat too. Or worse, he could be killed for protecting us.

Two minutes from takeoff and we were trapped.

I held my breath and stared at the seat in front of me. Vinnie filled my peripheral vision. Hell, he filled the whole aisle. I saw his hand drop onto the back of Gina's seat, then lift, swing past me to the back of mine. He hadn't slowed, hadn't paused. He just kept feeling his way down the aisle, seat by seat.

The second man passed, then the third. Ellen waited a beat, then wheeled around to look at my mother. She'd recognized Vinnie too.

"At the count of three," she whispered, "we'll get up."

My mother nodded. An attendant closed the cabin door.

"One. Two. Three."

The four of us stood up as one. I stepped into the aisle and back to let my mother out, then followed her to the front. The flight attendant had her hands up, like she was waving us back to our seats.

"I have to get off the plane," my mother said.

The attendant started to say something. My mother cut her off.

"Now," she said, adamant. "I'm going to be sick. I have to get off. I have to get off right now."

She was convincing. She was scared, almost panicking, which is exactly how people sound when they know they're an instant away from puking. The stewardess nodded, half annoyed and half sympathetic. Through the door, I could hear the hydraulics steering the jetway back into position. It seemed like an eternity. I felt eyes boring into the back of my head, but I didn't dare turn around and look Big Vinnie in the eye.

The door finally opened with a hiss, and we hurried off. My heart was racing. We couldn't tell if we'd been spotted, but it didn't matter. Vinnie was already sealed in the plane. We had time, a couple of hours before he landed in Vegas. My mother called our driver back, and he agreed to take us to Philadelphia, where we caught a direct flight to Seattle. Waiting for our bags was tense—they'd been sent ahead on Big Vinnie's flight, and we knew he would have had time to tip off someone by then. But there was no one around. Big Vinnie apparently hadn't recognized any of us.

My mother was relieved. We all were. But she saw it as a close call, a fluke, nothing more and nothing less.

I saw it for what it was. This would never end. There would be other flights and other Big Vinnies, other chance encounters with other wiseguys. We would always be in danger.

GINA: I woke up on the morning of my seventeenth birthday in July 1985 to the sound of my dad's voice calling me. I ignored him. It was midmorning, not early but not so late that I had to get out of bed on my birthday, even though I was excited because my dad had promised to buy me a car, a 1956 Ford with fat whitewalls and a pair of fuzzy dice hanging from the rearview mirror. It could wait, though. I tried to go back to sleep.

"Gina, goddammit. Get the fuck out here."

I put the pillow over my head. He'd been on a kick lately about my cleaning the barn. I knew that's what he wanted, but it was my birthday. If there was one day that I shouldn't have to shovel manure, this was it.

He called me again. And again. In between I could hear him talking to his friend Dwayne. He was a nice guy. A little dim, but nice.

"Gina! Get out here!"

I pulled the pillow off my head. "Fuck off," I yelled back. In my house, that kind of language wasn't considered extreme. I closed my eyes again.

Suddenly, my head was on fire, a searing pain, as if my scalp was being pulled from my skull. My father had his left hand wrapped around my hair, and he was pulling me out of bed, slapping me with his right hand. I rolled toward him and started swinging back, trying to deflect his blows. He shoved me to the floor, still holding on to my hair, and started dragging me across the carpet, out of my room and down the hallway into the living room.

Dwayne was there, slack-jawed and wide-eyed. "Jesus, Marty," I heard him say. "Stop it. You're gonna hurt her."

He let go of my hair but he kept slapping me. I managed to get to my knees, and I had my hands over my head to protect myself. I was crying hysterically, but he hadn't said a word. He was crazy, like in a psychotic rage.

I stood up, sobbing and trying to defend myself, keeping my hands and arms up around my head. Then he hauled off and threw a punch from his hip, a low one that hit me in the stomach. I'd never been hit that hard. The force lifted me off my feet and pushed me backward. My thighs caught the edge of the couch and I kept going, flipping backwards over it onto the floor.

"Marty, what the fuck, man. Stop it!"

I scrambled to my feet, dazed and barely able to breath. I ran for the door. I had a good lead on him, but he followed me outside, then detoured to his car. He fired the engine up, stepped on the gas, and spun the wheel so he was aiming straight for me. I sprinted into the horse paddock, praying he wouldn't plow through the fence or, if he did, that it would slow him down. I kept running to the far side and climbed the fence, but I got tangled on a string of barbed wire. A nasty cut opened on my leg, but I barely felt it. I landed in the field on the other side and ran to the closest house. I pounded on the door, wailing.

"Open up! Please, you've got to help me! Please, open up!"

I could hear the engine racing in the background. The door swung open. The guy standing there was young, in his twenties. I recognized him because I'd seen the band he played in. He had a horrified expression on his face.

"I live next door," I pleaded. "Please, you have to let me in."

He looked past me, toward my father who was

still raving. "Yeah, yeah, sure," he said, not taking his eyes off my father in the distance. "Get in here."

I was sobbing. My face was streaked with tears and blood was dripping from my nose and I could feel my lip starting to swell. There were welts on my cheeks and scratches on my face and arms and that cut on my leg.

My neighbor said his mom was a nurse, and he got her first aid kit. He dabbed the blood away and put antiseptic and bandages on the cuts, and then he got me an ice pack for my lip. He didn't ask what happened, and I didn't tell him. I was in shock. I couldn't speak.

My father beat me up. My father kicked the living shit out of me.

That bastard. I believed in him. All those years, I believed in him. I'd always forced myself to hold two different images of him in my mind, the good man I knew he was and the bad man the drugs and alcohol made him. I kept the good image alive, too, when no one else did, when the bad one was suffocating it.

He tried to kill me. He tried to run me down.

We had the nice house. We had the horses. He had the book coming. Why now? Was he high? Strung out?

Did I give a shit?

I stayed with the neighbor all day. I was too frightened to go home. So I stared at the television and tried not to think about what had just happened. I couldn't make sense of it. Who was that man? What happened to my dad?

The sun started to set at the far end of the valley before I got off the couch. I peeked out the window. Our house looked quiet. I couldn't see my father's car. Maybe he was gone.

I left and crept across the field, slowly, afraid he might see me first and I wouldn't have time to run. I got to the fence and stopped. I scanned the yard and the driveway. His car definitely wasn't there. I might be safe.

I climbed the fence and crossed the yard and started up the walk. I realized I was tiptoeing, like if I walked softly enough he wouldn't hear me coming. Then the door burst open and a man came charging through it. My heart leapt and a jolt of fear went through me.

I relaxed when I saw it was Chris. He was always around our house, just hanging out, but now he looked shaken, as if he'd seen a ghost. He saw my face, and his expression got darker.

"Jesus Christ," he said. He sounded relieved. "I thought you were dead."

"No, I'm all right." I sniffled. "I'm not dead."

"No, I'm serious," he said. "C'mere."

He took me by the hand and led me into the house, into the living room. On the mantel above the fireplace, there was a framed picture of me.

My father had shoved a butcher knife through it. I started to cry.

• • •

My father didn't come home that night or the next one. Two whole days passed before I saw him again. It was in the morning, but really early this time, before the sun had come up. I felt a gentle nudge on my shoulder and heard his voice in my ear.

"Princess. Psst. Princess, wake up."

My eyes shot open, and I reflexively rolled away. I'm sure I had a look of horror on my face, which was still bruised. "What do you . . ."

"I'm so sorry," he said. "Please, Princess, don't even talk about it. I was out of my mind. I'm so sorry. I'll never touch you again, I swear."

I stared at him. How does a girl process something like that? My father had become two people. Those competing images were still in my head, but they were colliding. It was so confusing.

But now he was being sweet. His tone was so soft, and I could tell he was sincere. He wasn't going to snap again, not right now.

I nodded at him and propped myself on my elbows.

"C'mon, get up," he said. "I've got a surprise for you."

A half hour later we were at a neighbor's house. My dad opened the garage, and there was my car, my '56 Ford. He said he'd already worked out a deal with the owner, but he didn't have the keys yet. So he hotwired it, and I drove my new car home.

GREGG: There were so many secrets in our family. We didn't keep them intentionally, I don't think, but there were just so many things we didn't know about my father. My mother would have her run-ins with him and Gina would have hers and I would have mine, but we didn't connect all the dots, didn't put all those events into one catalog. If we'd stuck together, if I'd been around on Gina's birthday or the day my mother beat him with a hammer, maybe we would have gotten out together. Instead, we disintegrated individually.

The summer of 1985 was over. Classes at UW had started, but I hadn't made up my mind yet if I was going back. Gina cruised around in her new car, my mother kept working, I waited tables at a restaurant called Garcia's in Bellevue. In a way, we were leading separate lives, connected only by the drunk in the house.

My father was actually in good spirits. Nicholas Pileggi had finished the book, and the publisher was getting ready to print it so it could be released around Christmas. My father was terrifically proud of the manuscript. Even though my father didn't write it, Pileggi told a lot of the story in long first-person quotes from him and my mother, so my father considered himself quite the storyteller. "It's fucking great," he told me. "It's gonna be huge. Fucking *huge*."

I wanted to be happy for him. I might have been too, if he'd just quietly accepted any success, just been satisfied knowing that he'd helped produce something good and then gone back to being Marty Scott. But he couldn't. That's not how he operates. His ego's too big. I was amazed that he'd ever managed to pull off a good score, like when he grabbed $480,000 from the Air France cargo warehouse, without bragging his way into an arrest.

He'd been boasting about the book for the last half of the summer. He'd told some people earlier, when the project was still being worked on, but once the manuscript got closer to completion, once he knew how good it was, he wanted the glory. He started telling his junkie friends that he had a book coming out that was going to be a best-seller. Then he'd push it further, saying it was about his old life. It seemed like with each passing week he added another, more dangerous detail. He didn't seem to worry about the wiseguys who had a reason to kill him or, worse, the wannabe wiseguys who might pop him simply for the notoriety.

Me, I'd have let him talk himself into the grave.

There was nothing I could do to stop him. But every little hint he gave out put my life in jeopardy, and my mother's and my sister's. I knew the danger was still real. I'd seen it, all three hundred pounds, waddling down the aisle of an airplane.

There were people at the house on the last Sunday night in September. I don't know who they were. My father's junkie friends, about a half dozen of them. I stayed out of the room; I hated being the only sober person in a crowd of drunks, and junkies were even worse. But I was in the kitchen, close enough to overhear everything, especially once my father got a couple of drinks in him.

"They're calling it 'Wiseguy,'" I heard him say. "'Life inside a Mafia family.'"

"No shit," one of the junkies said.

"Yeah, no fuckin' shit."

My fuse was lit.

". . . and I'm the fuckin' wiseguy . . ."

It was burning fast.

". . . it's the story of my fuckin' life. It's gonna be huge . . ."

I was hanging on his words, waiting to explode.

". . . I'll sign a copy for you . . ."

I charged out of the kitchen. "Shut the fuck up," I yelled at him, never breaking stride. "Just shut the fuck up!"

I dropped my shoulder into his chest and drove him to the floor, a hard, clean tackle. He landed on his side, and I twisted him onto his stomach, dropped a knee into his back, pinned him down, and pressed his head to the floor with my hand. "You're gonna get us all fucking killed. Just shut the fuck up!"

"You little fucker," he screamed at me. "I'll fuckin' kill you. Get the fuck off me, I'll fucking kill you."

He was pretty strong for a drunk. He was squirming, rolling back to his side, trying to get over on his back so he'd have a clear shot at me. I couldn't hold him, even with all my weight bearing down on him, and he was lifting himself off the floor.

I remembered a page from a book I got for my thirteenth birthday, *Deal the First Deadly Blow*. It was a military manual about hand-to-hand combat, overpowering bigger opponents quickly and lethally. A black-and-white illustration flashed through my mind, the exact details, like a blueprint.

I swung my arms out to either side, then brought my hands together fast, clapping my palms over his ears. The pressure change was supposed to be excruciating.

Apparently it was. My father let out an ungodly howl, like he'd been disemboweled. I felt a spark of satisfied surprise. *Holy shit! It worked!*

My father's whelps snapped me out of it. "Call the police!" I yelled to my mother. "Call the fucking police now!"

He was still squirming beneath me, but his strength was sapped. He was easier to hold, but I was exhausted, sweating, adrenaline forcing my muscles to keep pushing down on him hard, keep him in place, restrained so he couldn't get a good swing at me. It seemed liked an hour before I saw the lights of the cruisers flashing through the windows, but it was only a couple of long minutes. When the cops came through the door, one of them grabbed me by the shoulders and pulled me up while another one grabbed my father and dragged him to his feet.

I didn't resist, just took three big steps backward. My father was like an ember that had gotten a fresh puff from a bellows. He was raging again, swinging blindly. If the cops hadn't been sure which one of us to arrest, he made up their minds for them. Both of them grabbed him.

"I'll fuckin' kill you," he yelled. "You little fuck, you're dead. You little punk. You think you can fuck with me? You're dead. Fuckin' dead!"

His face was contorted into a mask of fury, and his limbs were jerking spastically, his feet at once trying to find solid footing and trying to kick, his arms yanking at the grip the cops had on him, trying to slip free so he could let loose a roundhouse. But the cops had him tight. One wrenched my father's left arm behind his back, clicked a steel handcuff over his wrist, then snapped his right down and behind for the other cuff. Then they dragged him out the front door by his throat.

"I'll fucking kill you. . . ."

That's all I could hear clearly. The officers ducked him into the backseat of a cruiser, slammed the door, and his words were muffled behind thick police glass.

I stood where the cops had left me, panting and sweating, my head buzzing. My mother was crying. The junkies were blank-faced. I heard someone mutter, "That's fucked up." My father's book party, his coming-out event, his wiseguy cotillion, broke up early.

• • •

I slept on the couch that night, the only reason being that that's where I finally sat down and by then I was too spent to walk to my bedroom.

I had to get out. I schemed, planned, calculated how much money I had saved, how much I could make at Garcia's, whom I could stay with for a few nights. Maybe Chris. Maybe Dwayne, my father's friend but a decent guy. I could take care of myself. I always had. I would have packed a few things that night if I'd had the strength. But I didn't. I fell into a restless sleep.

"Motherfucker!"

My eyes shot open. It was barely daylight. My father was upside down, standing at the end of the couch, behind my head, leaning over.

"You little cocksucker," he said. "You think you're gonna throw me outta my fucking house?"

There was a glint of metal. A hatchet. He had it in his right hand, and his arm was slightly cocked so the head of it was at his chest, poised to come down on my skull.

A jolt of adrenaline woke me up fast. I rolled to my right, pushing off the couch and onto the slate coffee table, then rolled again onto the floor. I reached for the first weapon I saw, the poker from the fireplace, twenty-eight inches of tempered steel with a point at the end and a small hook, like a gaffe, something you'd use to bring a small tuna on board a charter boat. I sprang to my feet, wheeled away, and swung as hard as I could into the front window. It shattered.

That was my warning shot. I spun back toward him and grimaced, the poker cocked like a Louisville Slugger. The next swing was going for his head.

My father's friend Dwayne stood in the

distance. My father with the hatchet in his hand. Me with the poker. *This was it.* It felt like a medieval death match. I had no thought at that moment other than to kill him.

I drew the poker back into a windup, ready to take a full swing. But then my father quit. He dropped the hatchet on the floor and turned toward the door. I struggled to stop my arms, like a batter checking his swing, lost my balance, caught myself.

I stared at my father, and he looked back at me. What was that look in his eyes? Fear? Self-loathing? Exhaustion? Regret?

I couldn't read it. I still don't know what it was, and I guess it doesn't matter. Then he turned and shuffled out the front door.

Dwayne was still standing by the door, watching. He might have even said something, might have tried to call off my father. But I'd never heard it. Combat focuses the mind pretty tightly. Now that it was over, I was still trembling with fear and rage. I turned and threw the poker with all my strength across the living room, as if my father was still standing there. It smashed into a fancy antique chair that my mom had reupholstered. I stood silently among the broken glass and furniture, struggling to catch my breath.

"You all right?" Dwayne asked.

I heard my father's car start out front.

"Yeah," I said.

"You got to get out of here. This is screwed up. You can stay with me if you want. Call me later." Then he followed my father out the door.

My mother came into the living room after they'd driven away. She'd slept through the battle, and now she was aghast at the destruction. "Oh, Matthew," she said. "The window. My chair. Oh, what happened?"

When I told her, I could tell she was upset with me, that she thought I'd overreacted, just as she had when I'd cut up my father's clothes and smashed all the patio furniture. That's what my mother seemed to focus on, her angry son instead of her lunatic husband.

"That's it, Mom," I told her. "Either he goes, or I go."

She just looked at me. I could tell by her expression what the answer was.

Later that day I threw my clothes into a duffel bag and some boxes, stuffed in a few other small things I thought I might need, and called Dwayne to pick me up. He took my bags and boxes, and I followed on my motorcycle, a 1971 Motor Guzzi 750 Ambassador that I got in a trade for the shotgun I once thought I'd use to blow off my father's head. I spent the rest of the night at his place figuring out what to do. I had to get away, far away.

At eleven o'clock I called American Airlines and booked a flight out of Seattle. In the morning I rode to Bellevue to tell the boss at Garcia's I was quitting and picked up my last check. The bank was next. I withdrew my life's savings, six hundred dollars, and closed the account. Then I rode to Chris's and left the motorcycle. It was still early and he was groggy. I told him I was leaving. I said goodbye and called a cab for SeaTac, and at 1:30 on the afternoon of October 3, 1985, I boarded a flight to someplace I'd never been, an unfamiliar city far away from my father.

Seattle is beautiful from the air. I looked down on the water surrounded by all those dark-green conifers, Mt. Rainier to the south, the city hugging the coast, the Space Needle, so big when you look up at it but no more than a fragile Tinkertoy from above. I realized how easy it was to leave, how I'd been conditioned to simply walk away from everything, from everyone. I'd had too much practice.

Was I doing the right thing? I was leaving Gina behind, leaving my mother behind without even saying goodbye. The government had finished its job. The marshals had kept my father alive, protected him from all those men who were now in jail. But in the end, it wasn't the Mob I had to run from.

It was my father.

The jet climbed higher into the sky, into the clouds that hung over Puget Sound, into the gray until I couldn't see anything at all.

GINA: I was devastated when Gregg left. So was my mom. At first we were worried because he didn't tell us he was leaving, but we figured he'd be back in a day or two after things calmed down. When days turned to weeks and he didn't even call, I finally asked Chris if he knew where he was. That's when I found out my brother had left for good.

I was crushed. Tears were rolling down my cheeks as I raced to tell my mom. I grabbed her tight and started crying uncontrollably. I was struggling to tell her what Chris had said, and before I'd even gotten out all the words, she was sobbing too. We cried in each other's arms for what seemed like an hour. We couldn't believe he was gone. He didn't even say goodbye.

I'd always loved Gregg, even when he was so serious. I'd never understood why he was so negative about everything. Now I wondered if he was just being realistic, if I was being naive, blind to how bad things were and always would be—if I just wouldn't accept that this was no longer a temporary situation.

My dad also left town days after Gregg, but that was for more government business. It was another trial, only this time he flew all the way to Milan, Italy, to testify against a financier named Michele Sindona. He wasn't there very long, just one day to get over his jet lag, one day to testify, and part of a third one waiting for a flight, but he found time to buy a Gucci bag for me and one for my friend Kathy. I thought that meant things might get better again. That was my dad, risking his life to testify in a foreign country—the world capital of the Mafia!—and yet being thoughtful at the same time.

And things really got better when the book about my dad came out in December 1985. He was right—it *was* huge. It made the *New York Times* best-seller list, and all the critics raved about it. *The Washington Post Book World* called it "entirely fascinating . . . cynical, violent, avaricious, lawless." The newspaper in Baltimore said it had "the kind of crude authenticity that we haven't had since *The Valachi Papers*," which I learned was a really big deal because Valachi told Congress all about the

Mafia back when the government officially denied there even was a Mafia. And *People* magazine said *Wiseguy* was "a chilling tale of human rot, all the more effective for its restrained tone."

I liked it too, which I know sounds strange because the rotting human in the book was my dad. My mom, to a stranger reading the book, didn't come across too well either. But I'd always been able to hold opposing views of my dad in my head. I knew the book was accurate, but it was about our old life back in New York, the years before I was born and when I was still a little girl. (Gregg and I weren't in the book at all. To help hide our family's new identity, Pileggi gave my parents two daughters, and they were only mentioned in passing.) And, in any case, my dad wasn't around those people anymore. They were all dead or in prison, and my dad was so far from the place where he'd committed those crimes that it was almost like reading about a different person.

If the book made him out to be a bad person, my dad didn't seem to care. You have to remember, that was probably the first honest money he'd made since his four years in the army, unless you want to count the stipend the government used to give us. That's funny: He got an honest paycheck by talking about all the dishonest things he did. He wasn't ashamed of anything he'd done. In fact, he was boasting about it, proud as a peacock, not even pretending to be Marty Scott. He flew to Hawaii and wore a fake beard to be interviewed on ABC's *20/20*. He signed copies of the book for his friends and my friends too. "To Kathy," he wrote in hers. "That names have been changed to protect the guilty. Ha ha. Love, Henry Hill."

Once he let the secret out, there was no stopping him. He was a celebrity, kind of an outlaw hero, and he played that role to the hilt. I went out with him one afternoon right before the book came out to look at a new car he wanted to buy, a teal Cadillac with a matching leather interior. It looked like a pimp mobile. He took it out for a test drive, and after riding around nowhere in particular, he went to Kathy's house. Her mom was home.

"Let's go out for a drink!" he said to Kathy's mom, like that would be the most fun thing anyone could do at three o'clock in the afternoon in Redmond, Washington.

Kathy's mom didn't know my dad very well. She certainly didn't know about the times he beat me up or the fights he had with my mom or the marijuana he grew in the basement. If she did, she never would have let Kathy anywhere near my house.

But she said okay, and we all got back in the Cadillac and drove to the Eagle's hall on Avondale Road on the outskirts of town. Kathy and I were only seventeen, so we had to stay in a separate part of the hall while my dad and her mom had a drink.

My dad told her everything, that his real name was Henry Hill and that he used to be in the Mob but now he was in the witness protection program and that there was going to be a book about it. Then he told her some things I'd never heard before, like how he wanted to be a priest when he was little and might have if he hadn't had such a hard time at school and ended up hanging out at Paulie's cabstand. Kathy's mom didn't believe any of it. How could she? My dad, before he got too drunk, was so charming and so gregarious that it was impossible to imagine his being a criminal or even associating with them. She would remember him almost like a cartoon character, a funny little man who could tell funny stories.

I didn't think of how dangerous it was, my dad telling people who he really was. I mean, it was Kathy's mom and some of our neighbors and his friends. Who were they going to tell? They didn't know any mobsters, and besides, we were all the way on the other side of the country. What bothered me, though, were all the other boundaries he started crossing. I'd always tried to keep my dad isolated from my friends mostly because he was so unpredictable and embarrassing but partly because he wasn't really Marty Scott. If anyone got too close to him in one of his stupors, there was always the chance he'd slip up or they'd figure it out on their own.

Everyone knew he was Henry Hill after the book. And that seemed to break down the last barrier. He had no shame left, nothing to hide.

Kathy came to pick me up one night in early 1986. I don't remember where we were going, but I wasn't ready. I was never ready on time. I never let anyone into my room because it was such a mess, so while I was getting dressed Kathy waited in the living room with my dad.

He was wearing his short robe and sitting on the couch rolling a joint on the coffee table. He lit it and took a puff, then held it out toward Kathy.

"Want some?"

Kathy thought about it for a millisecond. "Yeah, why not," she said.

Dad pulled the joint back. "If you tell her"—he jerked his head toward my closed door—"I'll deny it."

She took two big tokes off it and handed it back to my dad. When I came out of my bedroom, I smelled the weed and saw my dad, but I didn't think anything of it. I just hoped he hadn't hit on her. Dad flirted with Kathy so much my mom suspected they were having an affair (they weren't). They even got into a fight about it once.

I said, "Let's go" to Kathy and we went out the front door and got in her car. That's when it hit her. She suddenly had an uncontrollable giggle fit.

"What's wrong with you?" I asked.

She kept giggling. I figured it out pretty quickly.

"You're high," I said. "How did you get . . ."

I wasn't a genius at math, but I could put two and two together.

"You fucking bitch! You got high with my dad! I can't fucking believe you, you bitch!"

I let her have it for a good, long time, just screaming at her and calling her a bitch. Those two worlds—my world and my father's world—weren't supposed to collide like that. I was so angry I couldn't see straight. And the curious thing is, I was madder at Kathy than I was at my dad. She should have known better. I got out of the car and slammed the door. I didn't talk to her for three months.

GREGG: I was nineteen when I left Seattle. I finally had my freedom, but it had come at a steep price. I'd sacrificed everything and was beginning from scratch. Again. It was a familiar feeling, but lonelier this time, on my own, without my mother and Gina. It hurt more too.

I rented a cramped room in a boarding house for $150 a week and found a job as a waiter. My cardboard boxes and duffel bag sat unpacked on one side of the narrow room. I put my Big Ben windup alarm clock on the night table, but the ticking was so loud I had trouble sleeping. I lay awake on the twin bed, oblivious to the sound of a police siren nearby, pondering the choice I'd made.

I knew it had been the right decision. Things in Seattle had almost completely collapsed. My father seemed hell-bent on destruction. I didn't know the details then, but I didn't have to. I knew my father. Years later, though, I read through FBI file HQ 172-398, the heavily edited dossier on my father. It doesn't cover his whole life or even all of his time in the witness protection program. Any of his time in the program, actually, since the first memo is dated October 1, 1985, more than a year after he'd gotten us all bounced out of the program—and, coincidentally, two days before I left Seattle. A lot of it is blacked out in heavy marker, but what's there is both maddening and depressing.

The book my father was so proud of pissed off the feds pretty good. In an internal memo from October 22, whoever wrote it—it's unclear from the copy in the file—noted that "there will be widespread and possible national publicity concerning the book. . . . The Bureau should be aware that above publicity and attention that HILL and his family will receive will create additional security problems that are self-created."

No shit. At least my father was consistent. Even under armed guard he made problems for himself. When he flew to Italy to testify against Sindona, he made some calls back to Redmond that he billed to the hotel, which meant some

Milanese bellhop could grab the numbers off his bill. He placed some collect calls too which meant he would have had to give the operator the name he was known by in Washington, Marty Scott. That was a bad idea to begin with, and a worse one considering his Italian police guards—men he didn't know and couldn't trust—were in the room with him.

So who was he calling? The memos don't say. But a line in another memo gives a pretty good hint: According to a police detective in Washington (probably Redmond, but the town is blacked out), "Mr. Hill was under active investigation as a suspect in the trafficking of cocaine." And that, in turn, helps explain the anonymous phone call my mother received at 8:30 on the night of October 23. It was a man's voice with a local accent. He said, "Tell Marty he's dead." Then he hung up.

It was astonishing, really. The government had spent more than five years and untold thousands of dollars to keep the Mob from killing my father, and now some asshole in Washington wanted him dead.

GINA: My mother has a Florence Nightingale complex. She was always finding wounded creatures and bringing them home. In New York it was dogs and cats. In Washington it was people. There were always odd characters living in the house. For a while there was a bisexual crackhead who needed a place to stay. Derelicts my father knew or women whose husbands were in prison would be live-in housekeepers for a month or so. A family of Peruvians lived in the basement. My friends would be there for weeks at a time.

And then Dawn moved in. Dawn was married to Lee, who was a friend of my father's, and she had two children. Their marriage fell apart, and Dawn and her kids were suddenly homeless. I think the fact that Dawn was a junkie and an alcoholic had a lot to do with it. But my mother took pity on her and let her move in with her kids.

Of course my father got high with her. But everything came to a head when I found out he was fucking her. As far as I was concerned, she was a bumpkin from the wrong side of the tracks who was married to a crazy truck driver. I understood why my mom felt sorry for her and let her live with us. I'm sure she didn't guess that her generosity would lead to the end of everything.

Having Dawn in the house meant my dad had a regular drug buddy. They were high all the time, and pretty soon my dad had track marks all up and down his arms. Then he started disappearing more. He'd be gone for days at a time, weeks. If he was home, he was nodding off or passed out, and I'd find bloody needles around the house, or he'd be strung out and fighting with someone—a drug friend, a drinking buddy—in the driveway. The police came to our house a lot.

He was around less and less through the spring. By summer I hardly saw him anymore. Whatever money he got for the book was gone. Repo men were coming by the house every other day. It seemed like that, anyway. The horses were gone, even Bananas, because my father owed someone money and a horse was worth something. A jeweler came by one day and took a necklace my dad had given me, a gold Pegasus with a diamond eye. He took it right off my neck.

The dream I'd held onto all those years was shattered. I knew we'd never have that normal family because my father was a crazy fuck, a crazy, alcoholic, junkie fuck. It was too late, anyway. I was almost eighteen. We were broke. And my father was gone.

I went to the bank one day to withdraw some cash from the small savings I'd accumulated from working at Domino's. A woman I knew, whom my whole family knew, was there.

"Oh, I just saw your dad," she said. She was very pleasant about it, like she'd been happy to see him and wanted to let me know.

I hadn't seen him in weeks.

"Yes, he was up at our house for a barbecue," she said. "He's a wonderful cook, isn't he? We went waterskiing and just had the best time."

I tried to smile, but I could feel my blood starting to boil. Our lives were falling apart, and he was waterskiing? Jewelers were pulling chains off my neck, and he was having a party?

I went home with all my muscles tensed. I finally knew how Gregg felt when his fuse would start to burn.

Lee pulled up in his truck later that afternoon. I was still fuming.

"Lee, do you know where my dad is?"

"Probably with my wife," he said. His tone told me what I should have already known: My dad was sleeping with Dawn. "They're probably at that place on Redmond Way having lunch."

I snapped. "Give me your keys," I said.

"What?"

"You need to give me your keys. Now."

Lee handed them over. I think he was scared of me at that moment. I got in his truck and barreled down the driveway. I slowed when I got to the street. *A bat. I need a baseball bat.* I drove around the neighborhood looking at all the lawns, trying to find a bat. It was hard to see through the tears of rage flooding my eyes. But at a house around the corner, I saw the familiar shape, long and round, lying in the grass. I kept the truck running while I got out and grabbed the bat off the lawn.

I raced to the restaurant on Redmond Way. I

was crying hysterically. I hated my father and I was afraid of what I might be capable of. In the parking lot, the sane part of my brain kicked in—I left the bat on the front seat when I got out.

I burst through the front door. The place was packed with the lunchtime rush, but I spotted my father right away at a table in the middle of the dining room. Dawn was with him, and another woman. They were having a big Italian feast.

"Having fun?" I screamed.

The whole restaurant went quiet. I had Lee's keys in my hand, and I felt something heavy on the ring—a bottle opener of some kind, very dense and solid.

I was charging toward the table. My father got up and ran toward the back, so I turned my fury on Dawn. As I walked toward her, I brought the key ring forward and hit her square in the face. I hit her again and a third time. Then I straightened up and yelled to everyone else eating lunch.

"I want you to know this woman is a whore!" I said. "This woman gives blow jobs for drugs. She neglects her kids. She's a fucking whore!"

The woman eating with her, the one I didn't know, picked up her plate and moved over to the next table, like she was trying to pretend nothing was happening. Then I went after Dawn again with the keys. My father came rushing back and pulled me off her and grabbed the keys, so I went after him.

"Give me those keys, you piece of shit! You rotten fuck, you lousy motherfucker!" I was swinging wildly at him, but he wasn't fighting back. He was ducking and backing up. I spit on him. Then I spit on him again, got in close, and grabbed the keys. He took a step away. I turned back toward Dawn and spit on her too.

Then I heard clapping. My father was a regular at that place. People knew him. They'd just seen his daughter fly into a rage and curse and spit. And they were clapping.

I stormed out, got back in the truck, and drove home. I was exhausted, completely spent. I started to pull into the driveway, but then remembered the bat. I turned the corner instead and dropped it in the yard where I'd found it.

Then I went home and wept.

● ● ●

I don't know why I didn't leave after that. I guess it was because I didn't want to abandon my mom. I didn't understand then the role she'd played in everything, how if it hadn't been for her tolerating my father, always taking him back and believing his apologies, none of it ever would have happened. Maybe we never would have had to run from New York. Maybe we would have had a chance, a good chance, at the life I'd always wanted.

My father wasn't much of a factor in my life after that. He was basically gone. He went to detox a couple of times, but it never worked. He moved to California for a while and ended up panhandling on the streets, a real gutter junkie. Every few weeks or months, he'd come back or he'd call my mom and she would go get him and bring him home. I avoided him those times, or stayed somewhere else.

Almost a year went by before he seemed even remotely functional. He was back at the Ponderosa in the spring of 1987, maybe sober, probably still sleeping with Dawn. My mom tolerated it, though. She still took care of him. I assumed she would until he died. There was nothing I could do about it except stay out of the way.

On May 2, 1987, she grabbed her purse and her car keys from the kitchen counter.

"Where are you going?" I asked.

"Your father got arrested last night," she said. "I'm going to get him out of jail."

How many times had I heard that? I didn't understand why she bothered but it was her choice.

Two hours later her car screeched to a stop in the driveway. She came in the door, went right for the refrigerator. She pulled out a bottle of white wine, uncorked it, and took a long drink right from the bottle.

I hadn't seen my mother drink in years. She could get a buzz off a Gran Marnier chocolate. I was scared. I didn't know why, but I knew I should be.

"Mom, what's wrong?"

She took another long drink.

"Oh my God, everyone knows who we are."

"What? How?"

"I went to get your father, and he was standing in front of the judge and the prosecutor was behind him, and they were talking to the judge and I heard your father say, 'I'm Henry Hill.'"

She took another drink.

"And then I was bombarded by reporters."

My heart sank. This was the worst possible thing that could happen. It didn't matter if he boasted about it to the neighbors or his drug friends. That was different because it was limited. But to say it in court, with strangers listening, with reporters listening. . .

Reporters? Why, I thought, were reporters there? Oh, Christ—this must be serious.

It was in the papers the next day. My father and two other men had been arrested for selling eleven and a half ounces of cocaine to an undercover DEA agent in Kirkland, which was near Redmond, for $10,400. My father wasn't there, but the two men who made the delivery gave him up right away, and the agents arrested him at a restaurant.

We were right back where we started. My father was a drug dealer, the Mafia still wanted to kill him, and the newspapers were giving directions to our house.

This was the worst possible thing that could

happen. I knew it. Everyone knew it. Chris told me, "The Mafia always gets its man." His girlfriend, Diane, came by and gave me a pistol. I was horrified. "What am I going to do with this?" I asked.

"It's only a BB gun," she said. "But it looks real, doesn't it?"

Yes, it did. It would give a hired killer a good excuse to shoot me.

The reporters started swarming the Ponderosa the next day. Henry Hill, the wiseguy from *Wiseguy,* was a huge story in the Seattle papers. Newspaper writers knocked on the door and they interviewed the neighbors, and TV reporters did stand-ups next to their microwave trucks parked at the end of the driveway. One station even sent a helicopter to take pictures from the air. We didn't talk to any of them, except to scream obscenities. I stood on the deck— the lanai, back when the Ponderosa was going to be our dream house with horses in the barn and the family all around the table—and shook my fist at them. "Get the fuck off my property," I yelled.

It didn't look good on television. I was at a friend's house later that night, watching the news.

"God, Gina," one of the girls there said. "Look at you scream."

Like I needed more humiliation. The questions started right after that. What's it like? Are you really in danger? Did your dad ever kill anyone?

I rested my forehead on one hand.

"You don't want to know," is all I could say. "Don't even ask."

My father would be protected. I didn't know how, but I knew someone would step in, that the government would look after him.

But who would protect me?

"My life is such a mess," I whispered.

And for the first time, I believed it was true.

EPILOGUE

GINA: Ten years went by, a whole lifetime, or maybe it was the other way around, enough time to build a life, one that I wanted.

I'd finally left Redmond in the summer of 1987, not long after my father was arrested on the drug charges. It wasn't easy leaving my mom, but I knew I couldn't stay near my father. Whatever remained of my girlhood fantasy, my dream of a normal family, was torn away in those last few weeks.

At the end in Redmond, I had a strange kind of celebrity. I would go out to coffee shops with Kathy or Chris, and people I barely knew, even complete strangers, would hang at the edge of our booth and ask for my autograph. I hated it. I'd turn away and stare at the wall and not say a word, all the time feeling ashamed, until they got bored and walked away or Chris told them to get lost.

The irony was awful. I'd waited my entire life to be proud of my father. I was convinced that all those situations really were temporary, that someday the world would know the real Henry Hill or Peter Haymes or Marty Scott or whatever he was going to be called. And when the world did know, it turned out that I was the one who'd been wrong all along. My father became famous for all the things I'd come to hate and fear, all the things I endured and suffered. He was famous for being a criminal and a snitch. No, it was worse than that: Henry Hill became a famous *character,* not even a real gangster anymore who inspired fear and dread. Strangers felt free to harass his daughter in coffee shops.

I was right about his being protected, though. The government didn't rescue him, but things always seem to work out for my father. When he went to trial in September 1987, his lawyer argued that my father was actually a victim. The stress of witness protection, of being far from familiar places and constantly fearing for his life, led to drug and alcohol problems, which in turn caused his marriage to fall apart. The only reason he got involved with the conspiracy to sell cocaine, his lawyer said, was because he owed those drug dealers so much money that they were threatening him and molesting Dawn. "He was scared," the lawyer said.

It worked, sort of. My father was convicted, but the judge sentenced him to five years' probation. As long as he stayed out of trouble, he'd stay out of prison.

I didn't wait around for the trial. By then, I'd already flown east to, of all places, New York. I wasn't afraid. If anything, I knew I'd be more anonymous in Manhattan than I was in Redmond. So much had changed in the seven years since we'd left Rockville Centre anyway. The people we'd run from were dead or in prison, and none of them would recognize the pretty brunette adult I'd become as Henry's little girl anyway. And yet my roots were still there. I was still a New Yorker.

For ten years I thrived. I had a job planning meetings and events for a big financial firm that paid for my classes at New York University. I had a boyfriend and new girlfriends. I put three thousand miles between me and my father, and it seemed just far enough. In Manhattan I was Gina Scott, not Henry Hill's daughter.

I had only sporadic contact with him during those years. I knew about all the major events, like when my mom finally left him in 1988 and when he married Dawn a couple of years after that. In 1991 I flew out West to see their infant son, Justin, my half brother. He was beautiful. But that was about it. I needed the distance. I needed my own life.

But then my father called me one night in the fall of 1997. He told me Justin was in foster care. His mother was strung out on heroin, and my father was drinking heavily again, so the state of California took their son. My father was in a funk, depressed. He was afraid he'd lost Justin forever because this was the third time he'd been sent to foster parents. "He's not coming home," my father told me. "He has to get adopted."

I was numb. I didn't even know my brother, but my heart was broken. I knew what the boy must be thinking. Someone, probably a very nice social worker, had told him not to worry, that it was only temporary, that one day his dad would come for him and they'd be a normal family again.

I got off the phone and I wept.

The next day I tracked down the number for the foster home where Justin was staying. I called him just to tell him he had a big sister who would take care of him, who wanted to take care of him. Then I called him the next day and every day after that. A few weeks later I flew to California for his birthday and threw a party for him at Chuck E. Cheese.

When I saw his face for the first time, it was like looking into a mirror. Physically, he resembled Gregg—the same blonde hair, the same nose and eyes. But I saw myself too, pieces of both of us, and I could see his future because I could see my past. He was seven years old, and he believed his father was a wonderful prince, a smart and generous man who made incredible promises.

I couldn't leave him. I couldn't let that magnificent little boy live my life all over again. It took a year before I got custody of him, but I spoke to him every single one of those days. In 1998, Justin came to live with me. I raised him for four years, until California authorities decided his parents were fit to take him back.

It broke my heart all over again, knowing what he was going back to. But he still comes to see me, sometimes for a few weeks, sometimes for a few months. It's not just me he comes to see—it's us, me and my husband. He adores Justin, and Justin adores him. He's an exceptional man, my husband. He doesn't cheat on me or scream at me and he goes to work every day and he doesn't break the law. He's honest and loving and respectful. Together, we're normal, which doesn't sound glamorous, but it's still wonderful to me. The one thing I'd wanted all my life I found on my own. And I hope—no, I know—Justin understands how beautiful life can be when he's with us.

GREGG: I stood behind the one-way mirror looking into my son's preschool classroom. I came early to pick him up just so I could watch for a few minutes. The teachers all knew me, and some of the mothers touched my arm as they said hello. I nodded and smiled, but I never took my eyes off my boy.

He was four years old, and my wife said he looked like me. "His father's son," she'd say, and I'd feel a catch in my throat every time. Then I shifted my focus until I saw my own faint reflection in the glass.

His father's son. No one could ever say that about me.

Was I ever that young? I must have been. But it's hard to remember, or maybe just hard to reconcile. Was I really Henry's Kid, the boy with the crisp twenties tucked in his shirt pocket, the one waiting for his father to be paroled, the teenager fishing alone on a pier where the wise-guys wouldn't find him? Was that really me?

No one would believe it. I buried that boy long ago, back in 1985 when I flew off to a faraway city with nothing but my made-up name and my fictionalized past. I started over as Gregg Scott, alone and broke, and built a respectable life for myself, a good life. It was an act of will, of sheer determination. I went back to school and grad-uated with honors, and then I went on to law school. I'm a practicing attorney. I've never broken the law. I've never pulled a scam. I've never told anyone who my father is. Only my wife knows, and we don't talk much about it.

Class was over for the day. I watched my son

gather his few things, and then I moved toward the open doorway. He saw me and squealed. He ran toward me with his arms open wide, and I squatted down to catch him in a hug.

"Daddy!" Aidan buried his face in my chest for an instant, then tipped his head back so he could see me. I brushed a strand of hair away from his blue eyes. Such a beautiful boy. I wondered if my father ever looked at me like that. I wondered if he knew what he'd missed.

"I've got a surprise for you," I said.

"Really?" He was smiling, but he's always smiling. He's a happy kid.

"Really. Come on, let's go."

I stood up and took his hand and led my son out to the parking lot. It was a warm Friday afternoon, and the woods on either side of the school were still thick with leaves.

"Is it today?" Aidan asked. "Is it? Is it today?"

I looked down at him and winked. He's a smart kid, too. He'd been counting off the days, scratching off each one on the calendar on the refrigerator with a marker. I'd promised him it would be Friday. He knew I wouldn't break a promise.

I opened the hatch, slipped his backpack from his shoulder, and laid it inside, next to the overnight bags and the rods and reels. Aidan reached up just to touch his. He'd only practiced in the yard with a light weight tied to a rod almost twice as tall as him. He looked up at me and beamed. It was a brilliant Friday afternoon, and his dad was going to teach him how to fish.

I bent down on one knee and hugged him again. I hoped he would remember someday. More than that, I hoped he'd want to be his father's son.

Sleepers

Lorenzo Carcaterra

An unforgettable true story of friendship, loyalty and revenge

Lorenzo, Michael, John and Tommy shared everything – the laughter and the bruises of an impoverished childhood on New York's violent West Side. Until one of their pranks misfired and they were sent to a reformatory school.

Twelve months of systematic mental, physical and sexual abuse left the boys transformed for ever.

Eleven years later, one of them had become a journalist, one a lawyer – and the other two killers for the mob. In a chance encounter they came face to face with one of their torturers and shot him dead in front of several witnesses. The trial that followed brought the four friends together in one last, audacious stand – and a courtroom climax as gripping as any John Grisham novel.

'A compulsive true story'
The Times

'Undeniably powerful, an enormously affecting and intensely human story'
Washington Post

'Fabulous, unbelievably good'
Entertainment Weekly

'A brilliant, troubling, important book'
Jonathan Kellerman

arrow books

L.A. Confidential

James Ellroy

Christmas 1951, Los Angeles: a city where the police are as corrupt as the criminals. Six prisoners are beaten senseless in their cells by cops crazed on alcohol. For the three L.A.P.D. detectives involved, it will expose the guilty secrets on which they have built their corrupt and violent careers . . .

'Ellroy writes as if driven by demons. His brutal, staccato graffiti tips over into art'
Sunday Times

'No emotion is spared; the writing is sparse, the plotting controlled. Not for the faint of heart, this is a big, powerful crime novel and possibly the first important example of the genre in the 1990s'
Sunday Telegraph

'Empty of any unessentials and full of wise-cracking wit'
Mail on Sunday

'Unputdownable'
Time Out

ALSO AVAILABLE IN ARROW

Wilful Behaviour

Donna Leon

When a student visits Commissario Brunetti with a strange
interest in investigating the possibility of a pardon for a crime
committed by her grandfather many years ago, Brunetti thinks
little of it. But when the girl is found stabbed to death, Claudia
Leonardo suddenly becomes Brunetti's case, and no longer
his wife's student.

Claudia seems to have no discernable living family – her only
familial relationship is with an elderly Austrian woman, her
grandfather's lover. Brunetti is both intrigued and stunned by the
extraordinary art collection the old woman keeps in her small,
unprepossessing flat, and when she in turn is found dead, the
case seems to have been about to open up long buried secrets
of collaboration and the exploitation of Italian Jews during the
war, secrets few in Italy are happy to explore . . .

'A classic example of detective-book murder . . . Leon whips up
a briliant narrative storm'
Sunday Times

'Compelling . . . This is a powerful story, brilliantly evoking Venetian
atmosphere, and the characters of Brunetti and his family continue to deepen throughout this series'
The Times

'Donna Leon's novels have become successively more subtle,
more complex and perhaps more serious, without ever losing
their compelling power as narratives. This is especially true of
Wilful Behaviour; the story is wholly engrossing'
Evening Standard

arrow books

The Godfather

Mario Puzo

'A novel about the Mafia written on the grand scale with an admirable ring of authenticity and a remarkable degree of sympathy with the gangsters' own standards of justice'
Sunday Telegraph

'A splendid and distinguished blood saga of the Cosa Nostra, the American Mafia, and of the whirl created by five families of mafiosi at war in New York'
Sunday Times

'Mario Puzo is an extremely talented storyteller, and his tale moves at breakneck speed without ever losing its balance. More important, Puzo proves to be a genuine social historian. *The Godfather* is fiction, but it is still a valid and fascinating portrait of America's most powerful and least understood subculture, the Mafia'
Newsweek

arrow books

**Order further Arrow titles
from your local bookshop, or have them delivered
direct to your door by Bookpost**

☐	**Sleepers** Lorenzo Carcaterra	0 09 962871 6	£7.99
☐	**LA Confidential** James Ellroy	0 09 963371 1	£7.99
☐	**Wilful Behaviour** Donna Leon	0 09 941518 6	£6.99
☐	**Godfather** Mario Puzo	0 09 942928 4	£6.99

Free post and packing
Overseas customers allow £2 per paperback

Phone: 01624 677237

Post: Random House Books
c/o Bookpost, PO Box 29, Douglas, Isle of Man IM99 1BQ

Fax: 01624 670923

email: bookshop@enterprise.net

Cheques (payable to Bookpost) and credit cards accepted

Prices and availability subject to change without notice.
Allow 28 days for delivery.
When placing your order, please state if you do not wish to receive any
additional information.

www.randomhouse.co.uk/arrowbooks

arrow books